Read Your World

Alda Noronha-Nimmo

Kendall Hunt
publishing company

Kendall Hunt
publishing company

www.kendallhunt.com
Send all inquiries to:
4050 Westmark Drive
Dubuque, IA 52004-1840

Copyright © 2011 by Alda Noronha-Nimmo

ISBN 978-0-7575-8920-1

Printed in the United States of America
10 9 8 7 6 5 4 3 2

Contents

Let Me Introduce Myself...

1   There have been many texts written on reading processes, reading comprehension, and every other conceivable aspect of reading. And, although there have been paradigm shifts in what are considered best methodologies, or what comprises key competencies in reading, truth be told, no one really knows. What we do know for sure is that the more we read and comprehend, the better we become at reading comprehension. Similarly, the more we speak, the better we get at speaking; the more we write, the better we get at writing; and of course, the more we listen, the better we get at listening. Simplistic as these ideas may seem, reading is as basic as that premise.

2   Presenting reading comprehension as discrete skills/competencies often results in a piece-meal attitude about reading and a disjointed approach in processing reading. Reading comprehension is anything but! Although the general emphasis in most college circles is to teach discrete skills, in other systems of education, reading is approached more holistically. Books (such as novels and poetry) are bit off, chewed, and digested! New vocabulary is learned in the process. And, what is comprehension but understanding words that are strung together? And, how best to learn them, but in their natural contexts, such as in stories, conversations, lectures, or letters and e-mails? Based on these assumptions, this book is infused with general content knowledge about reading.

3   Some of the content is based on my own classroom experiences and observations and is not meant to serve as a research base. I hope to provide students with a practical and realistic approach to reading. This content can generate discussions in the classroom about reading. Often, classroom discussions center on generic reading material. Why not have discussions that center on the subject of reading?

4   I address such issues as reading from a learner's perspective, why reading comprehension sometimes fails, and the importance of motivation. I offer a common-sense approach to improve reading comprehension. This text handles the content of reading comprehension mostly through a real-life lens. In other words, how we comprehend in our natural environments is similar to how we comprehend while we read.

5   When nonreaders and/or developmental college reading students realize that there is no mystery surrounding reading comprehension, and that it is simply a natural progression from learning to decode, they learn to appreciate the act of reading to comprehend. Once students begin to feel successful, they are prone to read more, and the more they read, the more vocabulary they are likely to acquire.

6   Many reading texts have little content information about reading and mostly serve as workbooks. I want this text to be different. Part One of this book primarily provides some background information on the subjects of reading and, to some extent, writing. This section also serves to show the connections between reading, writing, speaking, and listening. It is important to me that students perceive themselves as critical thinkers at the center of the reading process and, thereby, discover the joys

Subject-Specific Vocabulary:

endowment: funds provided for the support of an institution, organization, etc.

royalties: payments to authors and composers for each copy of a work sold

holistic: relating to or concerned with wholes or with complete systems rather than with parts

discrete: consisting of distinct or unconnected elements

formulaic: a customary or set form or method allowing little room for originality

linear: relating to, or based or depending on sequential development

Non-Subject Specific Vocabulary:

conceivable, paradigm, intrinsically, relegated, permeates, diligent, amiss, perseverance, humble, insurmountable, overwhelming, comprises, assumptions, copious, inconsequential, vicariously, distinguishing, burgeoning of learning. Also, I hope students come to the realization that reading proficiency is intrinsically rewarding and satisfying, and that it is a journey of a lifetime.

7   Part Two primarily serves as a handbook for the discrete reading skills. For example, skills such as main ideas, inferences, and argument are addressed at length. In this section, too, I have made connections with writing, speaking, and listening skills where I thought necessary.

8   Although Parts One and Two do not serve as a traditional skills workbook, they nonetheless provide some critical thinking questions which help students to process content. It is best, therefore, that much of what is presented in these sections be read and "used." By "used" I mean that the chapters found in Parts One and Two can be used as reading material for students to practice their discrete skills, such as finding the main idea, major supporting details, and distinguishing fact from opinion. For example all of Part One, can be used to develop questions that require both inferential and critical thinking skills. Also, in this section, my opinions can be used to engage students in dialogue and discussion, thereby applying such skills as inferences, bias, tone, and argument. In other words reading about reading can provide the text for exercises. Instructors may choose to use the content from Parts One and Two to generate additional skills-based or content-area questions for their students. Furthermore, I hope that the understanding of the content itself will encourage students to initiate more reading from other sources.

9   Part Three contains a few selections of practice exercises and serves somewhat like a traditional skills workbook. It contains limited reading excerpts with some multiple-choice and short-answer questions. These selections are representative of a select number of genres and content-area texts that students are likely to encounter in the course of their studies, and that I hope will offer some indication of the type of thinking students will be required to engage in. Fortunately, there are copious amounts of current and relevant reading material that instructors can use to supplement Part Three, thereby customizing reading materials to fit the needs and interests of their student populations. Additionally, many post-secondary institution sites on the Internet offer many exercises in discrete reading skills (refer to Part Four for a select list of current websites). Adding lots of reading material when it may not be relevant (or current) to the population being taught would be of little instructional value and would increase the cost of the book. Furthermore, given our current focus on environmental issues, efficient use of resources makes sense.

10   Part Four contains a variety of material that I hope students will find both useful and interesting. For example, I have included a small section related to reading to young children. It is important to read to infants and children because then reading is demystified as children learn to both comprehend and appreciate reading. Often, I teach students who are parents or who care for young children. Therefore, I feel it is important to make sure that I address their need to ensure their children grow up to become successful readers. It has been the generous contributions of colleagues and friends that have made Part Four possible.

11   This book serves mostly as a holistic foundation about reading and less as a workbook. Addressing reading in a holistic fashion may be thought of as touching on literacy. But, it should! For someone to be literate, he or she must be able to read, write, speak, listen, and comprehend. Moreover, reading comprehension does not take place in a vacuum; neither is it relegated to the classrooms. Once students realize that reading permeates every aspect of their lives, it becomes a subject in which proficiency becomes a must—a much-desired and sought-after necessity.

12   Additionally, each chapter begins with the meanings of subject-specific vocabulary to provide background knowledge prior to reading. It is important to understand that this vocabulary is mostly specific to the concepts related to the subject of reading and writing. Nonsubject-specific words that students will encounter in the course of the reading have been addressed at the end of the chapters in the hope that students will first write the meaning they derived within context, and then look up the meaning in a dictionary to confirm this definition. If I have written definitions in the course of my discussions, I have referred to the Merriam-Webster dictionary, and in many instances, may have taken the liberty to write them down verbatim—particularly for the "subject-specific words." The definitions under the "subject-specific words" category are basic. Many of these words/terms are explained in more detail in their corresponding chapters.

13   As the reader navigates through this book, he may notice that he is asked to go to specific websites to read or refer to material to complete an activity. The reader should bear in mind that sometimes websites change or are shut down; therefore, if this happens I recommend finding another site that will provide the same information.

14   I have attempted to begin each chapter with a thought-provoking title with the expectation that it will catch the reader's attention. It is hoped that these titles—some of which have intentionally been created to cause debate—will engage the reader in a dialogue that will include activation of prior knowledge, and encourage her to think both creatively and critically. I am encouraged that by the end of each chapter the reader will come full circle, to understand the connection of the title to the content read.

15   This text serves as a conversation between the student and me. I trust that as I am "speaking in print" with students, they will be active in processing my message. Because of this conversational style, I have decided to use my creative license. For example, I chose to start many of my sentences with coordinating conjunctions like "and" and "but." Students may become confused about what is considered "good writing" as they may have been introduced to basic writing in their English courses in a formulaic and linear method. They may have not been introduced to the idea of "creative license" yet and, therefore, think that sentences beginning with conjunctions are grammatically wrong regardless of how they are used. This would be a natural teachable moment for instructors to explain to students what "creative license" implies. Furthermore, for practical purposes, I have taken the liberty to alternate *he* and *she* when referring to the reader or a third party. Additionally, I hope that students, as a result of the information and message in this book, will evolve to become avid readers and will someday pass on the gift of reading to someone else. At the risk of sounding like a cliché, reading is a gift that keeps on giving.

16   I do not claim that this book is complete by experts' standards. Like any such project, it is a work in progress. Most of what I have written is based on my years of experiences as an instructor of developmental reading in college. As I continue to grow in my knowledge of the convergence of students' needs and competencies of reading in academic settings, I hope this project will also evolve—after all, knowledge is naturally mercurial and keeping up with it is the objective of all authors of texts. I anticipate the book will serve as a guide for students to learn and as a blueprint for instructors to teach. It addresses more than the skills required in many reading courses. However, the chapters not dealing with skills are my own views that have evolved from educational and research experiences, and teaching over the course of many years. Additionally, working with students of diverse backgrounds not only influenced my writing style, but also made me realize that connecting reading skills and concepts to real life scenarios relates more intimately to my students.

17   Last, I trust that students can engage with me on this journey of discovery of self-as-reader, especially when they realize that, like many of them, I, too, have overcome many obstacles to achieve my goals. I am one of seven siblings born to parents who did not have a formal education yet who managed to learn enough English to teach me how to read in elementary school. I grew up poor where meals were not a guarantee, paper and pencils were a luxury, and being a member of a minority group often meant a lack of opportunities.

18   When I realize some of the overwhelming obstacles that many of my students face to attend college, I find that my experiences are inconsequential compared to what they are facing, and I am humbled. These students' successes despite the challenges they face are proof that, ultimately, we can overcome—that challenges are not a license for making excuses but instead are opportunities by which we measure our self-worth. Therefore, I hope that I have managed throughout this book to engage students enough to realize that gaining knowledge through reading is indeed a blessing that must not be taken for granted and a challenge that is not insurmountable. It is my intense desire to observe my students' process of becoming conscious of their burgeoning abilities and vicariously to share in their elation as they discover the joys of reading. Students' success in reading is possible!

My Blessings

19   Where do I start? Or rather with whom do I start? Ah, yes! I start with God, without whom nothing is possible. Then, I must mention my gratitude to my family who not only encouraged me, but also provided me with the space I needed to complete this work. Without them, this project would not have come to fruition. My friend and colleague, Karen Taghi Zoghi was diligent with editing and steadfast in her support. Most of the contributions in Part Four have been donated by people who are just as dedicated as I am to the success of a reading education. Also, I am thankful to my friends who provided me with invaluable feedback. Marla Swartz and Sarah Flynn, both with Kendall Hunt, were supportive and encouraging. They were patient with me as I have been recovering from illness, and as I still continue to grieve for the sudden loss of my father.

20   I would be remiss if I did not include my students—past, present, future—without whom, my own growth as a reading instructor would not have been possible. Their perseverance as they learn to read—and in many cases learn to read in a new language—provided me with the incentive to write this book. Students' personal struggles to overcome insurmountable odds just to attend a reading class keeps me humble and their progress as critical thinkers and readers gives me hope for the future.

21   Last, but certainly not least, I acknowledge the role of my parents in encouraging me to read and write early in life. I dedicate this book to my mom, Celina Noronha, and my dad, Felix Noronha. Dad passed away suddenly last year while I was working on this book. Although it has been difficult to focus on this project while grieving for my father, I

know that he would have wanted me to finish what I had started. And, I think that he is smiling down on me as I complete this project. Regardless of how little we had, Dad, or "Daddy" as I often called him, emphasized the importance of doing well in school. Therefore, it seems logical to state that without my dad's and mom's incredible influence on the way in which I view education, I would not have been in a position to write this book. It should not be surprising that I am establishing a memoral scholarship fund in Dad's name. All royalties (profits) that this book generates will help provide scholarships for college developmental reading students from low socioeconomic backgrounds. Consequently—although you may not have known about this at the time you purchased this book—you have participated in this scholarship project. I thank you for your contribution toward the success of others.

22   In these hard economic times and with my students' needs in mind, I have tried to keep the cost of this book to a minimum. When I realized that incorporating reading selections from other sources would add to the cost of this book (typically authors request monetary compensation), I avoided high-cost selections and kept borrowed material to a minimum. This decreased the cost of the book. Also, I know that instructors are extremely resourceful and will customize their instruction with supplemental material based on the needs of the student population they serve.

Contact Me

23   This text has been customized for my students. However, in the introduction I have included some suggestions for instructors who may wish to use this text. I encourage both instructors and students to e-mail me with their comments on what they found useful, not so useful, or what should have been included or excluded. Hopefully, there will be other editions of this book. I know that some students and instructors have their own written material that could possibly be included in the next edition. Therefore, I trust that you will contribute your best writings. You will be given credit and contacted if your writing is selected to be included in any future editions. You may e-mail me at aldanimmo@gmail.com. Please put "Read Your World" in the subject line.

Aeda

2011

Non-Subject Specific Words:

conceivable, paradigm, intrinsically, relegated, permeates, diligent, amiss, perseverance, humble, insurmountable, overwhelming, comprises, assumptions, copious, inconsequential, vicariously, distinguishing, burgeoning

Subject-Specific Vocabulary:

endowment: funds provided for the support of an institution, organization, etc.

royalties: payments to authors and composers for each copy of a work sold

holistic: relating to or concerned with wholes or with complete systems rather than with parts

discrete: consisting of distinct or unconnected elements

formulaic: a customary or set form or method allowing little room for originality

linear: relating to, or based or depending on sequential development

Dedicated to the memory of my Dad
Roque Vincente Felix Noronha (1926 - 2010)
The wind beneath my wings – yesterday, today, and tomorrow

Reason to Read

Part One

Your Attitude Counts

Chapter One

Do You Enjoy Reading?

1   If you are reading this text as a requirement prior to taking college-level courses, or if you have been informed that you scored low on the reading portion of a college entrance test or on the SAT/ACT, chances are that you probably share some similar attitudes and characteristics with the large number of students across the country who find themselves in similar circumstances. Often students do not like to read because they have experienced difficulty with reading, and/or perhaps they have never discovered the joys of reading. Other students may have been successful in reading in their native language but have difficulty with reading comprehension in English because of their limited English vocabulary.

2   It is **sobering** for me to find that many of my college students were never read to as young children and that some were not encouraged to read by the significant adults in their lives. Perhaps not learning of the immense pleasure reading can bring early on crippled many into having a negative attitude toward reading. That is why I have included "Reading MATTERS" in the appendices section (Part Four) of this book. In this section, Althea Duren addresses how to read to young children. Those of you who have young children or are influential in the upbringing of children may find this a valuable resource.

3   You will be happy to know that if you did like to read in your native language, and you did well in comprehending text in that language, the same problem-solving processes you used to make sense of the text are similar to the mental processes you will use to make sense of reading in English. You will quickly realize that we use similar reasoning to comprehend reading in any written language. How much vocabulary you know and your background information about the content in a reading selection will determine how efficiently you will be able to understand the type of written academic material you will have to read for your college-level courses. All of this, therefore, implies that if you do not like to read at all, you might have a more challenging task ahead of you.

Thinking, Reasoning, and Comprehension

4   However, all is not lost. If you are able to think critically, which means that you solve everyday problems that come your way after reasoning out possible solutions and reflecting on your actions, you will be able to comprehend reading. Comprehending what you read is the same process as thinking and reasoning through a solution to a problem. The only difference is that we have to be able to call out and identify the words when we are reading. In other words, we actually have to read the words (break words into sounds and syllables) so that we can then make sense

Subject-Specific Vocabulary:

decode: break words into sounds and syllables

of them, whereas thinking through a non-reading problem may simply require an analysis of information from our senses of touch, sound, sight, and/or intuition.

5   This means that if we are able to decode words, and we are familiar with the meaning of those words, our thinking brain is capable of comprehending what we read. For some of us, the process will be easier, but we all can comprehend what we read. First, we must approach reading with a positive attitude—an "I-can-do" attitude. Negative attitudes toward reading and/or learning will impede your ability to comprehend. For example, have you ever approached a task, such as learning to bake, in a negative frame of mind? You might have said to yourself, "I cannot bake," or "I will never get it right." And, then did the experience prove you right or wrong? Sometimes you will find that you are pleasantly surprised that despite your fear, you still were able to accomplish your goal. But, more often than not, you will find that your lack of confidence interfered with your ability to be successful. This becomes a self-fulfilling **prophecy**, which means that you have predicted the outcome with your negative attitude. However, we all know that some things—like changing long-held beliefs about ourselves—are easier said than done.

Your Attitude Can Change

6   It is crucial that you give yourself the opportunity to be successful. Only you can do that. Once you give reading a chance and you are successful, you will want to continue. We all know that success breeds success! We all also know that reading permeates our everyday lives. We do not just read for school or college (academic purposes); we read for other purposes that are just as important, such as directions on how to install a fan or how to prepare for the hurricane season.

7   If you have read thus far and have understood what you have read, you have comprehended my writing, and you are probably familiar with the vocabulary used. However, had this reading material been written using many words that were unfamiliar to you, your comprehension would have been severely **hindered**. This material is purposely written using a conversational style and everyday vocabulary so that you can feel success while reading and at the same time feel engaged with the material. However, you must understand that the kind of reading you will encounter in college courses is far from the conversational style that I am using. Therefore, it is crucial that you read, write, and listen for all purposes—including academic ones. This will build your vocabulary and background knowledge so that when the reading becomes more challenging, you will have a store of information to help you analyze and evaluate the reading material.

8   Keep in mind that even if you have a positive attitude toward reading, your attitude is likely to change depending on the purpose for your reading and the difficulty of the reading material. I love to read but if I had to read and study for a physics class, I know that I would be anything but happy! However, knowing that I will be challenged by my own attitude will help me in doing something about it instead of remaining frustrated and unhappy.

9   Now ask yourself, "Have I remained focused during this reading?" Was comprehension of the material easy for you? Did you connect and **integrate** this information while you were reading with information that you already have (from experiences and background knowledge)? Did you have to reread a lot? Did you find many vocabulary words that you did not know? How did you figure out the meanings of these unknown words? Did you find your attention straying from the material? Why? Did you like the style of writing? Why? If you are thinking about these kinds of questions, you are reflecting (thinking deeply).

Reading in a Variety of Forms

10   I want to focus your attention on something else. Before opening this book, did you look at the cover and wonder what the title meant? You can do this now if you did not do so before. What does *Read Your World* imply? Why do you think that I am suggesting some type of connection between reading text and reading your world? Do the illustrations on the cover and the back help you understand this idea? When you read, do you notice similarities with how you interpret music, graffiti, signs, symbols, and such? How so? By this time you must be thinking to yourself that I ask a lot of questions and that you were expecting a book where I would be giving the answers. Well, you are in for a surprise if you keep reading! Do I have your attention now? Here I go with the questions again …

11   Look at the back of the book cover. You see, among other things, musical notes and mathematical equations. Why do these belong on a reading book cover? Well, I think that we read those, too, and make sense of those symbols, do we not? In music, we not only read and play the notes, but if we are accomplished musicians, we also interpret them and play a little differently. In reading a language—in this case, English—we are interpreting the graphic representations

(for example, in English, letters of the alphabet) of the language, are we not? However, mathematics and music are often referred to as universal languages. What is meant by that? Well, it means that in most cases, you will understand music notes and mathematical symbols regardless of what language you speak.

12   English is not a universal language because there are many peoples of this world who are not familiar with it. You will agree that speakers of languages who use an alphabetic system that is similar to English (for example, Spanish and French) are at an advantage over those whose native language relies on totally different graphic representations (for example, Arabic and Hindi)—and, some languages use a symbol to represent an entire concept (for example, Chinese)! Many international students constantly tell me that English is difficult. But, of course, I do not think so! I suppose it is a matter of perspective—just as I would probably tell them that their language is difficult if I were unfamiliar with it!

13   I mentioned graphic representations earlier. Did you notice the graphic symbols on the front cover, especially those from ancient times? (Here I go with the questions again!) Were you able to identify them or at least some of them? Do any of them have personal significance to you? These are ways since ancient times that people have depicted meaning by using imagery, symbols, and graphics. We even have graffiti for the creative vandal, Braille for the person who is visually impaired, and sign language for the person who is hearing impaired. It just goes to show how human beings have used their imaginations to create a variety of systems in which they can communicate with each other.

Brief Survey

14   At the end of this passage is a reading survey. Please fill it out completely and truthfully. After you have completed the reading requirements for your course, you will complete another reading survey (two parts: A and B) at the end of Part Two. Then, you will be able to compare the two survey responses so that you can tell whether you have made progress in your attitude toward and knowledge of reading.

Rate from 1–42 (with 42 being the highest score) the importance of reading to your life goals __24__
Complete the following survey:

Pre-Reading Survey

Please circle the response that best describes you.

		Most of the time	Sometimes	Never
1.	I like being read to.	2	**Sometimes**	Never
2.	I enjoy reading in my native language.	3	**Most of the time**	Never
3.	My experiences with high school and/or college textbooks have been good.	2	**Sometimes**	Never
4.	I like class assignments that require me to read a book/novel.	1	Sometimes	**Never**
5.	I read even when I am not required to.	1	Sometimes	**Never**
6.	I would consider reading during my leisure time.	2	**Sometimes**	Never
7.	I know that reading can be fun.	1	Sometimes	**Never**
8.	I open a textbook expecting it to be interesting.	2	**Sometimes**	Never
9.	I preview textbooks before the course begins.	1	Sometimes	**Never**
10.	A course in reading is a good use of my time.	2	**Sometimes**	Never

11. I have read at least one book/novel in the last three months (not required for any class).	Yes	No
12. I have encouraged someone else to read.	Yes	No
13. I have discussed book(s) with my friend(s).	Yes	No
14. I am likely to discuss this textbook with my friend(s).	Yes	No

Analyze your responses: (Most of the time = 3; Sometimes = 2; Never = 1; Yes = 3; No = 1). For questions 1 through 14, add your scores based on your responses. The highest score is a 42 and the lowest score is a 14. The higher your score, the more likely that your attitude toward reading is positive. Now look at the number you put for the importance of reading to your life goals. If that number is 42 or close to 42, then what you are saying is that you know that reading is going to be an intrinsic part of your life. Now, reflect on the total survey score you received. If your survey score is high—which means that you have a fairly positive attitude toward reading—then you will have started your reading class "ahead of the game" and you are neck-and-neck with your life goals.

If your score on the reading survey was low, and your "life goals" score was high, this means you will have to work on improving your attitude so that your attitude can facilitate your learning and your appreciation of reading. This, in turn, will be in keeping with your life goals. This makes reading and learning so much more enjoyable! Even if your attitude toward reading is negative as you are getting started on this journey with me, I hope that by the time you complete your course and read this book, you will come to realize the powerful influence of reading in every aspect of your life.

Application:

A. Write what you think the following words mean in the context of your reading. Then, use the dictionary to check if you were right in your summation:

sobering, prophecy, hindered, integrate

B. Based on your comprehension of what you have read here, answer the following questions:

1. Why is your attitude toward reading important? Provide a personal example to explain.

2. How are reading comprehension and thinking the same?

3. What is the difference between decoding words while reading and reading comprehension?

4. In one sentence tell what you think this selection was about (Remember that a sentence is a complete thought and it should be written as such.).

5. What does "self-fulfilling prophecy" mean (do not use a dictionary)? Tell how you were able to make sense of the term.

If you have answered the above questions without much difficulty, this means that you easily comprehended the material. Kudos!! You are off to a wonderful experience in reading.

Why Bother to Read?

1   There are many reasons for reading. I think we all know that. We may not know what the categories are, but we all have read for many reasons. I know, for example, that I have read a magazine in the doctor's waiting room when I have become bored. I have read the newspaper either to follow up on a story that I first heard on the television, or sometimes to read just the cartoons or my horoscope. There are many times, of course, that I have had to read to learn for my school or college coursework. I think you know what I am talking about because you have done it, too. Later on in this text, you will find that I talk about the author's purpose for reading. However, for purposes of this discussion, I am referring to why you, the reader, may decide to read. Therefore, I have created the three basic categories below to describe why we read:

2   **Read for Utilitarian/Practical Purposes:** This type of reading is best described as reading for practical purposes. Examples are: newspapers, cookbooks, manuals, grocery lists, etc. Most of us read for practical purposes without consciously thinking that we are indeed reading or reflecting on the importance of being able to read and comprehend for everyday use. This type of reading we take for granted, almost like we take for granted our ability to communicate by speaking.

3   **Read for Enjoyment:** Even if you have not read an entire book, you might have picked up a magazine and read an article on something that interested you. For example, you might have read a passage on the latest fashions or on the current sports events. You have read for pleasure—again, without the **conscious** knowledge of your ability to make sense of what you have read. Others have read entire novels. These types of readings are for pleasure and, in many instances, people read as a hobby. Novels usually employ a narrative style – writing in the form of stories told. Since we are familiar with story grammar from as early as infancy when we heard stories in our environment, novels become easy to follow. Prayer and/or inspirational books also fill our need for pleasure.

4   **Read to Research:** This type of reading lends itself to the type of reading material you are going to be reading to either **garner** information for your own personal use (for example, reading about various ways to cook a green bean casserole) or for formal research. These kinds of readings also lend themselves to the **utilitarian**/practical purpose that I have already discussed with the exception that research implies more than one source of information. The other type of reading to research is the type of formal research we conduct to write formal papers (read to write) and to give formal presentations (read to speak/present). I have addressed this research-related reading in depth further along in this section.

5   **Read to Learn:** As in school and in college, we find that we have to read for information related to our subject areas. Most times, we do not like to read our textbooks even if we like the subject. (I hope that this is not the case with this textbook!) There are many reasons for this. First, textbooks are often written in a style that is

Subject-Specific Vocabulary:

narrative: something that is told or written, like a story

implies: involves or indicates by inference, association, or necessary consequence rather than by direct statement

synthesize: to make (something) by combining different things

cite: to refer to

scan: to glance from point to point, often hastily, casually, or in search of a particular item

skim: to glance through (as a book) for the chief ideas or the plot

paraphrase: to restate a text, passage, or work giving the meaning in another form

summarize: to re-tell (information) using fewer words

CliffsNotes: student study guides that contain summaries and some analyses of mostly literary work

not reader friendly. Second, textbooks are written in a formal style that many of us find unfamiliar. Third, we realize that what we read in these books—although it may be interesting—is usually information that we would not only have to understand thoroughly but also store in memory for future **retrieval** and testing. We intrinsically do not like that sort of pressure. And, if we add to this equation a general dislike of reading—if that is indeed the case—then, we have a challenging situation on our hands. These are some of the many reasons that we do not like this sort of reading.

6   At the very least, when we read for practical purposes, we usually see direct and immediate results. For example, there is an end product after following the directions on a recipe. With pleasure reading, we read as and when we please and if we do not understand what we have read, we do not worry about it. Besides, usually there is no reason to have to memorize anything. It is no wonder that we do not like textbook-type reading. However, the reality is that if we are going to be studying for academic purposes, comprehension of this type of reading will be crucial in determining our success.

7   Note: Although this is considered a formal text, I have purposefully kept my writing style informational yet conversational so that I do not further alienate those of you who do not like to read much. After all, who wants to learn about reading by reading a boring text about reading? It would defeat the purpose of this text! I especially want to reach the readers who have not yet discovered the joy and satisfaction of reading.

A Note on Research-Related Reading

8   You may think that only scholarly people **engage** in reading for research. However, most people research information whether they are in academic situations or not. This is especially true in today's technological world when information is at our fingertips just waiting to be discovered! For example, a mother who searches the Internet for information on the medication prescribed for her child's illness is researching. Furthermore, she may synthesize this information with the prescription "flyer" given to her by the pharmacist. Similarly, a person who plans to relocate to another state may read about the demographic profile, employment opportunities, and available housing from various books and articles, from the Internet, and from asking friends who live in the area. When we are researching for personal reasons, we usually do not have to authenticate the sources of our information although it would be advisable to check for accuracy, especially if you are making important personal decisions based on the information collected.

Academic Research

9   However, when we are researching for academic purposes, we must make sure that our sources are **credible** because the research we present will be scrutinized by experts. What this means is that we need to pay attention to who is saying what. Is the "Who" someone who is known to be an expert in the topic and therefore, someone who can shed credible light on the topic? Is the "What" **relevant** to the topic you are researching? The types of delivery systems (online sources, books, articles, etc.) from which you are obtaining your information are not important although in a good research paper you are expected to cite using all these types of information systems.

10   The current problem, in my opinion, is mostly related to our excessive reliance on the Internet and the information overload that we feel we are constantly bombarded with wherever we go. Because the younger generation is one that relies heavily on the Internet for not only information but also for the processing of information, and because many people in our society feel a need for instant gratification, people are tempted to solely use the Internet as their primary source of information. This is understandable given that so much information is only a mouse click away. However, keep in mind that for scholarly research, much of the embryonic information on the subject will probably be tucked away in some books in the library. This means that although you will be able to check via the Internet what library the book is located in, and if it is available, you will probably still have to have the book in your possession in order to read it. Of course, this does not mean that the Internet is not a good source of information. However, it is important to remember that it is not the only source of good information and that much of the information prior to the computer-age is not online and, to turn in a good research paper, you will be expected to cite sources in addition to those you find on the Internet.

Credible Websites

11   Good research means that you have read most of the right experts who have been published in all the right Internet sites, books, journals, and such. What are the right Internet sites? This depends. If you are doing scholarly research, and if you have library access, you can log into the library databases. You do not have to be physically present at the library.

You can log in from anywhere you have Internet access. Although some databases may require a fee, many are free. Library Internet databases are vast, and you can conduct your search in your subject area database (e.g., science, education, etc.) for journals, articles, newspapers, and such.

12   If you find full-text articles in these databases, you can read them online; however, many times you have to go to the library and find the material there. Sometimes on search engines, such as Google.com, Ask.com, or Bing.com, you may find full-text articles, and this may help you avoid a trip to the library, but you must know which expert's online article you want to read. Otherwise, you may have literally thousands of hits on the topic, but the authors may not be credible in your field of research. Alternatively, the piece could be written by a **prominent** researcher, but it may not be scholarly enough to be published on a professional database, and that is why it resides in public search engines only and not in the Internet archives of a credible site. Please note: Public search engines have links to some professional websites and nonprofessional websites. Usually credible sites on the Internet are the ones that give you access to information through libraries and major universities as well as federal, state, and local government sites.

13   Reading information from any site to research for personal reasons is your **prerogative**. However, please understand that because anyone or any group can post just about anything on the Internet, it becomes just as important for you to narrow your search by using credible sites. You are more likely to get accurate information from credible sites since that information has endured some **scrutiny** by experts in the field before it became worthy to be "published" online. How many times have you heard about someone self-prescribing supplemental medication based on something she read over the Internet? There are government sites, local community sites, and major news organization sites that you should get your information from. Government sites usually have *.gov* in their website addresses. Universities and other post-secondary institutions usually have *.edu* in their website addresses.

14   You must be vigilant in these matters, or you will not only get inaccurate information, but you will also get confused. Sometimes, websites may have official sounding titles, but you notice that the site is not as professional as you expected, or the text is too emotional, there are many grammar errors, and/or what is being said is not what you expected. Also, you may notice that these sites often do not post a location address or a phone number. These may be signs that you need to call the health department or the state government, or whatever agency oversees those particular affairs to check on the site's legitimacy. Sometimes, depending on the program your computer is run on, you may get a pop-up message warning, "This site has a poor reputation." Hopefully, you will avoid such a site! Again, I know that we are tempted to read the first thing that pops up on search engines and to consider that to be the gospel truth but—be forewarned—that is unwise! Much of the time, such information is misleading, and it is sometimes intended to spread misinformation (propaganda—you will read about this later).

15   Now that you have read all this good information about your research topic, how are you to synthesize and evaluate all the articles so that you have a better understanding of how the articles relate to each other and to the whole? This seems like a **daunting** task! The following are simple guidelines that I think should help you get organized and not feel terribly overwhelmed:

1. Narrow your topic of research as best you can.

2. Decide how many references you will need and what delivery systems you are going to use to get your information (Internet, books, articles, etc.).

3. Scan and skim for relevant information on your topic from these sources. Keep in mind what I said about credibility of sources and your criteria for #2 to select your reading material accordingly. Knowing key words (few words that express the topic) about your topic helps in expanding your online search for books, articles, etc. If you need assistance, check with your librarian.

4. Read and highlight subtopics and important concepts.

5. Summarize (paraphrase [put into your own words] main idea or implied main idea and major supporting details).

6. Notice information that is similar and dissimilar among the various readings on sub-concepts or subtitles and put into separate categories.

7. Explain the research topic and discuss how similar and different ideas have been presented and how your evaluation has added to your initial understanding. In some instances, such as critiques of literary material, you may be required to provide some response in the form of an opinion.

16   Keep in mind that libraries have many resources and that librarians are only too happy to assist you narrow your search or to find those key words. Moreover, most libraries have links on how to do research, what databases to use based on your topic, and other good information. Other good resources are the online dictionaries. Most times I use the online *Merriam-Webster Dictionary*. I particularly like that it has a link "defined for English-language learners" that provides a simplified version of definitions. When you have the time to surf the Internet, familiarize yourself with all these resources.

Online Reading

17   I have been asked how online reading differs—if at all—from reading a book. I have not done research on this subject; however, my observations have resulted in some definite opinions. First, I think there is little difference if you are reading an online book or a hardcover book. The difference is in the delivery system. I must admit that although technology has sometimes run **amok**, the convenience of online books is a definite plus! If you prefer reading books online, then, do so. It is wonderful that you are reading. A small but **negligible** difference may be that you cannot write on your online book. You see, even when I read for pleasure, I have the habit of simultaneously holding a pencil or a pen (when I am reading a text for information, then I most definitely am equipped with colored pencils and highlighters) because I like to process reading by writing comments and marking the text. This way, I feel that I am engaged with the author, the characters, and/or the material. Of course, I cannot do this on loaned books. However, if the books are mine, I oftentimes write in them. For example, I may circle a particularly powerful phrase or underline an interesting but unfamiliar word (You do not suppose that I know all the words in the English dictionary, now do you?). I would not be able to do this online. Otherwise, we would use the same mental processing online as we do while reading a hard copy. By the way (BTW—for those of you who are into text messaging!), I do not think that reading a novel online compares to romancing a book!!! I mean actually holding a book, turning the pages, all the while creating an intimate relationship between the author's words and your interpretation of them. As you can tell, I am from the old school!

18   Now, mental processing of other types of online reading, such as when researching articles or browsing through websites, is indeed different, in my opinion. I am unsure if online reading in such cases is somewhat **detrimental** to the development of our imagination and our brain's normal function of gathering information from its own databases. What I mean is this: If you are reading a hard copy of some information, you would probably have to rely on your prior knowledge or find other ways of solving comprehension problems that arise as you read material or words that may be unfamiliar to you. However, usually in online situations, there are links to unfamiliar words or links to more information on a topic; this tempting convenience is only a click away. Why would you, perhaps, agonize over what a term means when you can simply click on the link and probably be bombarded with more information on the topic than you can handle? And even if there are no links, since you are online, getting to search engines or resources such as the dictionary is so tempting that you automatically engage in this type of activity. Is this somewhat like using *CliffsNotes?* Do you give your brain a chance to figure out the problem? So then, what implication does this have in terms of reading comprehension or indeed critical thinking, which is the mother of all comprehension?

19   I have experienced—unfortunately too many times—when young adults cannot subtract, add, multiply, or divide because the computer is down, or they do not have access to a calculator. People have become over-reliant on these tools to do their thinking. Does the calculator have its uses? Of course it does, but that does not negate our learning to solve basic mathematical problems on our own using the tool at our disposal—our brain! So also, I find an over-reliance on the computer, and because many of you were probably born when computers were already a common household item like the television (unlike me!), the computer generation probably has had even less exposure to the type of critical thinking "older" generations had to do—without use of these convenient tools. I am not suggesting that this generation is incapable of thinking like previous generations. All I am suggesting is that perhaps some normal—and crucial—human thinking experiences have been taken over by artificial intelligence (computers)!

20   On a final note while we are discussing computers, think about how your formal writing may change because of your frequent use of "texting vocabulary." For example, what does "LOL" mean? When I first began to notice these sorts of terms in my e-mails, I was clueless! I had to ask when I could not figure them out in context. Of course, text messaging, because of its characteristic brevity, does not offer much context. For those of you who are clueless like I was, LOL means laugh out loud. My friend's 70-year-old mother explained to her daughter that it does not mean lots of love! What about "OMG" and "BFF"?

21   So, because we are now in an age where everything is a click of a mouse away and texting, etc., is the norm, I am beginning to see informal texting-type of writing in formal e-mails. When writing e-mails to friends or texting from our

cell phones, because of the very nature of this type of communication, we do not give any consideration to grammar or conventions of writing. We are doing so much of this type of writing that our formal writing is becoming **infused** with it, as well. This has caused much confusion for people who are still learning English. Another implication is that if most of the reading you do is of writing such as the one I have described, then it is like knowing nonstandard English but not standard English. You see, reading, writing, speaking, listening, texting, e-mailing, and surfing the Web are not only intricately and essentially interwoven into the fabric of our lives, but they also influence how effectively we process information within and across these modes of communication.

Application:

A. Write what you think the following words mean in the context of your reading. Then use the dictionary to check if you were right in your summation:

conscious, garner, utilitarian, retrieval, engage, credible, prominent, prerogative, scrutiny, daunting, relevant, amok, negligible, detrimental, infused

B. Based on your comprehension of what you have read here, answer the following questions:

1. In one sentence tell what you think this selection was about. (Remember that a sentence is a complete thought, and, therefore, you should write a sentence.)

2. In your own words, tell why you do or do not like textbook reading.

3. You have had to read textbooks before. What kind of strategies or techniques did you use to help you understand and study? Name at least two and tell how they helped.

4. Do you think that processing reading online is different from processing text in a book? Give reasons for your answers.

5. Tell in your own words why it is important to be selective about sources while doing research.

6. Tell what "intrinsically" means in this passage (Give yourself credit for trying to figure this out without the use of a dictionary.). Tell how you figured out the meaning.

7. Respond to my discussion on the influence of texting and e-mailing. Tell whether you agree or disagree and why.

Imaginary Vs. Real: Fiction Vs. Nonfiction

Chapter Three

Fiction

1   In a broad sense, written work is either characterized as a work of fiction or nonfiction. Fiction means made up. It is a work derived out of the author's imagination. It is usually written in prose form (the usual form of written and spoken language). Examples of fiction are romance novels and short stories. Danielle Steele's *Legacy* is an example of a romance novel while Edgar Allen Poe's *The Tell-Tale Heart* is an example of a short story. An example of fiction written in metered structure as in poetry or verse is William Shakespeare's play *The Merchant of Venice*. You will find that a narrative work—to tell a story or tell about event(s)—that is written in prose is usually much easier to comprehend than a written piece in meter because prose takes the form of ordinary language. Metered structure tends to incorporate many aspects of figurative language (refer to the separate section on literal and figurative language), which can lead to more than one interpretation.

Nonfiction

2   On the other hand, nonfiction is telling truthfully about a person, place, or thing. The authors present this information as if it were true. I say "as if" because there is no way for me to discover the truth of an author's writing. I can only judge whether something is truthfully written by perhaps the reputation of the author or my first-hand knowledge of the events/material presented. Therefore, whether the material presented is true or false would depend on the reader's knowledge of the material. This is why in literary circles there are often disputes about the **veracity** of biographical works (stories written about someone other than the author). In other words, you may read a book on Mother Teresa and find some inconsistencies. However, the author is considered to have written the book true to his/her knowledge of this person. Just because the book contains information that can be proven false does not make it fiction. Textbooks are examples of nonfiction, although we probably do not refer to them in this way. This text you are reading would be categorized as nonfiction. Perhaps there are some statements in this text whose veracity experts may find questionable. Nonetheless, the general rule of thumb is that I (the author) have written it because I believe that what I am telling is true.

Textbooks

3   Most textbooks are written in expository style rather than narrative. This makes sense since the purpose of expository writing is to **expound**, explain, describe, and/or inform. Textbooks provide information. Make the connection! However, what about

---

Subject-Specific Vocabulary:

prose: the ordinary language people use in speaking or writing

metered structure: systematically arranged and measured rhythm in verse

figurative language: used with a meaning that is different from the basic meaning; not literal

expository style: used to describe writing that is done to explain something

analogy: a comparison of two things based on their being alike in some way

history texts? Do they not sometimes use narration to tell about events? Of course they do; however, we do not discuss language in **absolutes**, and therefore we know that we may find narrative style in textbooks as well. The style will simply depend on the best format to present the information.

4   By now, you are probably asking yourself, "Why do I need to know all of this 'stuff'?" All you had signed up for was a reading course, and all you expected was to learn how to read and answer comprehension questions. And, from what you notice now, it seems that you are being **inundated** with a lot of mumbo jumbo about English. Well, my question to you is: Do you believe that thinking happens in a vacuum (no context)? It does not now, does it? Thinking happens within contexts of other things. Context would **encompass** all the sensory information we are receiving at any given time from our environments. Making sense of all this sensory input is what forces us to think. Similarly, reading and writing do not take place in a vacuum. They require thinking, and they encompass all that makes us literate, which is primarily our language, in this case, English.

Reading and Writing – Birds of a Feather

5   In most other English-speaking countries, reading and writing are not taught as separate subjects but are taught under the umbrella term of language arts or just plain English. In my opinion, it is because in this society we teach reading and writing as separate subjects that many students begin to think of them as two distinct subject areas, which they are not. That is why I keep discussing reading and writing terms and concepts and their interrelationship throughout this text. Therefore, for example, if you know the challenges in writing a book of nonfiction, you will understand the possible comprehension challenges you may face when reading nonfiction and vice versa.

6   Let us move on and discuss more terminology and concepts that we might encounter as we are required to read and write. As I have explained before, most of the reading you will encounter in college content-area subjects (such as science and physics) will be in textbooks written in mostly expository style. And, although expository style uses ordinary language to expound on a topic, academic language can be anything but ordinary! In other words, you will run into comprehension difficulty if you do not know sufficient vocabulary to make sense of the reading. Moreover, if you do not have sufficient background knowledge on content-specific vocabulary, you will have even greater comprehension challenges to overcome. For example, if you are reading a passage on the topic of football in the U.S.A. and, if you do not know what a Hail Mary is, you may run into a problem. When I first heard "Hail Mary" while my son was watching football, I thought that his team was not doing well and therefore, he was getting ready to pray! I did not have content-area or subject area background knowledge.

Some General Literature Terminology

7   However, in college English courses where the emphasis is on writing and responding to literature in its varied forms (such as drama and poetry), you will encounter the type of terminology I have found important to include in this text. A good understanding of reading is incomplete without discussing reading holistically. Therefore, you need to know the difference between fiction and nonfiction, and it would also **behoove** you to become familiar with the following terminology:

protagonist: central character in literary works, such as in works of fiction, who captures your imagination

antagonist: a character (or force) who struggles against or opposes the protagonist (central character)

genre: type of literary work, such as drama and poetry

elements of fiction/storyline/plot: problem or conflict, and resolution; the protagonist is the one who faces the conflict

point of view (POV): In English courses, *point of view* will likely refer to who is telling the story. It is defined by the pronouns (for example, *he, I, you,* and *they*) are used to tell the story. There are three types: first person, second person, and, third person (limited and unlimited omniscient). In first-person point of view, the narrator uses pronouns such as *I,* and *we* to draw the reader into experiencing the story through the narrator's eyes. It tends to create an intimacy between the author and reader. Second-person POV uses pronouns such as *you, your* and *yours* where the narrator speaks directly to another character or the reader. This usually makes the reader feel like he is a participant in the narrative. It is not commonly used in works of fiction. You may find the POV in interactive adventure stories, self-help books, and game books. Third person POV uses third person pronouns such as *he, she,* and *they.* The author writes the narrative as an outsider looking into the thoughts of character or characters. Third-person omniscient POV is when the narrator knows thoughts of all the characters and details of their worlds even before the characters do. In limited omniscient, the narrator has knowledge of all thoughts and motivations of one character. As you can tell in this book I have often used first person (I, we) to draw you into the discussion, and second person (you, your) to speak directly to you about reading. I have sometimes used third person (he, she) to make general statements about students.

8   You will realize that this preceding section is very basic and that my intent is to introduce you to these terms so that when you encounter them in your English courses, you will be somewhat familiar with them. During the course of your reading this book, you will notice that I have addressed point of view as perspective. In other words, whose point of view is being narrated?, or What perspective is the writer coming from? Perhaps this is one of the distinctions we make when we speak of POV in writing versus reading. It is my opinion that in writing courses POV is likely to be discussed as a style that an author uses to establish his intent, while in reading classes, we are likely to want to know whose perspective is being addressed.

9   Of course, the above are not all the possible terms specific to the content of literature. Far from it! I do not want you to be inundated with literature-specific vocabulary. You can examine literary terms on your own. You should be able to do so now that you know what sites are best to get this sort of information from.

Reading Literary Pieces

10   In English courses, you would probably be asked to analyze the literary piece that you have to read. Would you be able to figure out, if you have to, what motivated certain characters to react the way they did based on their behaviors and what they said? Would you be able to understand how they were essential to the plot/storyline? You may think that you may not be able to engage in such analyses. But, do you not analyze characters in movies in this way? What if the Joker were not part of the Batman movie plot? Would the movie still be viable? Was the Joker's character of equal importance or almost equal importance in the movie? Can a nemesis have equal importance to the story as the hero? Of course, you would have profound answers to all these questions. You do this all the time. You even talk about the people in your life and their motivations and their contributions to problems and solutions in their lives—and sometimes your own life! If you can analyze these "stories" (After all, everyone has a story to tell.), why would you not be able to analyze one that you read? Sometimes I think it is the fear of not being able to comprehend written material that results in a self-fulfilling prophecy.

11   The only challenge I think literary reading would present is if you had limited background knowledge about the figurative language and vocabulary used and even the author's style and background. I mention author's style because your analysis of the material is **facilitated** if you are familiar with the types of figures of speech (such as similes and metaphors) he uses and what point of view he is coming from. These sorts of analyses we do in our daily life subconsciously because we know what position the "storyteller" is coming from. Usually we understand the literal colloquial language the person is using. And, if we do not understand, we ask.

12   You may be familiar with the music of Bob Marley. If you are, would your analysis of Bob Marley's song lyrics be more in-depth than someone who is not as familiar with his work? (Refer to an analysis of Bob Marley's *Concrete Jungle* by Jeffrey Fraser in Part Four. Would you agree/disagree with his analysis? What would you delete or add to the discussion?) Moreover, can I not suggest that lyrics of songs are much like poetry given voice by being set to music? Song lyrics often employ the same types of figures of speech as do poems. This is also true for when we are reading. Again, I think I am making a case for the importance of background knowledge and vocabulary development. In the context of this discussion, you may also think of Tupac's song lyrics. Every time you listen to your favorite song, you may want to analyze the songwriter's use of words to convey message(s) and to establish a tone, as well as your own background knowledge that makes this sort of analysis possible.

13   In works of nonfiction, such as biographies and documentaries, would it be that difficult to understand the author's motivations for emphasizing some characteristics of the central figure and not others and/or to describe some events in greater detail than others? Perhaps some major events are left out. Why? A history book may, for example, have been

written from an author's **ethnocentric** point of view. In a history book about the United States, perhaps the Native American people's contributions to this country were either **glossed over** or not fully explained to the same extent as were the contributions of other ethnic groups. You would have to ask yourself such questions. You would have to be the judge of that when you are critiquing such works. When you learn about such skills as bias, fact and opinion, and argument later on in this text, you will be able to tie them all in to these types of higher-order analyses. One thing you must do: Always strive to look for the interconnectedness of the ideas presented in this book. Only then will you see reading in its entirety and understand your place as you evolve into a **proficient** reader.

Application:

A. Write what you think the following words mean in the context of your reading. Then use the dictionary to check if you were right in your summation:

veracity, absolutes, encompass, expound, behoove, inundated, facilitated, ethnocentric, glossed over, proficient

B. Based on your comprehension of the material have just read, answer the following questions:

1. Tell in your own words the differences between nonfiction versus fiction works. Why is it important to know this information? Give an example of each (book or other written piece).

Getting Wired: The Reading Brain

1   Throughout this book, you will notice that critical thinking is mentioned many times. This is because critical thinking is the umbrella under which fall all other types of comprehension matters, including reading comprehension. So, for the purposes of this reading course, what do I mean by critical thinking?

Critical Thinking, Metacognition, and Reading Comprehension

2   *Critical thinking* means to analyze, synthesize, evaluate, and thereby to interpret any given situation. Many times our interpretation leads us to reconstruct meaning. Therefore, a person thinks critically in order to construct and reconstruct meaning. Metacognition has a similar meaning and falls under the umbrella of critical thinking. It is a word often associated with reading and sometimes defined simply as thinking about thinking. When a reader is metacognitive, she not only analyzes and evaluates, but also monitors her understanding and fixes comprehension problems by drawing on a **repertoire** of strategies. In other words, while reading she knows when she does not know and tries to fix that problem by being resourceful.

3   As you probably have realized by now, I like to explain reading experiences or terms by relating them to real-life situations that you may encounter. Therefore, I oftentimes may use a word specific to reading, such as *metacognition,* and explain it using a nonreading example. The discussion about the car that follows is a nonreading example that explains how metacognition works while reading.

4   If you are working on the engine of your car, and you run into an unforeseen problem, you have to stop and analyze the situation to determine your next course of action to solve the problem. You may come up with several alternatives and you may try them one by one. You have engaged in critical thinking. Your mind has to process what you already know about car engines, what the car is "doing" (such as the way it drives, and how it sounds) as well as what you are doing. If you continue to work on the engine and find that what you tried does not fix the problem, you would then think of another way to fix the engine. One way of fixing the problem may be to call on a friend who is also a mechanic to ask for advice. The more ways you know of fixing the engine, the greater the likelihood that you will be successful in fixing the problem. This is similar to what we do when we read and run into reading comprehension difficulty—we use metacognition.

5   Suppose while driving, our car engine begins to make unfamiliar sounds. Do we not pull over to the side to determine our next course of action based on our prior knowledge about cars and driving? Similarly, when we come across something that we do not understand while reading, we stop to process it using prior knowledge. Prior knowledge encompasses all the experiences and memory that we have on any

Subject-Specific Vocabulary:

metacognition: awareness or analysis of one's own learning or thinking processes

dyslexia: a condition in the brain that makes it hard for a person to read, write, and spell

imprint: to fix indelibly or permanently (as on the memory)

given concept. Vocabulary is also prior knowledge. In other words, what words we already know are part of our knowledge base.

6   Again, continuing with the example of the car, if the car made a noise as though it were out of gas, and you have had such an experience before (your "background knowledge"), you would immediately be able to determine what that sound meant. However, if the car is making a sound that you have never heard before, you will have to pull over and figure it out. If you continue driving, the car may stall on you in traffic. In reading, if you continue to read without even knowing that you have not comprehended key concepts, your comprehension will likewise completely stall. Have you ever read something and suddenly found that you were clueless? During such times, you probably decoded (read) words without conscious realization that you were not paying any attention. Therefore, you comprehended very little, if anything at all. This may also happen when you are distracted with problems, worries, or illness.

Importance of Background Knowledge

7   How much background knowledge you have about anything will determine how effectively and efficiently you can solve a problem related to that particular situation. Similarly, how much background knowledge you have about a subject area is crucial to understanding a reading passage. Background knowledge in reading includes the amount and type of vocabulary you own. I say "own" because once you know what a word means, and you know its many uses, and therefore, you can use it in proper context, you own that word. You own it to use it as and how you please to express yourself in speech or in writing. Since reading involves words, and words translate to vocabulary, it is essential that you build your repertoire of vocabulary words. The more vocabulary you know, the more you will be able to comprehend. Similarly, if you wanted to be familiar with your car, you would have to know its mechanics; otherwise, you would have to rely on a mechanic to determine what is wrong.

8   Background knowledge includes **nuances** that are unique to the English language. It is important to understand that there is a language culture around which nuances form, and being immersed in the language and its cultural context will enable a reader—just like any other communicator—to interpret these nuances (refer to chapter on *Say What?!? The Nuances of English*).

A Note on Dyslexia

9   Some people have what is known as *dyslexia,* a neurological learning disorder that affects a person's ability to read despite his/her average or above-average intelligence. Dyslexia manifests itself in different ways and in various levels of intensity. Usually, a teacher during a person's early school years will notice a problem and will refer the child for testing to the school psychologist. Other times, people may become dyslexic due to illness, injury, or medications. Schools and colleges have services for people who think that they might have some sort of reading and/or learning disability. Students should check with their schools or colleges so that they can get evaluated and receive the support and assistance they deserve to be successful in their academic goals. Refer to Karen Taghi Zoghi's selection on learning disabilities (Part Four).

'Imprinting' (Memory)

10   Now I would like to discuss what I refer to as "imprinting. To explain, I would like to share with you something I used to do as a youngster. In those days—long ago—when I used to go to the beach with my parents, I loved stepping into my father's footsteps as he walked on the wet sand. I was fascinated at how his footprints got a little deeper as I stepped and re-stepped into them. Likewise, when we process the same information several times, we are able to *imprint* that memory on our brain. Therefore, because most of college reading is for academic purposes, we will need not only to comprehend but also remember by processing the information more than once (imprinting).

11   We make sense of new information by associating the new information with something we already are familiar with (our background knowledge), and then we integrate the new information with the old. However, in order to study or to learn, we must process that information several times, preferably by using different methods, such as body-kinesthetic, hands-on, or auditory systems to commit information to memory. For example, we could repeat information out loud so we can use our sense of hearing (auditory), "act out" concepts like playing charades (kinesthetic), or take notes/mark

our textbooks (hands-on). This is why many college reading texts also speak of study skills because implicit in this concept is the idea that we will read, review, and study, and therefore, commit new information to memory. Do you recall cramming information at the last hour for an exam and doing well on your test? I am sure that you have had at least one such experience or know someone who has. We may have all done this at one point or another. Do you remember that material now? Probably not! This is because you have failed to "imprint."

12   This is also why it is important to practice reading skills because, at some stage, they become automatic, and we are able to find the main idea, the tone, etc., without much conscious thought. You have often heard that practice makes perfect. Therefore, you will understand that as you are practicing the reading skills in this book, you are also fundamentally reading because you have to read and comprehend in order to answer a question. And, the more you read, the better you get at solving comprehension problems, and the more likely you are to enjoy reading. It only makes sense that because you are feeling successful at reading, the more apt you are to read, and of course, the rest is obvious. Michael Jordan, who is considered one of basketball's legends, was expected to show up to practice. Basketball does not just take talent, but also requires critical thinking to strategize when necessary and practice to the point of automaticity. So also with reading.

Strategies

13   So what are strategies? *Strategies* are techniques that we use to "fix" a problem. They are like when we improvise. Something does not work, so we make something else work. I think that this is a human condition. We want to make sense of our world, and we want to solve problems; otherwise, we feel discontented. This is why I always thought that people who know how to improvise are indeed very smart, even if they never had formal schooling. These people look for ways to solve everyday problems by using their intellect. We find these people not just in institutions of higher learning but also in remote villages and in tribes we have never heard of. It is just people putting their critical thinking skills to their best use.

14   What might be some common strategies we use to "fix" reading comprehension problems? Rereading is one; another is looking up vocabulary in the dictionary or on the Internet. We have all used these strategies at one point or another. The larger an inventory we have of strategies, and the more knowledgeable we are about when and how to use them, and in what circumstances, the more likely we are to apply them successfully to reading comprehension problems. However, we need to be *metacognitive*. It means that we have to monitor for success and evaluate our reading progress while applying strategies when comprehension breaks down. In other words, is the strategy working? How well is it working? Would another strategy or a slight adaptation to this one be more effective? To be metacognitive is to critically analyze your reasoning while mentally processing reading. There is some research that suggests that the difference between "good" and "poor" readers is that good readers are metacognitive.

15   Contrary to popular belief among some college students, thinking is not detrimental to your health. Instead, thinking is good exercise for your brain. If you can think, with a little help, you will be able to master these reading skills required for your course.

16   Note: Part Two of this book addresses specific reading skills. At the end of each of these skills is a thinking strategy of self-questioning which addresses one way of fixing a breakdown of reading comprehension.

Application:

A. Write what you think the following words mean in the context of your reading. Then use the dictionary to check if you were right in your summation:

repertoire, nuances

B. Based on your comprehension of the material you have just read, answer the following questions:

1. Write an example of when you had difficulty comprehending in any context, and what strategy/strategies you employed to "fix" the comprehension problem?

2. What is the difference between reading to comprehend and reading to study?

Not-So-Strange Bedfellows After All! Speaking, Listening, Reading, and Writing

Chapter Five

1   Before we enter into a discussion about the interconnectedness of reading, writing, speaking, and listening, it is important to address the significance of being able to function well in these areas. This brings us to the concept of literacy and to be "literate." What exactly does all of this mean?

2   Before you begin to read the chapter, it is important that you become familiar with some terminology that may cause you some confusion. You will see three words used in this book frequently. They look and sound similar, so they may be easily confused. *Literate* is an adjective that means *able to read and write*. If you say that someone is a literate person, you are saying that the person is educated and can read and write. *Literacy* has the same root as literate, but it is a noun and means *the ability to read and write*. Literacy is essential for getting a good job. *Literal* is an adjective and has a very different meaning. When we use a word or phrase in the most obvious, ordinary/common, or usual sense, we are using the literal meaning. The opposite of literal is figurative. If you tell someone to "go fly a kite," the literal meaning would involve going outside on a breezy day to fly a kite. Of course, this is an idiom. We do not mean it literally. We interpret it in its figurative sense: we want the person to stop bothering us and leave us alone.

Literacy

3   To be literate used to mean that one had the ability to read and write—and, in some circles it still does have that limited definition. However, with new realities some now believe that definition to include listening, speaking, and information literacy. Knowledge in specified fields such as **multicultural**, cultural, and **ecological** areas also falls under the literacy umbrella. Why is literacy so important?

4   In 1948 The United Nations (UN) adopted The Universal Declaration of Human Rights. Article 26 of this document refers to all people's right to an education.[1] Education implies literacy. Therefore, the UN considers literacy a human right. If we give this idea some thought, it makes sense. History shows us that many rulers **oppressed** the underprivileged in their societies by denying them the right to read and write. In North America, this was the case with African slaves. They were denied

[1]Retrieved on 6/4/11 from, http://www.un.org/en/documents/udhr/index.shtml

Subject-Specific Vocabulary:

literacy: the ability to read and write

access to an education and were severely punished—and in some instances put to death—if caught reading or writing. Whites who dared to teach slaves to read were also threatened with bodily harm and were oftentimes **ostracized** from their communities. Women, regardless of race, were considered second-class citizens at best and were denied access to a quality education if they were educated at all. These were ways to control the citizenry, and it ensured power to the privileged few.

5   Thus, the act of becoming literate should instill in a person the sense of **empowerment** and the ability to function within one's society. The definition of literacy resides within the cultural and political contexts of each society. For example, in some parts of the world, technological literacy may not be important to navigate the political and social systems. Therefore, literacy may be defined as the ability to read and write. However, for most westernized societies, such as the United States and Australia, literacy may encompass not only the ability to read and write, but also to speak, listen, be technologically savvy, and be culturally knowledgeable. I think that all definitions of literacy would include cultural literacy since language—whether written or oral—occurs within the context of a particular culture and must, therefore, be interpreted within this context.

6   Why was this discussion important? Well, because in your quest to become a more skilled reader, you are engaging in the act of becoming more than functionally literate. Also, because we are going to be talking about the interconnectedness of reading, writing, speaking, and listening, it is important for you to understand that all these factors enter into your becoming a more literate person. In a democratic society such as ours, we rely on an informed, literate citizenry to effect positive change and to become empowered to participate in our political process. In essence, this means having a part in running our country.

Speaking, Listening, and Reading Comprehension

7   Did you have to go to school to speak or listen? I think your answer is probably "no." We learn to speak and listen from the significant others in our environment. Do you remember any instance during your childhood when the significant adult in your life was talking to you, and you were not paying attention or could not understand what was being said? Usually, the adult would then ask you, "Are you listening to me?" If you pay attention to these words, you will notice that the person asked about "listening" and not about "hearing." This is because the assumption is that you could hear. In other words, the sounds the adult was making were being received by your hearing mechanism (ears). "Listening" implied whether you had comprehended what was being said. And, in order to comprehend, you would also have to have been paying attention. And, in order to pay attention, you would have had to have the purpose for and the **motivation** to listen.

8   Similarly, reading comprehension is like listening to speech, whereas just recognizing words in print and calling them out without any understanding (reading without comprehension) is like hearing speech without making sense of the spoken word. You would also need to have the purpose for and motivation to read and comprehend. By this time, you must also have realized that writing is somewhat like speaking in print. The writer's intention—like the speaker's intention—is to get his message across without causing confusion for the reader or the listener.

9   Sometimes, for example, when a teacher is giving a lecture, you might start off actively listening and comprehending, but if the lecture becomes boring or your attention drifts off, then you are hearing the words but not making any sense of them. This is why when you may have lost focus while actively reading, you ceased to understand—just like when you hear but do not comprehend (listen). Listening, therefore, implies actively making sense of what you hear, just like reading comprehension implies actively making sense of what you read. This of course does not mean that if you are actively engaged in making sense of spoken or written words that you are guaranteed comprehension. If you do not have enough background knowledge on the topic (remember this includes knowledge of vocabulary), your comprehension of the material will likely fail. This is when you use strategies to fix the comprehension gap. However, if your background knowledge is limited in the subject area, then strategies may not help, and you may need to first become familiar with the information that you should have had as prior knowledge before moving forward with the listening or the reading.

10   Unlike how we naturally pick up language in our home and social environments, we attend school to learn to read because we have to first recognize and then make sense of the symbols (our alphabet) that represent the sound system and other graphic representations of our language system. However, once we become familiar with this system of decoding, comprehension follows paths similar to listening comprehension. Therefore, I always state: ***Hearing is to reading words (decoding) as listening is to reading comprehension.***

11   By the time you have enrolled in a developmental college reading course, you should have already been familiar with the sounds and graphic representations of English. You should also have become familiar with some rules of our language. English rules for decoding, as many of us well know, do not apply in all circumstances. Therefore, becoming familiar with these rules and constantly "trying" the language in environments that are conducive to learning standard English will assist a nonnative speaker with pronunciation and spelling. Investing in and actively using an English dictionary would help immensely. Rules for pronunciation and spelling, among many other things, can be found in most dictionaries.

12   If you need to familiarize yourself with pronunciation, you will find a basic guide in Part Four.

13   Look at the relationships in the chart below. Does it help to make clear the intimate connections between reading, listening, speaking, and writing? Notice how the words *make sense* (comprehend) are found in all these relationships.

Connections between Reading, Listening, Speaking, & Writing				
	write/s; to make sense	speak/s; to make sense	read/s; to make sense	listen/s; to make sense
you	✓			
reader			✓	
you		✓		
listener				✓
you				✓
speaker		✓		
you			✓	
writer	✓			

Application:

A. Write what you think the following words mean in the context of your reading. Then use the dictionary to check if you were right in your summation:

multicultural, ecological, oppressed, ostracized, empowerment, vernacular, motivation, coherent

B. Based on your comprehension of the material you have just read, answer the following questions:

1. Write a five-sentence summary on this section. Use your own words to express the ideas.

2. How can you apply the concept of "imprinting" on the brain when reading to study?

An Intimate Love Affair: Reading and Writing

14   When you read something that is written well, do you not think that it is an example of how to write well? Reading comprehension and writing coherently are like the two sides of a coin. One is heads and the other tails. I suppose whether we think of reading as heads or tails will depend on whether we are **partial** toward reading or writing. However, both are equally important and equally dependent on each other. The author depends on the reader to make sense of her words. The reader depends on the writer to write coherently enough for the reader to make sense. I know this only too well, and that is why I am writing in a way that I hope facilitates your comprehension of what I want you to read and comprehend in this book.

15   When you write a topic sentence, are you not writing the main idea of a paragraph? When you are asked to identify the tone of a written piece, do you not understand that you, too, inject tone in your own writing? When we speak of relationships as a skill in reading, are we not talking about transitions in writing? If you really want to know how interrelated reading and writing are, you should go over some of your written work (after you have read this book) and identify examples of some of the skills that you will have learned in your reading course. You will be amazed!

16   On another note, have you not noticed how speaking and writing have much in common? When we speak, we have to make sense so that the listener can comprehend. Similarly, when we write, we have to write coherently so that the reader can comprehend. In both speaking and writing, we need to string words together for our audience (listener or reader) to make sense. Without **coherence**, neither our speech nor our writing will make any sense. Therefore, when you are not sure if there is coherence in your writing, read your text to someone. You will be able to **gauge** if it makes sense or not. This is why oftentimes before turning in a written assignment or giving a speech, many people have someone else read or listen to it so that with feedback, the writing or speech can be made more understandable.

Application:

A. Write what you think the following words mean in the context of your reading. Then use the dictionary to check if you were right in your summation:

partial, coherence, gauge

B. Based on your comprehension of the material you have just read, answer the following questions:

1. Did the chart in this chapter help with your understanding of the connections among reading, writing, speaking, and listening? Give reasons.

2. Why do you think I referred to the relationship between reading and writing as "an intimate love affair"?

3. Write at least 10 sentences about your opinion of what you have read in this chapter. Now read what you have written. If someone else reads your written piece, would he/she understand it easily? Give reasons why.

A PPAT Down! Purpose, Place, Attitude, and Time

1 Before you read anything, understand the purpose for it. If you are reading for enjoyment, it will not matter if you are tired or forgetful. However, if you are reading for academic purposes, chances are that you will be required to study the material. Therefore, it would behoove you to pay particular attention to purpose, place, attitude, and time (PPAT).

Purpose

2 Your purpose for reading in college is mostly going to be for study. You will be reading this book to gain knowledge and to comprehend material you must read for academic or job-related purposes. Therefore, you would want to remember material from this course, especially how to apply the skills that you have learned. In other courses, you would probably have to memorize information for recall on exams and possibly for use in future courses and your career.

Place

3 Second, consider the place where you can read and study with the least amount of distraction. It helps if you have one special place in your home with a table and chair that you can call your own. It could be a corner in the room. Any time you go to that place, you will be reminded that you are going to be engaged in academic work, whether it be reading, studying, working on homework, or working on assignments. The place serves as a reminder of your purpose. It also takes the guesswork out of looking for a place to focus.

Attitude

4 Third, your attitude before and during reading is important. If you are overly tired, are sick, worried about a personal problem, or otherwise distracted, this will interfere with your attention span and the time it will take for you to complete your academic task. It will take you longer. Also, it will affect your motivation to learn because you will not be in the mood to read. Therefore, if you can afford to revisit your study time when you are in a better frame of mind, it would be a more efficient use of your time. However, if you do not have a choice, then you might want to try

Subject-Specific Vocabulary:

motivation: the act or process of giving someone a reason for doing something

some relaxation techniques before you approach your reading task. You may want to take some short (five to 10 minutes) reading or study breaks when you find that your thoughts are wandering off, and you have stopped effectively processing what you have been reading. Keep in mind that worrying about your problems while doing academic work is not going to solve your problems; instead, worrying will simply **exacerbate** the situation, making it worse with the additional problem of not comprehending because your worrisome thoughts are interfering with your reading process. Additionally, let us not forget that simply having a negative attitude toward reading will **impede** your learning.

Time

5   Last, you must take inventory of your schedule. When is the best time for you to read this material and/or to do your homework (Homework is another form of studying.)? You may be the head-of-household, work a full-time job, and have to take care of children. I hear students complaining that they do not have time to do their college work. Unfortunately, there is no way to get around doing homework or class assignments. These activities are designed to **enhance** your learning experience. So, where are you to find the time?

6   We all know that sometimes we spend a great deal of time waiting. When was the last time you went to a scheduled doctor's appointment only to find that you had to wait for hours before you were seen? Could you not read or study during this time? What about waiting in line at the bank? Or on the long bus ride home? What about the time between your two classes? What about the time when a class got cancelled? Think of all the opportunities when you could have read but did not; instead, you waited, becoming increasingly bored, or you just simply listened to your iPod or talked on your cellphone. As a college student, you will have to prioritize, and if you have limited time because of your personal circumstances, you will have to use these opportunities to your advantage.

7   Some people have the time but do not know how to manage it. Make a daily to-do list and prioritize. The list should have only those activities on it that you know you will realistically be able to accomplish; otherwise, the list will only serve to overwhelm and disappoint you because you could not accomplish your objectives. All of this is called "time management." Also, knowing what sort of attention span you have for reading activities should help you plan such assignments during the time you are most likely to feel alert, and perhaps in small but frequent periods of time, so that you do not feel **overwhelmed**, since this would only serve to re-establish your firm belief that you do not or cannot read.

8   Most of what I have discussed here probably seems like common sense. And, it is! Figure out what works for you. This may involve some trial and error, but that is also a way to learn. When something does not work, we must stop and try other ways, but to continue with what is clearly not working for us is unwise. However, just giving up is not an option. You have enrolled in this course. This means that you took the first step to becoming successful in college. And, keep reminding yourself that you can. Your success or failure does not depend on others—it depends on your effort and your perseverance. It will not be easy; you will have to work at it!

Motivation

9   One last bit of advice: Do not expect your instructors to motivate and encourage you. Most instructors do, but their primary job is to instruct you in the subject area. Instructors cannot be expected to constantly motivate you to become engaged with subject matter just because you may require much encouragement. Motivation should come from within. You are an adult—or very near an adult now—and it is unrealistic for you to assume that in "real" life you will have other adults motivating you. If you are employed, consider your job situation. Does your supervisor have to motivate you in order for you to perform your job adequately? Therefore, you must rely on yourself and take responsibility to keep yourself motivated and to understand that you determine your own success or failure. Do not give any one else that power!

Application:

A. Write what you think the following words mean in the context of your reading. Then use the dictionary to check if you were right in your summation:

exacerbate, impede, enhance, overwhelmed

B. Based on your comprehension of the material you have just read, please answer the following questions:

    1. How are you going to incorporate the PPAT (purpose, place, attitude, time) concepts into your life as a student?

    2. In one sentence (a complete thought) tell what this chapter was about.

    3. Tell how you were able to make sense of exacerbate in question A above.

Sink or Swim! English Language Learner and Reading Strategies

Chapter Seven

Subject-Specific Vocabulary:

fluency: the ability to read accurately, quickly, and with expression

strategies: a careful plan or method for achieving a particular goal

"My English is not very good."

1   I hear this statement so many times that I can almost predict with some accuracy which students are going to say this and when. Let us analyze that statement. When you say that your English is not good, what you probably mean is that you do not have all the vocabulary that you need at this moment to be successful in listening, reading, writing, or speaking, or in all or in a combination of these communication skills. You think that this is because English is your second—third, fourth, etc.—language, and therefore it is difficult. In other words, it is not your native language—the one you learned from infancy, and therefore probably the one you do most of your thinking in. Yes, English—like any other "new" language for you—will be challenging until you master it. It takes about seven years before we can master a new language academically. This is an approximate figure, of course. No one can really determine how long it would take a person to become proficient in a language since these determinations would have to include such factors as how **immersed** a person is in a new language. Suffice it to say that in general it takes several years to learn a language well. After all, it takes a child many years to learn his mother tongue well, and he is immersed in language from childbirth (at least that is the hope). Moreover, if you are past **adolescence**, and you have had no other experience in learning a second language, this challenge will be even more **daunting**, but not insurmountable.

2   The more languages you know, the more marketable you are in this global society. Therefore, kudos to all of you who have **ventured** into learning a new language! Trust me—like most things, it gets easier with practice.

3   I am multilingual, which means that I speak more than two languages. I heard three languages spoken in my environment. Therefore, familiarity with the spoken form of all three languages helped me learn these languages in their written forms when I began to attend school. However, I heard English most often, and this soon became the primary language I communicated with both at home and at school. Therefore, I do most of my thinking in English, and I am most comfortable communicating in English. What language do you think in? What language do you dream in? And, are they the same language?

Learning Another Language

4   Some advice for those of you who are parents and in bilingual households with young children: If you want your child to be familiar with both languages from an

early age (a very good idea!), then it would probably be best for one parent to communicate with the child in the one language while the other parent communicates using the other language. In this way, the child does not become terribly confused, especially if the languages are vastly different (for example, French and Arabic). However, the language that is predominantly present in the child's environment will probably determine his primary language. In other words, if you are communicating with your child in Arabic while your spouse is speaking to him in French, and you live in Saudi Arabia, your child will probably become more fluent in Arabic sooner than in French because he probably will be influenced by all the Arabic language in his environment. Notice how I use the word "probably" a lot. This is because I have based my advice on my observations and experiences. Also, I know that there are no absolutes when we discuss language.

5   Please realize that English can be difficult even for native speakers of English. How is this possible? Well, if you are only familiar with nonstandard English (Ebonics, Spanglish, etc.) and/or you do not have the vocabulary to be successful in your particular environment (academic, technical, etc.), then you, too, will have difficulty with standard English (the kind of English found in textbooks, used in academic settings, and in business and professional careers). However, know that nonstandard English has its uses. A community language (nonstandard form of language) has its advantages in that it allows us to successfully communicate in our social environments. And, this is good because, after all, the purpose for speaking is to engage others and to communicate with them. We must keep in mind, though, that when we interview for a job and when we communicate for academic purposes, we are required to use standard English. Therefore, we must become familiar with the sort of vocabulary that is used in these settings.

Translating to Assist in Comprehension

6   In my opinion, "new" English language learners translate English words into their native language in order to comprehend. In other words, if you speak Creole (Haiti) as your first language, then you are likely to take English words and translate them mentally into Creole so that you can make sense of what you are hearing or reading. This is because our brain likes to feel comfortable; once we understand what we are supposed to understand, our brain's sense of well being is restored. Therefore, we revert to comprehending in our mother tongue, and then translate that comprehension back into English to respond to reading and/or the speaker. This extra step is sometimes the reason why it takes a reader longer to complete reading comprehension tests. This back and forth translation will affect the reader's reading fluency (reading fluency includes reading rate) and comprehension. We can make an argument for this when anyone is learning any new language.

7   As we become more and more familiar with English—or with any other language for that matter—and are reading with fluency and comprehension, the less we are likely to **rely** on our native tongue to make sense of what we are reading. This means that we are becoming more proficient in reading in English which translates into quicker processing of test questions or responding in a conversation. Sometimes, we may find that we continue to rely on translation to make sense of difficult material, and this is perfectly normal. We rely on whatever means we have at our **disposal** to make sense of our world, and even after we become proficient in English, we may revert to translating in our native tongue when we encounter emotional situations or language that is difficult.

Subvocalization

8   A subconscious technique that I notice both nonnative and native speakers use when making sense of written material that is difficult to comprehend is reading aloud enough for themselves to hear. This is called subvocalization. I have news for you. I do it, too! It is almost a reflex action of the brain that has become uneasy or uncomfortable with noncomprehension. Let us say instead that the brain has lost its sense of equilibrium—a sense of well being. Remember how often we have been told that the more senses we use in making sense of something, the more we are likely not only to understand it better, but also to remember it? Well, the same situation occurs here except that we do this subconsciously. The brain feels that if it can hear the words, then it is more likely to understand the written material better and to remember it more for future retrieval. This is also why sometimes when we are trying to memorize something, we have a tendency to repeat it aloud to ourselves over and over. It is a valid strategy that works! Use it when you proofread and edit your own writing, too!

What Can Be Done?

9   What can you do to become more proficient in reading? Well, for one thing, you can read more so that you become more familiar with vocabulary and its uses that you do not now know. If you do not have time to read, you can listen to audio books, and you can do this while you are doing household chores, driving to and from places, riding the bus, or waiting in line. You can make the acquaintance of someone who knows and uses more English vocabulary than you, and who speaks in standard English, and you can make sure that you speak only in English with this person. This gives you practice and exposure to the type of vocabulary you may see in written text. You can listen to television programs that you know will provide you with vocabulary as well as formal ways of speaking, such as news stations or the Discovery Channel. You can begin by reading simple stories and articles of interest and then move on to more difficult reading so that you continue to increase your vocabulary. The more you are immersed in English and the more you practice it, the better you will be in processing written material. I would say this is probably true of most languages.

10   You ask me: "All this advice is good, but where and when do I find the time to read and do homework (practice)? I have two jobs, a family to raise, and other pressing obligations." In this society and during this time in our history, we all face more challenges in our lives than ever before. We find ourselves having to prioritize and to reanalyze our situation many times over which often involves reshuffling our priorities. However, it would be safe to assume that learning to read is a priority for you, because you are taking this course.

11   First, I want to give you a tip on how to get started with reading. Find a space in whatever environment you want to read. If you can, set that space up with a simple table or desk and a chair—even if this happens to be in your bedroom. This will be your little "corner of the world" where you can go and focus on academic activities such as reading. Whenever you go to this "space," you will be going there with one or more of the following purposes in mind—to read, to do homework, to work on an assignment, or to study.

12   Second, we are going to talk about when you can find the time to read—perhaps after everyone has gone to bed so that you are not disturbed. What about when you go to a doctor's appointment, and you know that you will have to wait to be seen? What about when you have to go to the bank on a busy day such as a Friday when people are cashing their paychecks, and you know that you will have to wait in line? Think of every time that you have had to wait for this or that, or for this person or that person. Would it not, therefore, make sense to carry your reading with you? This serves two purposes: One, you get something accomplished (reading) while you are waiting, and second, you do not get bored and impatient while waiting. If you are having a strong feeling of déjà vu—you are not wrong! I have addressed these same issues at length in an earlier section (this is fantastic—it means that you were actively processing what you have been reading). I suggest that you read or reread the preceding chapter of this book, "A PPAT Down! Purpose, Place, Attitude, and Time."

13   I suggest that once you become comfortable with reading you should "stretch" your mind with more challenging reading. What exactly do I mean by this? "More challenging reading" means the kind of reading that will take you out of your comfort zone, will stretch your thinking in problem-solving situations (such as some unfamiliar vocabulary, and some very complex sentences), and will advance your comprehension skills. In other words, reading that will challenge you to think critically! This is not to say that reading at your comfort level with familiar vocabulary does not challenge you to think critically. It can and often it does. Many times profound ideas are expressed in simple language. For example, in Part Four you will find quotes (courtesy of Karen Taghi Zoghi), some of which express profound thoughts with simple words.

14   Sometimes, students who consider themselves "readers" are surprised that they are taking a developmental reading course. According to them, they do like to read and have been reading. Therefore, when I ask them if they are readers, they tell me: "I am a reader because I read a lot." If you fall in this category of students and feel that you do not belong in this class because you are a reader, then you must ask yourself about the kind of written material that you have read. Have you read only material that keeps your brain comfortable and does not stretch your thoughts? In other words, have you mostly read material that does not contain or has only a few unknown vocabulary words here and there? If the answer is yes, then this may be one of the reasons why you have had to take this course. You have not given yourself the opportunity to increase your vocabulary by reading more challenging text. You have become comfortable with the vocabulary you know, which may not be adequate to be successful in an academic setting. Therefore, you should be reading at least one level above the level you are comfortable reading at now.

Readability Levels

15   How do you find out at what level you are reading? If you were in school, reading specialists would have administered certain kinds of tests, such as informal reading inventories, that would help them determine your reading level. For college students, I have found (courtesy of my friend, Althea Duren) an informal way to estimate a reading level. If you go to http://homeschooling.gomilpitas.com/articles/060899.htm, you will find that there are two tests: the Reading Skills Assessment Tool and the San Diego Quick Assessment test. Both of these tests estimate your reading level. The directions are easy to follow. You may decide to take either one of the tests or both. In my opinion, taking both tests and averaging the results may give you a better estimate. Remember that these are informal ways to check for reading levels.

16   On this website, you will encounter terms such as "independent level" and "instructional level." Also, there is a term in reading circles called "frustration level." "Independent level" refers to the level at which you can read and comprehend with comfort. "Instructional level" (your learning level) is the level one grade level above your "independent level" (your comfort level). It is the level at which you are likely to learn new vocabulary and stretch your thinking. The "frustration" level is the level at which reading becomes so challenging that it interferes with comprehension.

17   Let us suppose that you took these tests and determined that your independent reading level is at 6.2 grade level. This means that you can comfortably read text that would be appropriate for a reader in the second month of his sixth-grade school year. If you are reading often, but only at your comfort level of 6.0 grade material, then you are not likely learning new vocabulary, which is crucial to your success in college. Therefore, you would start reading material at the next grade level of 7.0 (your "learning" level) until that level of reading becomes comfortable for you. Once 7.0 grade material becomes your "independent level," then you could move up to 8.0 grade reading.

Finding Reading Material

18   This advice is not carved in stone. In other words, just because you are reading at a 6.0 grade reading level does not mean that that is the only level you can read. In high school and in college we often have to deal with texts that are written at or above the 12th grade reading level and we manage to get through the content because we are resourceful when it comes to learning. Sometimes we are not conscious about how resourceful we can be. We do not have a choice to match the reading levels of our textbooks to our "learning" level. That is why sometimes we find these texts so challenging that we become frustrated and stop reading and therefore, learning. However, what is important to remember is that we can and often do control the type of reading we engage in for pleasure. Knowledge of your independent reading level will help you select reading material based on its readability levels.

19   Therefore, if you want to develop your vocabulary, you should read material in which you will encounter some unfamiliar vocabulary. In this section I have only provided you with a **rudimentary** way to find your learning level (instructional level). I know that in high school and college, you may not have had or have a choice with difficult text. Therefore, at least outside of the academic setting, you can choose to read material using the advice I have given you. Now, it is up to you to do something about it. One thing is for sure: You will not be able to avoid reading in college!

20   To give you some idea of what levels of comprehension are associated with these varying levels of readability, I had to do some research. Although this book is not research oriented, this was specific information I did not remember and had to seek it from another source. I found out that according to Gunning (2006), students are successful when they know at least 95 percent of the words and they comprehend text at 70 percent or more (p. 22). This is what I referred to as your learning level. Gunning also states that when students know at least 98 percent of the words and comprehend text at 80 percent, they are reading independently (p. 22). This is what I referred to as your "comfort" level.[2]

21   What if you are reading at an elementary or middle school grade-level? Do not be discouraged. We all have to start somewhere! How can you find material to read that is interesting for adults (whatever your age) that is just right for you? In some schools, the reading specialist has the *Accelerated Reader List*, which is a compilation of fiction and nonfiction books—with their corresponding reading level—for kindergarten through 12th grade. This list also gives interest levels. You can go to the following website to find books related to different reading and interest levels: http://www.arbookfind.com/UserType.aspx.

[2]Gunning, T. G. (2006). *Closing the literacy gap.* Boston: Pearson.

Libraries

22   We are fortunate that we have libraries in our learning institutions and in our communities. All you have to do is ask your librarian. Librarians are wonderful resources, and they are happy to help you find reading material. They like nothing better than for you to check out books and to give you advice about the type of reading material they have. Tell the librarian what sort of subject/topic you are interested in and also inform him that you want reading material at a certain readability level. I am sure that the librarian will be able to direct you to such material, and then you can make up your own mind. If the librarian cannot help you, ask your instructor(s). If a community has a large population of ELL (English Language Learner) students, community libraries as well as college libraries stock their shelves with books for adult interests at varying readability levels. Library services are free—make use of them. First, begin by getting a library card and checking out a book! You will instantly feel like a reader.

23   While we are on the subject of libraries, please understand that the modern library is anything but just a repository for books and magazines. You can find audio books, videos/DVDs, music CDs, etc. Libraries have workshops and elaborate websites with links that help students with their understanding of how to do research, how to look for books, and how to check out books. And, fortunately for us, most of these services are free.

Readability in Writing

24   You probably have guessed by now that your own writing has a readability level. How do you find that out? If you have Microsoft Word 2007 or 2010, you can click on the help link http://office.microsoft.com/en-us/word-help/test-your-document-s-readability-HP010148506.aspx and follow the instructions there to set your program to automatically provide you with the reading level of your written work. In this way, every time you write, you can click on "Review" on your toolbar and then click on "Spelling and grammar." This should give you an estimate of your written sample's readability level. Keep in mind that the readability level will only show after the text has been checked for spelling and grammar. You could also choose to put in sample text from your textbook to ascertain the book's readability level. However, this is not usually practical because it means that you would probably first have to type in this information – unless, of course, this is "Copy-and-paste" text from Internet sources.

25   You may obtain this sort of information at other Internet sites as well. Follow the directions below (courtesy of Karen Taghi Zoghi):

Step 1: Open your Internet browser and type in the following web address: http://www.addedbytes.com/lab/readability-score

Step 2: Type in a sample paragraph from the book you are reading, or copy and paste a paragraph of your own writing.

Step 3: Click on the button "Check Text Readability."

Step 4: Scroll down the page of the results "Text Readability Scores" until you see the "Readability Formula – Average Grade Level." This is the average of all the formulas used—the approximate grade level of your text. (These formulas are not only easy to use, but are also the ones frequently used.)

Just as some restaurants and businesses close down, so may a website. If you cannot access the above site, try one of the following:
http://bluecentauri.com/tools/writer/sample.php
http://www.online-utility.org/english/readability_test_and_improve.jsp

26   According to the directions provided, you could input some of your written work to find out its readability level. This means the grade level at which other readers are able to read and understand your written material without too much difficulty (their independent reading level).

Reading Material

27   Another important factor in developing your reading skills and vocabulary is the kind of reading material you decide to experience. For example, if all you read is about sports—even if you are reading at your learning level—then your background knowledge and vocabulary, which are so important for reading comprehension, will probably mostly be sports-related vocabulary. If you want to pursue an undergraduate degree in business, you are not likely to find much vocabulary or background knowledge that is business-related in your knowledge base if you only read about sports. Therefore, you should add to your reading selections some reading material from business articles found in sources such as magazines, journals, and newspapers. This content-area knowledge (This refers to background knowledge, and vocabulary and terms that are particular to a subject area.) would help you later when you encounter written material in business textbooks.

28   However, just because you are a business major, does not mean that you are only going to encounter business textbooks during your studies. You will have to take core courses from areas such as the humanities and the sciences. I suggest that you expand your reading experiences to include more than one area of interest. Moreover, also understand that just because you have been reading material in sports at your learning level does not mean that you are not learning vocabulary that is **generic** across subject areas and that is crucial to your understanding of any written text. This type of vocabulary is nonsubject-specific or noncontent-specific vocabulary.

29   What about all the reading you do surfing the Internet and reading e-mails, text messages, and ads? Again, it depends on what kind of material you are reading. If the material you are reading is poorly written and/or if the reading has links for every concept, you may miss out on experiences that require solving real comprehension problems that you will encounter when you read textbooks. Usually, in books you will not find convenient links to make problem solving easier for you, although footnotes in textbooks could be broadly compared to links found in computer reading. Reading e-mails can also cause confusion about good writing. I have noticed that some people do not pay attention to grammar, syntax (the way words are put together in sentences), or spelling when writing e-mails. E-mails seem to be written in a sort of nonstandard way. If you get accustomed to reading these and writing e-mails like these, you are likely to write like that when you write formally for college or your job. While I am on the subject, remember that it is best for you to look for information on secure websites. Just like you would look for information on an illness in a medical dictionary/encyclopedia, similarly you would browse the Internet to look for this information on an official government medical website or library database. I addressed this at length in the chapter "Why Bother to Read?"

Some Reading Strategies

30   The following is a discussion on some reading strategies that you are either familiar with, are using subconsciously, or are not familiar with. In Part Four, you will find additional strategies to help you with reading. Please understand that some reading strategies also serve as study strategies (or learning strategies) and vice versa. For purposes of this reading course, realize that the difference between a reading strategy and a study strategy is that a study strategy should also help you remember what you read. In many instances, you will find that what you had encountered as a reading strategy has been defined as a study strategy elsewhere. When you are reading for this course and answering reading comprehension questions, you have the reading material to go over and reread as you please; whereas, in studying, you not only read for understanding, but you must also retain those concepts in memory.

31   We know one thing without a doubt: We must first read and comprehend in order to study. As you take time to read and thoroughly analyze these strategies, think of the times that you may have had to use one or more strategies to aid in your reading comprehension. In your analyses, you must also consider in what circumstances a strategy would not be useful, or how a strategy could be adapted to fit your comprehension needs. To use strategies, you have to become *metacognitive*. This means that you need to be an active reader. You need to know when you know something, and when you do not know something. You have to **monitor** your own comprehension, and try to fix comprehension difficulties using strategies. You have to evaluate what strategy would be best to use to fix a given comprehension problem. If that strategy does not work, you have to use another one. In other words, you have to constantly monitor and evaluate your comprehension and adapt strategies to aid in your comprehension. By engaging in such thinking activities, you become metacognitive (Remember this word?). The following are some strategies that I think you might find useful:

---

[3]Ogle, D. 1986. K-W-L: A teaching model that develops active reading of expository text. The Reading Teacher 39: 564-570.

1. KWL (What do I Know? What do I Want to know? What have I Learned?) (Ogle, D, 1986):[3] I think that asking ourselves the first two questions after reading the title/topic and prior to reading the material helps us to jumpstart our active engagement with the reading material. Just like we have to rev up a car before we put it in gear and take off—especially on cold days—so, too, we have to rev up our brain (by answering the first two questions) and prepare to put it into gear for smooth processing—especially when we are tired and distracted. The first question helps you predict. So what if you find out when you start to read that you are way off the mark? Is your instructor going to have a harsh consequence for you? No, this conversation is only taking place in your head! The second question helps you know about the purpose for your reading. You are reading because you want something, are you not? The last question is particularly useful for learning. Having to regroup your thoughts (sort of like paraphrasing some of the important information that you have read and wanted to know) helps with remembering the material for future study experiences.

   The first two questions could also be asked as you are beginning to read new information or as you encounter subtopics in the reading material. Its use is not limited to the main title. Remember that if you are actively reading, then you are actively predicting what is going to come next. Try this: Have someone read out loud from a passage. Usually, if a person is reading fluently and with comprehension, you will notice that he has occasionally substituted one word for another, but the words are synonymous (same or similar meaning), and therefore it is okay to continue reading without correcting the reader. For example, the written sentence may state: The students were going to school to learn. The reader may read: The students were going to school to study. There is not that much difference between learn and study. This is why if there were just a blank in the place of learn, chances are that the reader would have put in either one of those words. This is because the brain thinks ahead and it is predicting as we go along when we are engaged with the reading. I have addressed this in some detail in the next chapter under the subheading, "Some Insight into the Reading Process."

2. Rereading: This is one of the strategies we commonly use on mostly a subconscious level. We reread the material that has caused us some confusion, and we may even reread it a little more slowly. When you reread, try to understand particularly long and complex sentences in parts. Break them into smaller thoughts, because often many thoughts are expressed in one difficult-to-understand, long sentence. Then, put all these smaller chunks of thoughts into the one overarching thought. Sometimes when we are rereading, we also may want to read out loud if we can. The additional sensory input of hearing assists in comprehension.

3. Paraphrasing: This means you put information read in your own words. If you run into difficulty, try to go back and reread, and then put this information into your own words from sentence to sentence as you check for understanding. If you have a short attention span and/or an attention deficit, you may benefit from making a conscious effort to paraphrase information in small chunks. This act will help you focus in order to work. Paraphrasing is another great way to study for tests because it helps you retain material.

4. Self-Questioning: When you run into comprehension difficulty, stop and reason it out by asking yourself logical questions to aid in your comprehension. When we understand, our brains have already self-questioned and answered (reasoned) and therefore comprehended, but this was done on a subconscious level. Thus, we cannot always verbalize how we know that an answer to a comprehension question is right. All we know is that it is right! It is when we run into difficulty that we have to slow down our thoughts and have a dialogue with ourselves.

   If you run into comprehension difficulty when you are trying to apply a reading skill to a comprehension question, I have provided you with a self-questioning technique that can aid you in answering that comprehension question. You will find this self-questioning technique at the end of every skill chapter. It is not all inclusive of the type of questions you may ask yourself. Therefore, you may add to those questions or you can delete from them. Alternatively, you may make a list of your own questions. It is important for you to have a strategy to address a skill-based question instead of becoming frustrated when faced with a question that you perceive as difficult.

5. APRILE (Activate, Predict, Read, Integrate, Locate, Evidence) is an acronym that I created to give you an idea as to the kind of "steps" you can take when having to read a selection and answer questions for a class. Please understand that there is no one, precise way to process reading. We all have our own way to approach reading. However, sometimes—especially when we do not want to read for an academic purpose—following simple

guidelines like APRILE can make the task a little easier. It works like a to-do list strategy. Also, keep in mind that whether you read the questions at the end of a selection prior to or after reading the passage is a personal decision. I prefer to read the passage first; otherwise, I find that the pressure of having to look for answers sometimes overcomes my need to comprehend what I am reading. Of course, if I am reading for a timed test, and time is of the essence, I may have to revert to reading the questions before the passage and then skimming (looking for main idea) and scanning (looking for specific information) for answers.

1. Activate prior knowledge by reading title

2. Predict what the selection is about

3. Read the passage and the questions

4. Integrate information from selection with prior knowledge

5. Locate evidence in selection that will answer the questions

6. Confirm Evidence in text

Application:

A. Write what you think the following words mean in the context of your reading. Then use the dictionary to check if you were right in your summation:

adolescence, daunting, ventured, rely, disposal, immersed, clarification, rudimentary, disheartened, generic, monitor, activate

B. Based on your comprehension of the material you have just read, answer the following questions:

1. (This question may not be applicable to all students.) Listen to someone speak to you in English. Do you find that while people are speaking to you in English that you are first translating what was said into your native language before you can respond in English? Why?

2. Describe one strategy/technique (not listed in this chapter) that you use when you run into reading comprehension difficulties.

3. List two things that you can do to become more proficient in English.

How and Why Does It Matter Anyway? Pronunciation, Reading Rate, Fluency

Chapter Eight

1 Many of my students speak English as a second language. They often ask me for help with pronunciation. Some tell me that they read slowly and have much difficulty with comprehension. Perhaps a discussion about pronunciation, reading rate, and fluency will shed some light on these issues and give students confidence that they will, in time, become proficient readers. They will learn that although proficiency in reading is a process that takes time, proficiency is achievable.

Pronunciation

2 When we speak of pronunciation, we are talking about applying sound-symbol relationships in a language to sound out a word correctly. To learn the rules of pronunciation, you will first need to have a basic understanding of phonics. Because you are either in a high school or in a college reading comprehension course now, pronunciation is an area of reading that your instructor will probably not address. Moreover, you are taking a reading comprehension course, which is different than reading words aloud. It is assumed that you know how to string together sounds to identify written words. Phonics instruction is usually the initial instruction in learning English. I want to give you a little background and tips on pronunciation. These are general and very basic. For more of an understanding of how to pronounce, refer to the pronunciation guide in Part Four.

3 First, you can refer to any **elementary** reading book to learn phonics-related rules governing the English language. As you read more, and with practice, you begin to subconsciously and automatically apply phonic rules to spelling, pronunciation, and decoding written language. This is similar to how we learn to walk by putting one foot in front of the other. As toddlers, we had to learn to do this consciously. However, once we were skilled at walking, we no longer had to think through the steps. This is also why you are reading this material more or less effortlessly unless perhaps you encounter a word that you have difficulty decoding. Remember that the problem with pronunciation is not whether you are familiar or unfamiliar with the meaning of the word, but that you are having difficulty with applying the phonetic rules to decode the word (break words into sounds and syllables). In other words,

Subject-Specific Vocabulary:

phonics: a method of teaching beginners to read and pronounce words

alliteration: the use of several words together that begin with the same sound; for example, Peter Piper picked a peck of peppers

syntax: the way in which words are put together to form phrases, clauses, or sentences

semantics: the meaning or relationship of meanings

[1] Retrieved on 6/4/11 from, http://www.un.org/en/documents/udhr/index.shtml

you may not be familiar with a word, but you may be able to pronounce it accurately. On the other hand, you may be familiar with the word and not be able to pronounce it. Being able to accurately decode a word and pronounce it does not guarantee that you know what the word means. This is why I emphasize that knowing a word is not the same as speaking the word correctly.

4   Second, if you do not know the pronunciation of a word, and you are not sure what rules to apply, check in the dictionary. Another way to check is to go on the Internet to Webster.com and type in the word. You can get a pronunciation that way as long as you have speakers for your computer.

5   Third, you can always ask someone to help you pronounce the word. However, you should make sure that the person you are requesting help from has good English pronunciation skills, or you may learn to pronounce the word incorrectly!

6   Finally, understand that English—and probably most other languages, too—operates on the simple notion that we need to string sounds, then syllables, then words together so **harmoniously** and efficiently that when we speak, it is like a musical symphony. We speak quickly in almost any language since we need to get our thoughts out almost as fast as we think. Therefore, for us to go from one sound to another and from one syllable to another, all our speech mechanisms have to work together.

7   Our nose, mouth, lips, tongue, teeth, and palate (upper roof of the mouth) are essential in forming the sounds needed in language. For instance, in English, to make the sound for the letter "m," the lips have to come together, but for the letter "l" the lips are open, and the tip of the tongue touches the upper front palate of the mouth. When talking with a friend over the telephone, we may ask, "Do you have a cold?" without his telling us that he is sick. Why do we make this **assumption**? We do this because his speech has started to sound uncharacteristically nasal (We need to have uninterrupted breathing to sound out words properly.). Similarly, when our grandmother forgets to put in her artificial teeth, she sounds strange, and it is difficult to understand her. This is because we need our teeth to make many sounds. Therefore, most words in English go from one sound position (When I refer to position, I mean the position of our tongue, lips, etc.) to another effortlessly—otherwise it would take longer to say the word. For example, if your tongue had to go from the back of your palate to the front and then the back again to string sounds of a word together, it would be laborious and would take longer than the milliseconds it should take. Therefore, words are constructed in such a way as to facilitate and **expedite** speech. If you must resort to contorting your mouth or your face, or if you find it physically uncomfortable to sound out a word—provided that you do not have a speech **impediment**—a general rule of thumb is that you most probably are pronouncing the word incorrectly. Stop and find the correct pronunciation in the dictionary or by asking someone. Of course, this discussion does not always apply to proper names. Sometimes names—especially foreign names—may prove difficult to pronounce unless we are familiar with that language's vernacular.

8   Say the following sentence quickly: "She sells seashells on the seashore." Sentences such as these are commonly called "tongue twisters." In literary terms, this is an example of alliteration. These tongue twisters make us appreciate the efficiency and speed with which we communicate in speech—most of the time!

9   When I come across a word that is difficult to pronounce, I check for the correct pronunciation and then insert forward slashes (see examples below) to separate the syllables (Syllables are small "chunks" of sounds.). This way, I do not have to repeatedly ask someone or go to the Internet to remember how to pronounce the word. I realize that this is basic advice and that pronunciation is complicated, but as I mentioned before, the assumption is that you know the basics of pronunciation already. Perhaps most of your pronunciation problems will be that of deciding where a syllable begins and ends, and what syllable needs to be stressed. By "stressed," I mean emphasized. Therefore, a useful and simple way would be to learn to separate syllables with slashes and to put stress marks for syllable emphasis when you are aware of how to pronounce the word. An illustration of what I am suggesting is as follows:

Word: police	po/lice'	(correct pronunciation)
	po'/lice	(incorrect pronunciation)
Word: academic	a/ca/de'/mic	(correct pronunciation)
	a/cad'/em/ic	(incorrect pronunciation)
Word: hotel	ho/tel'	(correct pronunciation)
	ho'/tel	(incorrect pronunciation)

Accents

10   Many English Language Learners (ELL) may hesitate to pronounce words or even to speak in English because of their accents. I, too, have an accent. Having come from another country, I have and will continue to have an accent. If I had come to this country before adolescence, I would probably have had no **discernible** accent by now. However, I came here as a young adult and although English is my mother tongue, I will continue to have an accent. For those of you who have been learning English for the past few years and for whom English is not your native language, there should be no surprise that you have a strong accent. And, remember that the older you were when you first began to learn English, the more likely you are to keep your accent although accents may soften with time.

11   However, keep in mind that people who come from English-speaking countries also have accents! Have you ever heard an English person speak? What about people from English-speaking Caribbean countries? They all have accents, too! Also keep in mind that the English spoken by people from England and by people coming from ex-English colonies is likely to be what we often term "the Queen's English." Here in the United States, we speak American English. There are some differences in spelling and in the pronunciation of some words. You never thought that English could be quite so **intriguing** did you?

12   Even though your accent will become less noticeable in time, it will probably never go away entirely, and others will know that you are originally from a different place. Accents are lovely and make us unique and add to our mystique! If you find that despite your efforts, most people who speak English have a difficult time understanding your verbal communication, you may want to sign up for accent-reduction workshops or classes. Check with academic institutions in your area if these types of classes are offered. After all, you speak to communicate with others, and if you find that people have difficulty understanding you, it may mean that you have to **resolve** that situation.

13   Becoming proficient and independent in reading is a process and for many of us a life-long journey. You may wonder what your status is now in this process. As you probably know, we first begin our reading journey by making the connections between the sounds we hear in speech and their corresponding representation in symbols (for example, our alphabets). Then we progress to understand the relationships between sounds and words, and we learn to decode (break words into sounds and syllables). Once we learn to decode, we begin to read (decode) with increasing speed (reading rate), accuracy, and with appropriate pauses and expressions. At this "stage", our reading is becoming more fluent. This fluency aids us in comprehending what we read. Fluency in reading then allows for us to become proficient and independent readers. During this entire process of becoming proficient in reading—and throughout our lives—we learn meanings of new words in context. It is important to note that reading is a process and, therefore, it takes time to become proficient. With increasing experience with reading, we get better at reading. Moreover, we all progress in our own time and in our own way. Some of you are probably at the "reading fluency" stage where you are improving your reading rate with accuracy and with expression, which helps you comprehend. Since reading fluency includes reading rate, a basic explanation of reading rate and reading fluency may be important to you.

14   In the following discussion on reading rate and reading fluency, note that although I have presented this material as two separate subsections, reading rate is a component of reading fluency. In reading fluency, you read quickly (reading rate) and accurately and with appropriate pauses and expressions.

Reading Rate

15   This term refers to the number of words you can read per minute. You could time yourself reading silently for five minutes and then divide the number of words read by five to calculate your reading rate per minute. Of course when you read silently there is no way to know whether you are reading accurately or not. And sometimes you may substitute one word with its synonym without changing the meaning of the text. This is why reading rates are estimates at best.

16   By the time you get to college, your silent reading rate, by some estimates, should range from 250–300 words per minute. However, the score for oral reading is 150 words per minute—usually "established" by eighth grade. This rate holds steady and is usually matched by adults, as well. It is important to note that I am only providing you estimates based on my experience and background knowledge. Although your silent and oral reading rates will depend on such factors as purpose and difficulty of text, remember that there are no absolutes. You should not be **alarmed** if your reading rate does not meet the mark. Like all things learned, this takes time. The more you read, the likelihood of your reading faster and with accuracy will increase. Think about how long it took you to speak English when you first started. You spoke fewer words a minute than you do now, did you not? What if you were to read in your native language? Your reading rate would be higher than when you read in English if you are a nonnative speaker of English.

17   However, even if you are proficient in reading, it may take you longer to read certain texts than others if you run into difficult or unfamiliar vocabulary, and if you have limited background knowledge on the subject. This would slow down your reading rate, would it not? Besides, what good is it to read fast with no attention to comprehension, since this will only mean that you have to reread, and the rereading will take up more time? Suppose a surgeon is reading complicated written directions crucial to the success of a complicated surgical procedure. She will probably need to read very carefully at very near 100 percent comprehension, and this would perhaps slow down her reading rate. On the other hand, if you are skimming the newspaper, you are not reading every word, are you? Good readers know that they must adjust their reading rates to match the purpose for their reading.

You will find many exercises to improve your reading rate. Two techniques that help me to read faster are:

1. predicting the content from the title and subtitles so you can take advantage of background knowledge before you start; this should not take longer than a few seconds depending on the length of the passage

2. skimming for main ideas within the title and subtitles so you form a basic summary in your head before you start

18   From the information you gathered from (1) and (2) above, you are now ready to read, but you will begin to do so with more speed because you have some predictive knowledge of what you are reading, and therefore, do not have to read every word. This way you are not literally reading every word but are reading only select words to make sense of written thoughts.

Some Insight into the Reading Process

19   Keep in mind that most times when we read, our eyes scan a few words at a time and lock in on the important word. When you scan, you are looking for specific information, and in this case, looking for specific words to fix your eyes on. Of course, when you first learn to read, your eyes will actually focus on every word. Pay attention to a 4-year old reading for the first time. She will read every word. However, when you read out loud, you will notice that you not only skip certain words sometimes, but that you use synonyms for the words that you have not even looked at yet. The word could be a word in a sentence that is on the next page. Before you even turn the page, you have probably correctly predicted a word or a synonym for it. This means that you are not simply reading words, but that you are also comprehending the material. Our brain realizes, at some point when we are becoming proficient, that we do not have to fix our eyes on every word. Instead we focus only on important words that we then string together in our head to make sense. Look at the following sentence:

She went to the party and had a good time.

20   Was it important for you to read every word? Perhaps at this stage in your reading development it is. However, if while you were reading your eyes registered the words "She went," "party" and "good time," you would probably have understood the idea as a complete sentence although your eyes fixed only on some of the words. You brain did the rest. Look at the following sentences and fill in the missing words:

She went to the party and had a good time.

It was _____ when she got _____. She was surprised when her mother _____ the door.

21   What words did you add, and why did it make sense to do so? Most people will put in similar words in these blanks not only based on knowledge of syntax (way words are put together in a sentence) but also semantics (meaning). However, our brain processes more than our eyes are seeing! My completion of the above sentence is: *It was late when she got home. She was surprised when her mother opened the door.* You probably had something similar that did not detract from the meaning.

22   Semantics and syntax are learned to the point of becoming subconscious analyses and only familiarity with the language provides for this level of automaticity. Therefore, the speed at which you can read will also partially depend on these kinds of factors. You will increase your reading rate and comprehension with knowledge and practice of the language, but you already know this, do you not?

23   Be careful: During reading, your mind can make sense of a sentence that is missing words (like the example given earlier); similarly, when proofreading your own writing, you are likely to process your incomplete written thoughts in the same way, and perhaps forget to add the missing words to your writing.

Reading Fluency

24   When we speak of being fluent in English, we mean that we are able to speak English easily and well. When we speak of reading fluency, we refer to our ability to decode accurately and read with expression (as well as to read quickly as I have explained before). When we are fluent, our brain is automatically decoding words, and our thinking processes are free to focus on meaning; therefore, we are able to read with expression. Reading fluency also means that you are reading accurately, quickly, and with natural pauses. If we were still having problems with decoding every other word, our focus would not be on meaning but on identifying the words, and we would not be making sense of what we were reading but merely calling out the words. Therefore, reading fluency serves as a bridge between decoding words and reading comprehension.

25   You could check for fluency by recording your reading for five minutes. Analyze how often you hesitate with words while your brain is trying to figure out how to decode and pronounce them. Then, ask yourself whether you easily understood the thoughts expressed, or if you had to reread. If you are an English Language Learner, then you will also probably be translating the information into your native language in order to process meaning. This, too, will interfere with your reading fluency. A strategy to improve fluency may be to listen to a CD while following along and reading the book (Some books are accompanied by CDs). As mentioned before, the more you read with fluency, the better you will be able to comprehend, and the more proficient you will become at reading. This is no big secret. However, do not forget that even if you are proficient at reading, your reading rate may slow down for a particularly difficult reading passage.

Application:

A. Write what you think the following words mean in the context of your reading. Then use the dictionary to check if you were right in your summation:

elementary, alternatively, harmoniously, assumption, expedite, impediment, discernible, intriguing, resolve, alarmed

B. Based on your comprehension of the material you have just read, answer the following questions:

1. How important is pronunciation to you? Why?

2. List two challenges you think you (or others) face in your journey toward language fluency.

Seductive, Elusive, and Versatile Vocabulary

1   Did the topic catch your attention? I hope so! It was meant to grab your focus and make you wonder why I referred to vocabulary as **seductive, elusive,** and **versatile**.

Seductive

2   Well, I think of words—and I hope that by the end of your experience in this reading course, you will think so, too—as tempting the senses (Therefore, I call them seductive.). Do we not use words to make a certain **impact** and to **appeal** to, for example, someone's sense of fairness, or sense of logic, or sense of love? What words we choose and when and how we choose to use them to communicate our message is what causes reactions in others, whether those reactions are unpleasant (for example, when someone gets angry or feels hurt) or pleasant (for example, when someone agrees to go out on a date with us or to give us what we asked for).

Elusive

3   Words are elusive. By elusive I mean that sometimes when we are communicating, either by speaking or in writing, we find that we cannot think of a particular word that we know would best represent our thoughts. It teases us by **barely** existing on the tip of our consciousness—sort of like a word on the tip of our tongue, but we cannot say it. It is almost like saying, "so close and yet so far." Has this happened to you? Now that I am getting old, I find this happens to me a lot and, trust me, it is not much fun!

4   (I hope that you realize the thought that went into this topic and all the topics in this book. Take the time to analyze each topic and after reading the chapter, relate the material back to the chapter topic to make the connections.)

Versatile

5   Words are so versatile! This means that they take on different flavors and can be used in many creative ways. There are words that are spelled and pronounced the same but have different meanings. These are called homonyms. For example, the word *bear*. *Bear* could mean the animal, or it could mean *to carry a burden*—the meaning depends on the **context**. Then there are words that are spelled the same, but have different meanings or pronunciations (homographs). An example is *bow* as in "Will you tie this bow tie for me please?" and bow as in "He had to bow before the queen." Then there are words that are pronounced the same such as *read* (past tense

---

Subject-Specific Vocabulary:

synonym: word that has the same or similar meaning as another word in the same language

antonym: a word of opposite meaning as another word in the same language

prefix: a group of letters at the beginning of a word to change its meaning

suffix: a group of letters at the end of a word to change its meaning

of 'to read') and the color *red*, but have different meanings or spellings. These are called homophones. What about *bear* and *bare*? You decide.

6   Sometimes words are given human characteristics, especially in literary works (For example, *The wind beckoned for my hat.*). We refer to this as "personification." Other times, words are given meanings that are not literal and whose meanings have to be discovered in the context of the message (For example, *The dark clouds of uncertainty settled in her mind.*). "Dark clouds" in this context symbolize unsettled and confusing thoughts. And, of course, words have other words that mean the same or very nearly the same (synonyms). Then people use words as puns. You may often hear people say, "Pardon the pun, but …" Puns are used when people want to make a play on words, usually with the intent to be witty. For example, I may say, "Pardon the pun, but it finally hit me why it was important to hit the ball so hard!" I am sure you noticed the play on the word "hit" with the first "hit" referring to understanding and the second "hit" referring to physical contact with a ball. Think of any puns that you have used or heard of lately. How can we not be in love with a language so fascinating and so much fun!

7   English is a living and fluid (another way to say "versatile") language, which means that it has always been evolving and will continue to **evolve**. This means that every year, the dictionary has new words added or adds new meanings for existing words. Take for example, the word *mouse*. "Mouse" means a small rodent and can also be used to refer to a timid person. While referring to the the Merriam-Webster dictionary, I was surprised to find that this word also means a dark-colored swelling around the eye caused by a blow. However, in contemporary times the use of the word *mouse* has evolved to include the manual device that we manipulate to control movement of the cursor and selection of functions on a computer. In fact, for this generation of students the primary meaning of *mouse* is probably the meaning associated with the computer. Some students—especially those from western societies—are unlikely to have seen a mouse (rodent) in real life and therefore, probably do not associate the primary meaning of mouse with a rodent. Then, there are words that were considered slang or substandard (not acceptable English) but are included in the dictionary such as *ain't* as in *I ain't going with you*. Although *ain't* appears in the dictionary, most people in academic settings still consider it unacceptable. I admit that I have difficulty using *ain't*, like I suppose most people from my generation, as I grew up knowing that the word was unacceptable.

8   Words are so powerful that besides representing their own meanings, they have the ability to evoke much emotion in us based on our own experiences with those words. For example, the word "father" has taken on a whole new character for me after my own father's passing away. I cannot process the word without thinking about my father even if the context in which the word is used has no connection with my father.

Words and Culture

9   Words also have cultural significance. Addressing my father as "Father" would be too formal in my culture and "Pops" would be too informal and considered disrespectful. "Dad" or "Daddy" is acceptable within my cultural circles and therefore, for my siblings and me, our father was referred to as "Daddy" when we were youngsters which later evolved to "Dad" as adults. Therefore, although every time I encounter the word "Father" I think of my dad and the void his passing has left in my life, it is the word "Dad" (or "Daddy") that packs the most emotional impact. Speechwriters and public relations people are familiar with the personal and cultural impact of words. For example, politicians (especially persons in high positions like the president) and advertisers rely heavily on the impact of words. Attorneys and judges are well versed in language because the way a word is used can determine the fate of a trial.

10   With all these amazing and truly fascinating characteristics of words, how can we afford to ignore them? Keep in mind, too, that language is power. In most countries, speaking the standard form of the official language of the country—the language in which business is conducted—is considered "smart." People judge others by their command of the language. Therefore, those who can express themselves well are perceived as intelligent, educated, upper class, and sometimes even of good moral character. For example, in Haiti, French and not Creole, is the language of power. In Germany, speaking High German is the language of power and an indication of education. Think of your country. How do you perceive people who speak well in your language?

Academic and Technical Vocabulary

11   You have heard about vocabulary enough to know that it is not only important for your academic success but for communication in general. For purposes of this text, any word that you do not know is vocabulary. There are two types of vocabulary: academic vocabulary and technical vocabulary. I like the term "academic" vocabulary because knowledge of this type of vocabulary is especially crucial in academic settings. However, I use this term interchangeably with "nonsubject-specific vocabulary" or "noncontent-specific vocabulary." Academic vocabulary is the vocabulary that makes you good in general English. Throughout this book, you will see that I have listed academic vocabulary from my writings in the "nonsubject-specific" category.

12   Technical vocabulary (or "subject-specific vocabulary" or "content-specific vocabulary") are words specific to a particular subject or field. For example, *hypotenuse* is a word that is specific to the subject of geometry. At your job, you may have specific words/terms that refer to certain **inventory** that the regular shopper may not know. Other examples of technical vocabulary can be found in the "subject-specific words" listed at the beginning of each chapter in this book. These words are mostly specific to the subject of reading. However, whenever I address the importance of increasing your vocabulary background, I am mostly referring to academic vocabulary, and I will **delineate** some ways of learning these. These strategies can be applied to learning technical vocabulary or even for learning vocabulary of any other written language.

13   How do we learn vocabulary? The answer is so simple that you probably have the answer to it. We learn vocabulary naturally in our everyday surroundings. Just as babies learn words from their environments and learn what these mean, so too, as we continue to grow, we pick up words from our surroundings. When we go to school, we pick up more words from the class and school environments. Teachers start to give us a list of words and their definitions and test us on them. However, in order for us to "own" these words, we must remember what they mean, how to use them, and in what contexts. For us to remember meanings of words, we have to use them in proper context over and over again. How do we use these words? We use them in our verbal and written communication with others.

Imprinting and Associating

14   We have to "imprint" these words on our brains (refer to my discussion about "imprinting" in the chapter "Getting Wired! The Reading Brain"). If I ask you how your teacher taught you to learn the new words she gave you, you might say that the teacher told you to write the definition over and over or to repeat the definition over and over and, therefore, commit it to memory. Someone else in class may say that his teacher had his class write sentences using the word. Others may say that they had to think of synonyms and antonyms of the word. Still others may say that they had to learn about root words and prefixes and suffixes. All these ways of learning vocabulary words, except for the ones suggesting that somehow repetition will help with long-term **retention**, are good. If you simply memorize by repeating, you may pass the **imminent** test, but you will probably not remember most of the words the next week or the week after.

15   To learn something, you must be able to associate it with something you already know. That is how most of us learn. Of course, there are those of us who can memorize anything; however, does that mean we really know it? For example, if you show me an ordinary photo and tell me to look at it for a little while and then ask me to close my eyes and tell you what was on the photo, I would probably be able to tell you, but I am not likely to remember the photo the following week. Because I have not given that photo any other thought, I will not be able to tell you what it meant, or even why I was looking at it. Similarly, we have to process vocabulary words we want to know more deeply than the superficiality involved in merely memorizing to do well on tests, especially if our purpose is to learn and use these words during our lifetime.

Ways to Learn Vocabulary

16   There are other ways to learn vocabulary. Knowing root words and prefixes and suffixes is one way. For example, "trans" is the basic root meaning "across." When we say "transatlantic" flight, we mean across the Atlantic Ocean. Prefixes are word parts used at the beginning of some words to change their meanings. For example, "re" means to "do over." Therefore, when we say "reread" or "rewrite," we mean that we have to do these over. So suffixes are … you may have guessed right, or maybe you already know! They are word parts that are added to the end of some words to change

their meaning. For example, "er" means "one who." Therefore, when we say "teacher" we mean one who teaches. For more information on vocabulary in general, fast forward to the chapter in Part Two, "It's a Piece of Cake! Unfamiliar Vocabulary in Context."

17   Another way is to draw a word map like the one below:

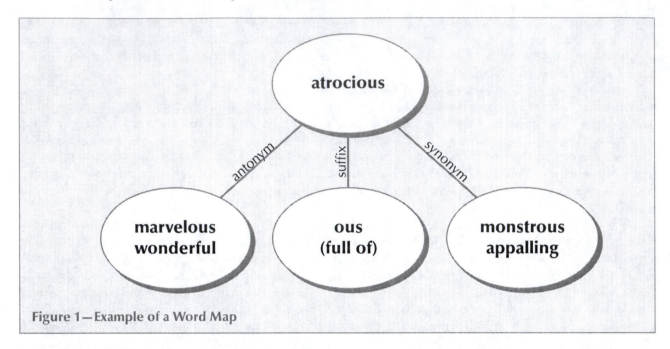

Figure 1—Example of a Word Map

18   One way that I particularly enjoy learning vocabulary is by using vocabulary index cards. However, these are more than your ordinary index cards on which all you have written is the word and definition—something you could have done just as easily on paper. An example of the front and back of a 5x7 vocabulary index card is as follows:

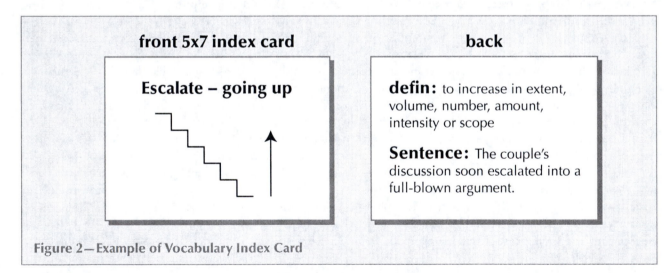

Figure 2—Example of Vocabulary Index Card

19   As you can see, the word to be learned is "escalate." Now, according to the Merriam-Webster dictionary, this word means "to increase in extent, volume, number, amount, intensity or scope." Therefore, I understand that this word means to go up. Instead of memorizing the meaning of the word, I can think of a way to illustrate the meaning because it is so much easier for me to associate something new (escalate) with something from my background knowledge (escalator). Thus, I drew an escalator with an arrow pointing upward (since an escalator goes up and down). On the reverse side of the card, I wrote the definition, and then I wrote a sentence using the word in context.

20   Similarly, you can draw or cut pictures or have someone else draw for you. Even if you go around thinking about the meaning of the word and how to illustrate it, you will be subconsciously learning since you will be "working" with it

in your head and asking others about it. The more you work with a word, the better you will learn it and, therefore, will more likely use it. Similarly, you could draw cartoons or write a joke or **anecdote** using the word. Anything that will help you learn the word at a deeper level will help. These techniques may initially take time to do; however, the long-term results are worth the time and energy you put into doing them.

21   I recall one single mother in her 20s who was a student of mine few years ago. She had a nine-year-old daughter who assisted her with making vocabulary cards—like the one I illustrated before—for every one of the 200 vocabulary words that were presented in class. In order to study for the vocabulary tests, my student made a deal with her daughter. The child would shuffle the cards, and then ask the mother the definition. If the mother answered incorrectly, she had to pay her daughter a certain sum of money. This sort of interaction with vocabulary words lasted throughout the semester. It is not hard to imagine that this student received high marks on her vocabulary tests. We could probably also surmise that she recalled the definitions long after other students who might have crammed for the vocabulary tests. What surprised her most, though, was that her nine-year-old daughter knew all the 200 words as well! This child learned these vocabulary words in their natural settings (her mother's homework), and she learned them without realizing that she was learning them. What better way is there to learn? Mother and daughter not only had fun, but they also spent quality time together. This resulted in the child gaining confidence and self-esteem in her own ability to help her mother as well as to develop her own vocabulary. How empowering is that for a 9-year-old?

22   There are many workbooks published on vocabulary. You can look them up on the Internet or your bookstore or ask your instructor to recommend one for you. These books are usually relatively inexpensive. Another alternative is to look at lists of words in the SAT and/or ACT preparation books. **Perusing** these books will give you an idea of the kind of words that you ought to know in college. However, keep in mind that the best way to become familiar with vocabulary is to read on your learning level and to immerse yourself in listening to and speaking with people who have a large **repertoire** of rich vocabulary whether this be in person or through television, radio, or the Internet. In Part Four of this book, I have included a list of words that have been contributed by a dear colleague of mine, Cherie Canon. These words were **compiled** by consulting SAT, ACT, vocabulary books, and her personal experience working in an academic setting for many years. You will probably encounter these words frequently in your academic settings and, like my student's 9-year-old daughter, feel empowered when you understand them!

Application:

A. Write what you think the following words mean in the context of your reading. Then use the dictionary to check if you were right in your summation:

seductive, elusive, impact, appeal, barely, perspective, versatile, evolve, devolve, inventory, delineate, retention, imminent, context, anecdote, perusing, repertoire, compiled

B. Based on your comprehension of the material you have just read, answer the following questions:

1. In your own words, tell why vocabulary is so critical to your success in college.

2. How do you learn new vocabulary words? Does your way of learning new words help you remember them long after you are tested on them? Tell why.

Are You Ready? Testing for Reading Comprehension Skills

Chapter Ten

We have all had the opportunity to answer questions after reading a passage. Many times, especially with narrative text, we have been asked for our opinions. For example, you might recall a question like this: If you were the protagonist, how would you have handled the problem? Questions like these, although they require you to comprehend the material, are not specific. Usually there are no incorrect answers because you are being asked for your opinion.

Tests relating to courses such as the one you are enrolled in require you to answer specific questions that have right and wrong answers. These are usually multiple-choice questions, and therefore, there is no partial credit. For example, you may be asked what the meaning of a specific word is in context of the passage. If the question is developed right, there is usually one correct answer. Therefore, reading comprehension tests should be handled logically and with common sense. Your opinion about a passage or the author is **irrelevant**. Your **intuition** might mislead you! If you can justify your answer with evidence from the written passage, your answer is probably correct.

Like most instructors, I learn as much from my students as they do from me. What I am going to share with you next is one such learning experience for me that I think will emphasize the importance of what I have just said about keeping emotion out of a reading comprehension test.

Several years ago I had a senior student. Although she was well into her 70s, and had faced many personal challenges in her life, she **persevered** in my reading course. She was **diligent** with her homework and her assignments. However, she was struggling with English as it was not her first language. One evening—it was an evening class—we were going over the answers to questions on central point (main idea of a long selection). After class, this student came to me quite confused. She told me that she had initially selected the correct response, but after thinking about it, decided that it was untrue and too rude to even be considered! The central point referred to women as second-class citizens. This concept did not sit well with this student's view of the world, and therefore, she chose not to select this response.

My student's error provided me with the opportunity to teach her what I have been stating in this chapter—that our emotions are irrelevant, and that reason **reigns**! I explained to the student that the central point was from a selection that discussed the status of women in the 18th century and that women were **perceived** differently then. I explained to her that, similarly, she might come across reading material written by a **bigot**, in which the main idea may be a **derogatory** statement about immigrants or people of color. The main idea is what it is. By selecting an

Subject-Specific Vocabulary:

multiple-choice question: a question that has more than one answer choice; the test-taker must select one of the choices

answer—however **repulsive** it may be to our good nature—we are not stating that we are agreeing with the author. It is not our opinion that is being sought. We are simply being asked to think **rationally**.

Good News

The good news about reading comprehension tests is that you do not have to memorize any content information like you do for a science course or a psychology course. Your reading material is with you during testing, is it not? You could read and re-read the material if you have the time. However, this does not mean that you will not need to remember key concepts in reading. For example, if you do not know the difference between a fact and an opinion, you will not be able to apply that knowledge to identify fact and opinion statements. However, what you need to remember is minimal. How many times you applied a reading skill by completing class and homework assignments and how many times you were able to consciously apply your skills in real-life situations will determine how successful you will be on these tests. After all, questions on these tests are not going to ask you to define fact and opinion; instead, they will ask you to identify a particular statement or statements from the passage as a fact or an opinion or both. However, you will agree that you first need to know what a fact and an opinion are. Working with these sorts of questions in reading exercises prepares us to answer these questions accurately and almost instinctively (automatically) because we will have applied the skill to so many reading experiences. This is why "drill and practice" are necessary to some kinds of learning. Also, experience in transferring these skills to real-life situations is crucial.

On a final note, understand that reading test questions carefully and understanding what is being required of you are important. Sometimes, we are so anxious during testing that we do not properly **scrutinize** directions or test questions. Therefore, sometimes we answer incorrectly not because we do not know, but because we failed to interpret the question correctly or to specifically follow the directions. We must read the questions just as carefully as we read the passage. For example, think of how easy it is to miss the word *except* in a question, and as you know, that word will make a difference in our response.

Application:

A. Write what you think the following words mean in the context of your reading. Then use the dictionary to check if you were right in your summation:

intuition, irrelevant, persevered, diligent, perceived, derogatory, reigns, bigot, repulsive, rationally, authentic, scrutinize

B. Based on your comprehension of the material you have just read, answer the following questions:

1. Why do you think answering reading comprehension questions in an exam situation requires reasoning and not your opinions?

2. What have you learned in this chapter that you did not know before?

Reflection

When you *reflect*, you are thinking profoundly (deeply) about an idea, a thing, or a person. It means that you have consciously decided to think further into whatever it is that you need to reflect on. Throughout life, we reflect on many things. For the purposes of this course, you are to reflect in writing about the kind of ideas and thoughts expressed by me in this first part of your text. What sort of ideas jumped out at you, and what sort of deeper thinking did these ideas lead you to? Write out your thoughts as you are thinking them. Then, after you have written about these thoughts, go back and read what you have written. Ask yourself if someone else would be able to read what you wrote and make sense of your thinking.

Fix your written communication to make it easier for the reader to go into your head and know what, how, and why you are reflecting. You can use transitions (for example: "also," "similarly," "after," "next") to show connections between your thought processes. Always put your thoughts in complete sentences. Remember that a complete sentence is a complete thought. You can also put a collection of similar thoughts into paragraphs. All of this makes it easier for the reader to comprehend.

This exercise should not only get you to think critically about what you have read and hopefully comprehended thus far, but also help you to establish a purpose for your writing and to put yourself in the reader's shoes while you are writing. You are not receiving a grade for this assignment. Therefore, do not stress over it. You are the one who will evaluate your own writing.

Read to Reason

Part Two

The Chemistry of Reading

(Do not forget to check titles and subtitles in this reading material and to predict what the reading material is going to be about. Bring to mind all that you know about the topic and all that you would want to know so that you begin reading as an active reader.)

Your prediction based on topic and background knowledge:

What do you hope to gain from this reading material?

1   Look at the illustration (Figure 3). What can you make of it? How would you interpret it? Can you draw any conclusions? Do you agree that communication requires comprehension and that critical thinking involves comprehension? Would you agree or disagree that there is no communication taking place when you are not comprehending? Comprehension is a **component** of critical thinking, since in order to critically think you have to first understand. Understanding takes place in **varying** degrees. However, to comprehend critically, we must integrate this new knowledge with our preexisting knowledge and then analyze and evaluate it, thereby interpreting it. In some instances our interpretation leads us to reconstruct meaning. For example, can you explain a concept using your own examples rather than those presented to you at the time of learning? Can you apply a concept to other seemingly unrelated concepts and make sense of them? Are you able to apply skills learned in this reading course to when you are listening and/or taking notes? This type of transfer means that you have deeply processed the material. You will be required to engage in this sort of analysis in your English courses, especially with literary works such as poems. Are you ready for that?

2   Note: The knowledge of self as a critical thinker and reader, who is constantly immersed in making sense of language, is crucial to your success in college.

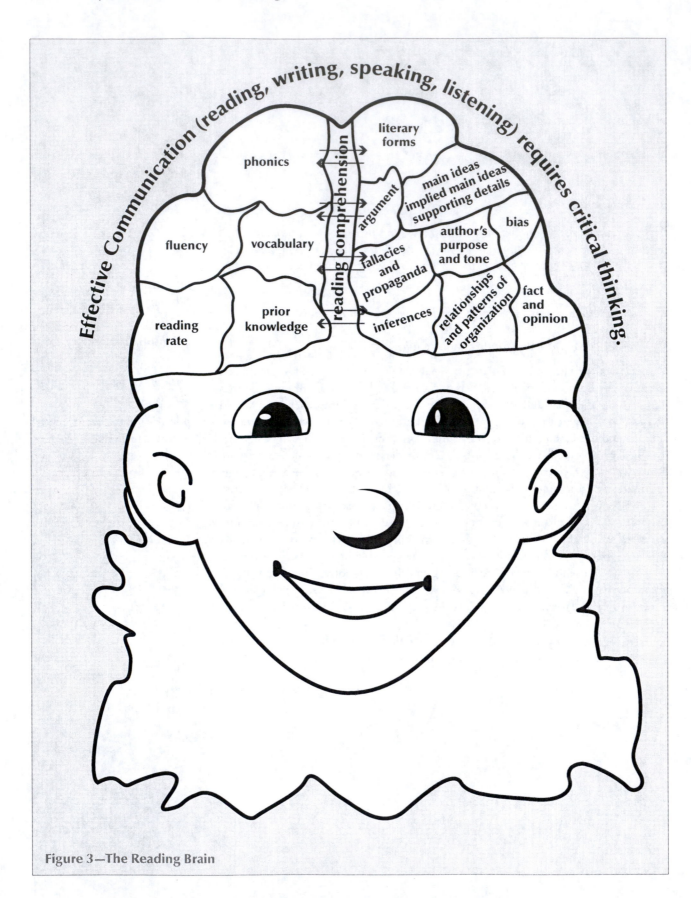

Figure 3—The Reading Brain

Explanation of Illustration

3   Look at the illustration again (Figure 3). All the skills you are going to be learning are represented as pieces of a jigsaw puzzle that fit neatly in the area of the brain. It is as though your entire brain is involved in reading. I wish! This may be the fantasy of most reading instructors, but you know that the brain is involved with lots of other functions. Although this megacomputer—as I sometimes refer to our brain—is so complex that it has fascinated scientists down the ages; no one has yet been able to completely discover the secrets in its many "storerooms." One such storeroom deals with language. It is not important to know all the details. It is important to know that this is simply an illustration to show you the various components of becoming proficient in a language such as English and that although these components may seem separate, they are parts of a larger picture—the reading experience. And that although in the following chapters, these parts (skills) are addressed separately, it is hoped that you will see how all these parts fit into the entire whole. We do not comprehend in parts but as a whole!

4   You may also look at the illustration and notice that "phonics," "vocabulary," "fluency," "reading rate," and "prior knowledge" are **depicted** on one side of the brain whereas all the other skills that you are expected to learn in this course like "main idea" and "inferences" are on the other side of the brain. I do not want you to think that these all are unrelated because they are—very much so! The purpose for showing the separation of skills is so that you can tell at first glance what sort of material you can expect to learn in a reading comprehension course. Do you also notice the arrows going back and forth? This implies that we integrate new information with old information (for example, background knowledge and vocabulary) all the time—and for all types of communication—to make sense of our world and our personal lives.

Processing Reading

5   In Part One of this book, there was a lot of discussion on what facilitates reading comprehension and some important features of reading. However, truth be told, exactly how our brains process reading is still somewhat of a mystery. As humans, we all process information differently, and sometimes we arrive at different conclusions based on our unique perspectives, past experiences, and motivations. Most times, however, most of us draw similar conclusions; otherwise, there would be total chaos in our language. I speculate that there is no one way to process reading efficiently that works for everyone. What research about reading has found is that some things work better than others. But again, that does not mean that they will work for you. We do know, however, that the more we read with comprehension and the more we are immersed in vocabulary-rich environments, the more our comprehension of reading material is facilitated.

6   As mentioned in Part One, recall that reading comprehension tests/exams ask you to identify, analyze, interpret, and evaluate written text. Certain reading skills like the ones this book focuses on, such as main idea, fact and opinion, and patterns of organization, are only pieces of the reading jigsaw puzzle. And, for the purposes of this course, we will focus on these skills. Although these reading skills are of equal importance, you will find that certain skills such as bias, argument, and inference require more analytical thinking, and therefore they may be considered as higher-order thinking skills.

7   I think of phonics and vocabulary as literal comprehension skills. These require basic reasoning. Main idea, supporting details, implied main idea, relationship between and within sentences, pattern of organization, and inferences I usually group under inferential comprehension skills. These require some analytic reasoning. Author's purpose, tone, fact and opinion, bias, argument, and analysis of figurative language I usually refer to as critical comprehension skills. These require both analytic and evaluative thinking. (Refer to Figure 4)

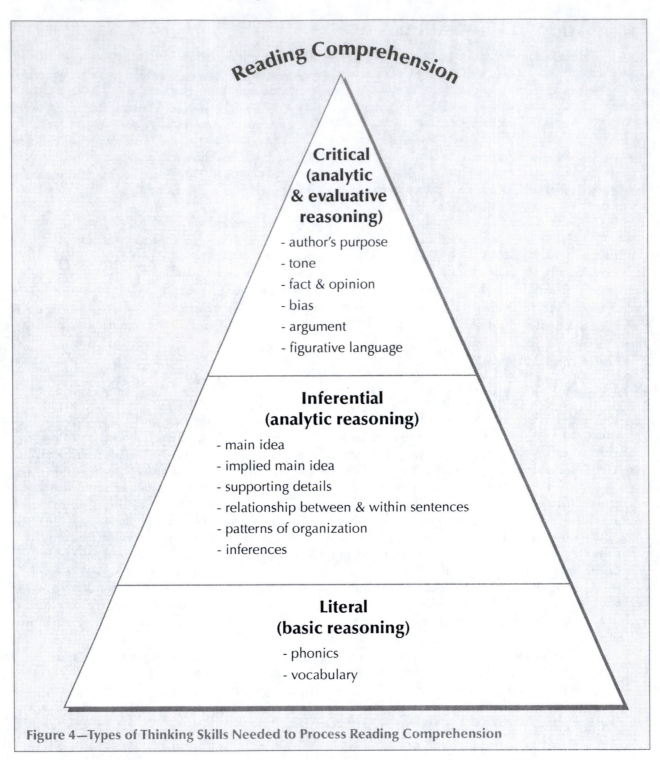

Figure 4—Types of Thinking Skills Needed to Process Reading Comprehension

8   Therefore, when you test and receive feedback, reflect (think profoundly/deeply) about the kind of questions you got wrong. What category would the majority of your incorrect answers fall within (literal, inferential, critical)? This sort of reflection will not only give you an idea as to what skills you are having difficulty with, but also whether you need further practice in **honing** your analytical skills to apply to comprehension questions.

Application:

A. Write what you think the following words mean in the context of your reading. Then use the dictionary to check if you were right in your summation:

component, varying, depicted, interrelated, honing

B. Based on your comprehension of the material you have just read, answer the following questions:

1. What was confusing? What would you like to know more about?

2. Refer to the pyramid diagram and analyze it. Can you see the relationships and the complexities involving reading comprehension? Would you add to or delete from this diagram? How so?

Say What?!? The Nuances of English

(Do not forget to check titles and subtitles in this reading material and to predict what the reading material is going to be about. Bring to mind all that you know about the topic and all that you would want to know so that you begin reading as an active reader.)

Your prediction based on topic and background knowledge:

What do you hope to gain from this reading material?

1   If you were actively **engaged** and had a purpose for reading this, you might have paused when you read the word "nuances." There is not much in the title to give you any idea as to this word's meaning. If you do not know what this word means, understand that as long as you know that you do not know, you are one step ahead of the game. Realize that when you are **vigilant** while reading, you are engaged. If you like learning new words and find this particular word exotic sounding (I know that I do!), then you are either proud that you know the word or are happily **anticipating** knowing this word. Moreover, your background knowledge probably tells you that this word is important to know for the understanding of this material since you know that usually the words in a topic have a direct connection to the written material.

Nuance

2   So what are nuances? *Nuances* are shades of meanings of words and nonliteral interpretation of language. Therefore, when words are strung together to produce a thought, how words are used and in what context would determine the shade or shades of meaning. This makes for **undertones** in language. Many words can be used expressively as neutral, positive, or negative. Therefore, you as the reader would have to understand the expression in the context of what is being said. You cannot let your guard down and read looking solely for literal meaning. Sometimes the meanings of ideas and thoughts are indeed basic and superficial (literal interpretation). However, most times in good writing, the writer expresses himself using all the expressive tools at his disposal (all the nuances of language—especially used in poems and song lyrics). He may use language in a way that a literal interpretation will not work. Therefore, understanding the nuances helps you avoid misinterpreting his message. This brings us to the discussion of connotative and denotative meanings of words.

Subject-Specific Vocabulary:

evaluate: to determine the significance or worth of something by careful appraisal

interpret: to explain the meaning of (something)

Connotative and Denotative Meanings

3   All words have denotative meanings. This means the literal, explicit, dictionary meaning of a word. On the other hand, the connotation of a word is how it is associated in the context of what is being said and is usually associated with figurative language. Read the example below:

She is a sister.

4   We all know the literal definition of the word "sister." What if I were to tell you that this sentence was written by an African-American woman while discussing an acquaintance? Now, if you had background knowledge about the culture within which this expression was used, would you not realize that the author wants the reader to know that the person she is referring to is also an African-American woman (connotation)? If you were not familiar with this culture, you might be puzzled, especially if you knew from the context of the material that the woman did not have a **familial** tie (denotation) with the author. Also, it is important to understand that many other members of groups that want to express their close bonds with each other may use sister in a similar context. This word's reach has become more inclusive. Note: In the context of this discussion, the use of sister is informal.

5   It makes sense to suggest that you would probably know the literal meaning of a word before you start to understand its connotative uses in varying literary and cultural contexts. Therefore, students who have limited English proficiency and/or limited multicultural experiences might have difficulty with interpretation since they are still learning literal meanings of words. Proficiency in a language takes time and a conscious effort to immerse oneself in the language whenever the opportunity arises. And, let us not forget the importance of interpreting language within a culture!

Synonyms

6   Many times students think that synonyms are words that mean the same, but this is not always true. Synonyms are words that mean the same or almost the same. Although most times the literal definition (dictionary definition) of words and their synonyms are similar, their connotative meanings are different. In other words, what words we choose to express from an array of synonyms assists the reader in interpreting our message correctly. Read the following:

My brother is frugal.

My brother is thrifty.

My brother is cheap.

My brother is careful about spending money.

7   The words "frugal," "thrifty," and "cheap" have similar denotative (literal) meanings of someone who spends money carefully. However, "frugal" and "thrifty" have positive connotations because being frugal or thrifty is considered a good characteristic in a person. It means that the person does not spend money unnecessarily or unwisely. However, "cheap" in this context has a negative connotation. Also, "cheap" is an informal word in this context, but I took the liberty to use it in this example because I realize that many of us either use it or have heard it in everyday situations. Think about the last time you might have been tempted to call someone "cheap" and decided against it. You might have thought that it would hurt the person's feelings. It connotes that the person may be stingy or selfish. The last sentence is phrased to be neutral. Let us look at some other examples below:

The mentally retarded student ran out of the classroom.

The mentally handicapped student ran out of the classroom.

The mentally disabled student ran out of the classroom.

The mentally challenged student ran out of the classroom.

The intellectually challenged student ran out of the classroom.

8   Which sentence do you interpret as the positive, negative, not-so-negative, and neutral? In your decision, you weighed the connotative meanings and the associations these evoked in you. As you know, we no longer call intellectually challenged people "retarded" or "handicapped." These words carry with them negative connotations, and our experiences lead us to believe that no person—regardless of his/her challenges—needs to be labeled in a negative manner.

9   But wait—What about stating, "people with intellectual challenges" as opposed to "intellectually challenged people"? In the latter, it would appear that the challenge defines a person. A positive spin on this would be that a person is an individual first and his challenge becomes secondary. This way we are likely to view the person first and not define him by some characteristic. After all, we do not say, "HIV person," but rather "a person with HIV," do we not? Perhaps you never thought of our sometimes casual use of seemingly neutral words.

10   This idea of denotation and connotation is also applied in everyday life to interpret symbols. For example, a Confederate flag is a symbol of the Confederacy during the U.S. Civil War. This is the literal interpretation of the flag. For descendants of Confederate soldiers, it may be a symbol of pride and honor. However, for minority groups, particularly African-Americans, it is a symbol of slavery, bigotry, and prejudice. Go on the Internet, do a search on the Confederate flag, and read about some of the heated arguments and **controversies** that this symbol has **generated**.

Implications

11   By this time, you must have realized some of the implications of all this. For one, you cannot just know the literal meaning of a word, but you need to know how and when to use it for varying purposes and contexts. You can learn this only by experiencing the word in text, in speech, and in different situations. The more contexts and interpretive ways a word is used correctly will determine how well you know that word. Second, you can tell that having background knowledge about the culture in which a language exists is extremely important to understand these kinds of nuances. Therefore, for students who are English Language Learners and who are fairly new to the American culture, connotations will take longer to realize. Even those who speak English as a first language, but do not have experiences with the use of academic vocabulary, may have difficulty with interpretation. Being immersed in the language whenever you can is one way of eventually overcoming this obstacle. After all, it takes many years to become proficient in a language. Take a moment to process the relationships in Figure 5:

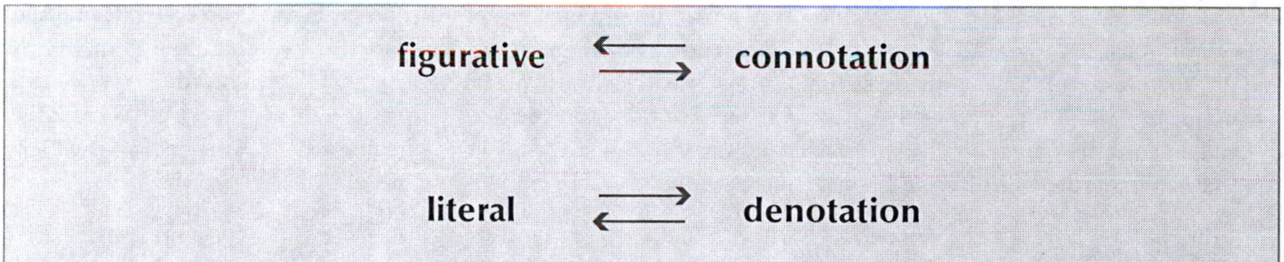

figurative ⇄ **connotation**

literal ⇄ **denotation**

Figure 5

12   Note: Most times we first learn the denotative meanings of words and then we progress—based on our experiences—to knowing the many connotative implications of words. However, sometimes we could first learn the connotative meanings of words and then their denotative meanings. Whether we first learn the denotative or connotative meaning of a word will depend on the context in which we first encountered the word. As mentioned before, connotative meanings are associated with figurative language whereas denotative meanings are associated with literal language. These relationships have been illustrated in Figure 5 denoted by arrows that point both right and left.

Opinion on Use of Thesaurus

13   I want to comment about the use of a thesaurus. I have noticed that many students rely heavily on its content. Students do this because they have been instructed that their written pieces are not effective if they overuse words. Instead, they should use appropriate synonyms. So students use their thesaurus to find any synonym for the word that looks or sounds good and inject it into their writing. Also, because much of the writing that we do, we now do on computers, the thesaurus is a click of a button away and becomes a tempting and convenient tool. The problem with simply **injecting** synonyms in place of another word is that language is nuanced, and words have both connotative and denotative

meanings. If you replace one word with the other, you may cause the reader to misinterpret your message. Read the following sentences:

Last night, my neighbor was murdered.

Last night, my neighbor was assassinated.

14   Both "murdered" and "assassinated" literally mean to be killed. However, unless your neighbor was someone in political office and/or a prominent person, you would not use the word "assassinated." This word is generally reserved for the "murder" of prominent people, often for political gain. When you are trying to impress your instructor with a written piece, and you are injecting it with all these words from the thesaurus that look and sound very important, and you think it makes you seem like an accomplished writer, you may create an opposite reaction. Your instructor knows from your writing whether you have any knowledge about how to use these words. If you do not, then your paper becomes a dead giveaway that you have generously used the thesaurus. Your message becomes **convoluted**, and interpretation becomes difficult. That is why I am going to keep advising you: Words have a certain place in your writing and different shades of meaning depending on what message you are trying to convey. If you misuse them, especially if you consistently misuse them in your writing, any instructor will be able to discern that you did not give your writing much thought, or that you are not yet proficient in the language. You are better off using simple language to express yourself correctly than to use "big" words that you are not familiar with.

15   I have an admission: I seldom use the thesaurus function on the computer. I prefer to search in my head the old-fashioned way. What I am trying to say is that, in my opinion, the thesaurus and its easy accessibility may cause people to think less about the significance of their word choices. Does this mean that a thesaurus is not useful? Of course not! Even I have used it—seldom though that may be. I use it when I cannot recall a word, but I will not simply select a word and use it without knowing whether it will represent the association I want to evoke in the reader.

Literal Interpretation

Some textbooks are **conducive** to mostly literal interpretation, and therefore, even if you are not proficient in the language, you will probably still be able to make sense of the material if the language is simple. For example, you are likely to find that science and math textbooks are geared toward literal interpretation because they use literal language. This makes sense because while explaining the circulatory system, the author's intention is for you to gain information, and not for you to inject denotative meanings into words. Therefore, most of the text will likely use words with neutral meanings. In tests, you will probably be asked to recall information and not interpret the author's message. What kinds of texts do you think are more likely to favor the use of connotative language? Literary texts like the ones you will encounter in a literature course, or an English course, are good examples.

What Do You Really Mean? Literal Vs. Figurative Language

You already know what literal language means; now let us talk about figurative language. What does that mean? You may want to refer to Figure 4 in the last chapter. Figurative language is a type of communication that often engages the reader's imagination in interpreting subtle layers of meanings. Figurative language compares ideas in imaginative ways. The reader is required to analyze and to interpret the words, and to evaluate what is meant in unique ways. Sometimes, as in the case of poetry, many layers of interpretation are possible.

Although you may not find figurative language used in most of your college textbooks, especially the ones geared to content areas such as earth science or math, how well you can analyze figurative language probably almost always determines your level of proficiency in English. You are required to use your interpretive abilities to analyze, apply, synthesize, and evaluate. There are different aspects of figurative language, and these are called figures of speech. Writers use figures of speech as literary devices (tools) to engage the readers in interpreting the written message. Therefore, you will need to hone your critical thinking skills and your background knowledge to identify the literary tools used by the writer to interpret and evaluate the reading. I am going to list some of the most common ones with examples so you are able to recognize them when you encounter them. As your journey through language progresses, you will find other figures of speech to add to your background knowledge.

For Your Information: A student surprised me by asking me what sort of courses in college would present the most challenges to students like him, given his developmental reading background. Without pause, I expressed my opinion. I stated that I think that the English and English Literature courses would pack the most challenges, especially for students who are in the process of becoming proficient in English. I went on to explain that English and English Literature coursework typically involves analyses and interpretation of nuanced language, which means that students must be able to apply their knowledge of figures of speech to analyze, interpret, and evaluate figurative language (such as in poems). Although typically English courses are encountered in students' first year of college and a content-area course such as anatomy in their second year, the English course would require more critical thinking—in my opinion—than the anatomy course. The anatomy course will deal primarily with information that needs to be memorized and not necessarily interpreted and evaluated. Therefore, students who have good strategies to memorize information may do better and receive better grades in the anatomy course than in an English course that requires interpretation but little memorization (for example, definition of words like "simile").

Some Figures of Speech

It figures that figures of speech would figure into language so figuratively! What was that? You will figure it out, I am sure. Continue reading and then come back to it!

Simile: A simile uses "like" or "as" to compare two seemingly unlike ideas or things in a unique way. For example, "This huge man was as gentle as a lamb." Lambs are usually associated with being gentle creatures, and a man's behavior is being compared to that of a lamb, thereby suggesting the gentleness of this man. Other examples include: As sharp as a needle, As hard as nails, Her betrayal was like a stab in my back.

Metaphor: A metaphor is like a simile but does not use the words "like" or "as." It simply expresses a state of being. For example, "She was a breath of fresh air." This means that the person in question was recognized as a welcome diversion. Other examples include: Her home is a pigpen, Her classroom is a zoo.

Alliteration: Alliteration is when the same initial or other-position sounds of words are used over and over to establish a rhythm or mood. A tongue twister would fall in this category. For example, She sells seashells by the seashore. What about the sentence I made up? "It figures that figures of speech would figure into language so figuratively." Do you think it qualifies as an "alliteration"?

Personification: Personification is used when an author gives a human characteristic to an animal, idea, or object to allow the reader to interpret the author's perception. For example, how often have you heard "Diamonds are a girl's best friend."? "The wind beckoned for my hat" is another example.

Idioms: Idioms are phrases that together have meaning, but if each individual word were to be separately analyzed and put together, the phrase would not make sense. For example, The decision to foreclose has been a "bone of contention" between us. "A bone of contention" (idiom) means a problem. I think that the implication is that of two dogs who would fight over a bone. Do you know this idiom: to kick the bucket? It means to die; yet, you could never have made sense of it by just analyzing each of the words and putting them together and coming up with "to die," now, would you? Do you realize that you may not have this idiom in your language or in your culture? Idioms are, therefore, usually particular in that they are associated with a culture. Even among English speakers, those who speak British English may be unfamiliar with some idioms that are particular to American English. Therefore, always understand that language is not learned in a vacuum. It is best learned in context of its culture because, after all, language is used to communicate within our societies. In Part Four of this book, Jennifer Nimmo has provided you with some common idioms for your reading pleasure. Take a look at them and enjoy them!

Oxymoron: This is a combination of words that have opposite or very different meanings and are sometimes purposely created to reveal a paradox (for example, jumbo shrimp, genuine imitation, and living dead).

Euphemism: This is when we substitute an offensive term with one that is more acceptable. Pre-owned (used); put to sleep (euthanize); and vertically challenged (short) are some examples.

Hyperbole: This means that a statement has been exaggerated to give the message emphasis. For example, "The lawnmover cut off on me a million times." Obviously, the author wants you to understand that the lawnmower broke down many times—breaking down a million times is possible but highly improbable.

Other Expressions and What They Mean

Clichés: These are phrases and expressions that have been overused and have, therefore, lost their initial impact to influence the imagination, for example, "as easy as pie". This means that whatever act is being referred to, is quite easy to achieve. "There is no place like home" is another example. You have probably heard these expressions many times and perhaps even used them yourself. It is difficult for people who are not proficient in English to determine if a set of words is a cliché or not. Suffice it to say that with experience with the language comes wisdom! This means that when you hear an expression over and over, it is probably a cliché.

Proverbs: Proverbs are sayings that briefly express a long-held truth, wisdom, or advice. Many English proverbs are not original but come from other languages and cultures. Therefore, a proverb in English may be identical or similar to an existing proverb in another language. Some examples of proverbs are: "A bird in hand is worth two in a bush;" "Necessity is the mother of invention;" "All that glitters is not gold." The first proverb means that it is better to keep a sure thing than to go after more things that are not guaranteed. The second proverb means that it is when we find ourselves in need of something, we improvise, which often leads to a useful invention. The last proverb warns about being fooled about the value of an item by its outward appearance. What do you think "Do not judge a book by its cover" means? It means that you do not judge people or things by their outward appearances. You did look at the cover of this book, did you not? Based on your recollection, did you anticipate the book to be interesting or not? Was your judgment right? In Part Four of this book, another dear colleague of mine, Robert Mathews, has provided you with some proverbs for your reading pleasure. By now you have probably inferred that I have quite a few very dear colleagues – and some you are yet to read about - who not only believed in this book project, but also in their own ability to make a difference in your journey of discovery. I hope that you will refer to their contributions and learn from them.

Analogy: This is a comparison of two things based on their being alike in some way. A comparison between the heart and a car engine is an example.

Much of what I have listed in this chapter under "Some Figures of Speech" and "Other Expressions and What They Mean" are also expressions that we use in our spoken conversation. It is important for you to be familiar with these figures of speech and other expressions so that your comprehension of literary material is facilitated. Knowing what these expressions mean is almost like having to learn unfamiliar vocabulary words. As I have mentioned before, you are not likely to find these types of expressions in a chemistry text. However, you are most likely to not only find them in everyday speech, but also in your literary texts, and in magazines, novels, and such. You will notice that in narrative text, many times these expressions appear in the dialogue between characters. It would not hurt to reread or review the section on "Seductive, Elusive, and Versatile Vocabulary" in Part One of this book. It will enhance your understanding of this section.

Application:

A. Write what you think the following words mean in the context of your reading. Then use the dictionary to check if you were right in your summation:

engaged, vigilant, anticipating, undertones, familial, controversies, generated, injecting, convoluted, conducive

B. Based on your comprehension of the material you have just read, answer the following questions:

1. Why is it important to know the difference between literal and figurative language?

2. Research two figures of speech not listed in this chapter. Provide their definitions and an example of each.

3. Look at the diagram below and write in at least two examples for each of the figures of speech listed.

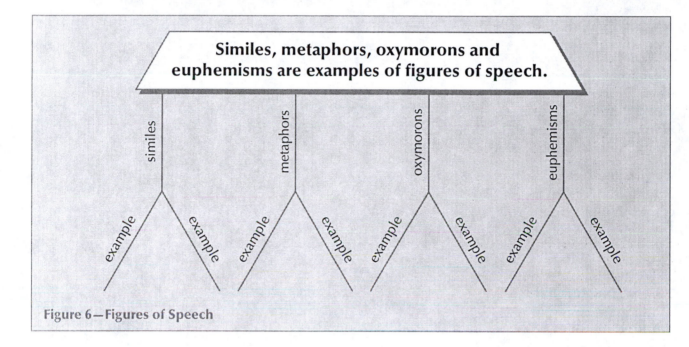

Similes, metaphors, oxymorons and euphemisms are examples of figures of speech.

similes — example / example
metaphors — example / example
oxymorons — example / example
euphemisms — example / example

Figure 6—Figures of Speech

It's a Piece of Cake! Unfamiliar Vocabulary in Context

Chapter Three

(Do not forget to check titles and subtitles in this reading material and to predict what the reading material is going to be about. Bring to mind all that you know about the topic and all that you would want to know so that you begin reading as an active reader.)

Your prediction based on topic and background knowledge:

What do you hope to gain from this reading material?

1   I have already discussed the importance of vocabulary and some ways of learning new words in Part One of this book. Also, in Part Four, I have provided you with a listing of collegiate-level vocabulary words, confused or misused words and commonly misspelled words (courtesy of Cherie Canon).

2   In this section, I address roots, prefixes, and suffixes of words that can give you a clue about the meaning of the word (Part Four has more information on this subject.). Knowledge of roots, prefixes, and suffixes unlocks the meanings to thousands of words. Also, we discuss some of the ways we can figure out the meaning of unknown words.

Roots:

3   Just like a tree has roots, so also many words in English have roots. These are the base components of the word. In English, these roots usually come from Latin or Greek and exist in those languages as a complete word. When the root is attached to the beginning of a word, it is called a prefix. On the other hand, when it is attached to the end of a word, it is called a suffix. Here are some examples:

Roots	Example
aqua(water)	aqueduct, aquarium, aquatic
octo(eight)	octopus, octagon, October

Prefixes:

Prefixes	Example
trans(across)	transatlantic, transport, transpose, transfer
anti(against)	antigovernment, anti-aircraft, anti-Semitic

Subject-Specific Vocabulary:

connotation: an idea or quality that a word makes you think about in addition to its meaning

denotation: the literal meaning of a word or phrase

Suffixes:

Suffixes	Example
ous(full of)	glamorous, famous, atrocious
er(one who)	teacher, manager, abuser

4   Most times we hear unfamiliar words in context. After all, we do not speak using one-word ideas. Our thoughts are expressed by a string of words so that our idea is communicated. When we are reading or listening, we may come across an unfamiliar word(s). It would not make a difference if the unfamiliar spoken or written word is a foreign word. The fact is that we do not know the word. However, our **ingenious** brain realizes that we do not understand and works within milliseconds to "fix" the problem. For example, I requested of my student who had just entered the classroom, "Please remove your 'cap' from your head before you take a seat." The student complied with my request. What is amazing though is that I did not use the English word for *cap*; instead, I substituted it with the Hindi (a language of India) word for *cap*. The student quickly understood what I meant in context without hesitation.

5   We analyze the idea(s) and the other words and sentences surrounding this unfamiliar word, and we make sense of it. We may not be able to determine a dictionary definition of the word, but we would know somewhat the meaning of the word. You see, our brain, while comprehending (This means that we must be focused in order to comprehend and, therefore, know when we do not know.) any kind of communication, does not like to feel what I call "uncomfortable." And, the brain becomes uncomfortable when it realizes it cannot make sense of words or a situation. (Think of the brain sort of frowning on the inside just like you find yourself frowning on the outside when you do not understand.) Therefore, thinking gets intensified to solve the problem word or phrase, and then the brain reverts back to feeling okay.

Unfamiliar Words in Conversation

6   Now, your brain has engaged itself in this sort of processing of an unfamiliar word many times. Think of the last time someone was having a conversation with you, and she used a word that you were unfamiliar with. Did you stop her mid sentence or mid thought to ask what the word meant? Chances are that you did no such thing. Instead, because we string words together quickly, the speaker continued with her message, **impervious** to your lack of comprehension of the word. If you were paying attention to her, you realized that you did not understand, but you kept up with trying to make sense of the message. In the context of everything that the person said around that word, you were able to figure out the meaning of the word although you never heard it before. It might have even been a foreign word that the speaker inadvertently used, **reverting** back to her native-language because her brain could not find that word's translation in English. The important thing is that you made sense of the word.

7   It is possible that the word was used again during this same conversation, but this time you thought its meaning did not quite apply in the new context. Now, you may still not have engaged the speaker in a discussion about the word's meaning. However, if you experienced the same sort of discomfort when the word was used again, and it still did not make sense based on your analysis of it, it was then time to ask the speaker, especially if the word was important to your understanding of the message. In other words, sometimes we may not know a word, and it may not be important for us to know its meaning since it is not important to the speaker's message. Therefore, we continue listening. However, once the word interferes with our comprehension of the message, then we must ask or go to the dictionary for assistance.

Unfamiliar Words in Text

8   Similarly, when we read, we come across words we do not know. We use the same type of reasoning to figure out their meanings, and if we continue not to get it right, then we refer to a dictionary or to an expert-other (for example, an English instructor). We do this in every spoken language. Therefore, if you can figure out meanings of words while someone speaks to you, you will use that same approach when you read.

9   Sometimes, when you are paying close attention to someone's message, and he gets "stuck" on coming up with a word to complete his thought, have you not provided that word for the speaker? How did you know what word or its

synonym would come next? You knew because you were paying attention, and only that word would make sense. The same principle applies when we can fill-in-the-blank in a reading selection (refer to the section on "Some Insight into the Reading Process" in Chapter 8, Part One). However, you should realize that the more words you are unfamiliar with in a written selection or a lecture, the more difficult this process becomes. Fortunately, in reading selections, we can reread to figure out meaning, whereas in a conversation or in a lecture, unless we are recording it, such back and forth is not easily facilitated.

10   Fortunately, in most reading comprehension tests, you are required to identify the correct meaning of a vocabulary word in context. Without context, this **proposition** is difficult. This is why standardized tests such as the SAT and the ACT often ask for meanings of words that have been provided with no context. It is no wonder that many test-takers who lack a rich vocabulary do not score well on the reading portion of these tests.

Context Clues

11   Since we already know how to process unknown words in context while listening, and we apply these same processes to reading, it would make sense then to infer that we do not need to know more. But, we do. For example, there are some context clues that we need to be aware of that can **facilitate** our encounter with unfamiliar vocabulary, especially when we feel that we are "stuck." In a reading comprehension test, you will not be asked to name the context clues. However, you will and should apply them to answer questions on vocabulary. The context clues are as follows:

Synonyms and Antonyms

12   First you must know what these words mean. *Synonym* is a word with the same or a similar meaning. Remember that many words have different shades of meaning, and therefore they are not always the same. An example is: angry – irate. They may be similar but are not the same. For instance in this case, *irate* represents a much stronger state of emotional upset than *angry*.

On the other hand, an *antonym* is a word that has the opposite meaning of a given word. Again, the antonym may not be the exact opposite of a given word, but it will be close. An example of an antonym is: thrifty – spendthrift.

Read the simple sentences below:

My aunt is <u>beautiful</u>. Similarly, my mother is <u>gorgeous</u>.

13   Now suppose that you knew the meanings of *beautiful* and *similarly* but you did not know the meaning of *gorgeous*. Would you not be able to **deduce** that because the second sentence or idea is similar to the first sentence that the writer must be writing about a similar characteristic? Of course you would. Therefore, you would conclude that *gorgeous* must mean something similar to *beautiful*, which is like the state of being pretty. I realize that these sentences are **elementary**, but I use them to demonstrate the logical thinking that allows for this sort of interpretation.

14   Suppose you did not know the meaning of the word *similarly*, would you have been able to solve the word problem? Probably not! Without knowledge of the word *similarly*, you would not have known that the second sentence had a similar thought. And, of course, if you did not know what *beautiful* meant, it would not have mattered that the second sentence had a similar thought. You would not have been able to know the meaning of *gorgeous*. Therefore, just knowing that there is a synonym clue does not guarantee that you will figure out the vocabulary word. This all depends on how many words you do not know in those sentences, and also whether you know the meaning of the transition words, in this case, the word *similarly*. Some examples of other transition words that show a synonym relationship between the ideas are *likewise* and *in the same way*.

Now, read the simple sentences below:

My aunt is beautiful. However, her husband is hideous.

15   Now suppose that you knew the meaning of *beautiful*, but you did not know the meaning of *hideous*. Would you not be able to deduce that because the second sentence or idea is in contrast to the first sentence that the writer must be writing about a dissimilar characteristic? And, what word is the clue for you? Of course, you realized that the transition "however" usually introduces an opposite or different idea. The same sort of logic that you would use for the synonym clue, you would use for the antonym clue. Some examples of other transition words that show an antonym relationship between ideas are *on the other hand, unlike,* and *but*. Keep in mind that transition words such as "however" and "on the

other hand," do not always introduce an opposite concept. These words may very well introduce a difference in the level, grade, or intensity. Read the following example:

My aunt is <u>beautiful</u>. However, my mother is <u>gorgeous</u>.

16   In the above example, "beautiful" and "gorgeous" mean good looking; but *"gorgeous"* implies better than "beautiful." It is not an antonym for "beautiful." Therefore, an antonym clue is not going to be very helpful here. This is why in English there are no absolutes, and there is a risk of solely relying on clue words to critically think through a reading. Remember my mantra: There is no substitute for thinking!

Example/Illustration:

17   You probably know what *example* means. However, I want to explain the word *illustration* in this context. When we illustrate, we draw either visual pictures, or we describe an idea or concept so well that our brain can visualize the meaning. Now, read the simple sentences below:

<u>Serial killers</u>, such as Ted Bundy and Jeffrey Dahmer, murdered a number of people.

<u>Hallucinogenic</u> drugs, like peyote and LSD, can cause serious mental distortions.

18   In my opinion, this is the easiest clue in reading. Why? Well, simply put, it helps explain the terms *serial killers* and *hallucinogenic* by providing examples of serial killers and hallucinogenic drugs. These examples in turn are followed by what the killers and the drugs do. Now, read the simple sentences below:

She is <u>schizophrenic</u>. She talks to imaginary people and hears voices.

19   This last sentence provides illustrations of two common behaviors manifested by a person with schizophrenia. There are no examples of the word *schizophrenic* like in the previous set of sentences. However, her behaviors illustrate (describe) a mental disorder of some sort. We may not be able to provide a specific definition of the disorder as stated in psychology literature, but we would know that it is some sort of mental disorder because of the abnormal behaviors described.

Question to Infer Meaning:

20   If the context clues discussed thus far are not available, then the next best option is to self-question. This is where the ability to reason is important. What questions you ask yourself will determine whether you arrive at the correct answer. Look at the following sentence:

To keep her participant's identity confidential, the researcher used a pseudonym instead.

21   The logical question you will ask yourself will probably be something like, "If someone's name is to be kept confidential, what can be used instead?" The answer could be another made-up name and that is what *pseudonym* means. However, if you ask yourself, "Why can't the participant's identity be disclosed?" you may come up with a logical answer, but you would not have asked the correct question for determining the meaning of the word "pseudonym."

A Note on Connotation of Words and Figurative Language

22   You have read before where I stated that it is important not only to know the meaning of a word but to know how and when it is appropriate to use it. In other words, you have to make a word your own by knowing how best it can be used. This means you have to hear and see the words being used in varying contexts. Knowing the connotation of a word helps make the word your own. Connotation speaks of the nuances in language that I discussed before—the kind of "stuff" in language that you know just by trying and experiencing the language. For example, we know that some words have positive or negative connotations, and that some are neutral. Some synonyms of words have stronger positive or negative connotations, and therefore it is important to determine just what word fits right. This is why synonyms do not solely **imply** words that mean "the same"; instead, sometimes synonyms also are words that are similar in meaning.

23   If you have forgotten my discussion on connotations and denotations, it will be useful for you to refer to that section (Chapter 2: "Say What?!? The Nuances of English") to review and familiarize yourself with the material. It will be helpful to recall the relationships of denotative to literal language and connotative to figurative language (refer to Figure 5).

24   Refer to the following self-questioning technique that you can use to facilitate your understanding of unfamiliar words when you run into difficulty.

Self-Questioning Technique

It's a Piece of Cake! Unfamiliar Vocabulary in Context

- Read passage for general comprehension.

- Read for understanding of the specific vocabulary word.

- To figure out the unknown word, it is important to also read at least the sentence before, and the one after.

- If I substitute the vocabulary word with what I think the word means, will the word still make sense in context?

- If it makes sense, is there a response like it among the answer choices?

- If not, are there any clues (antonym, synonym, example/illustration) in the context in which the vocabulary word is used?

- If I find a clue and figure out the unknown word from among the choices, will the answer choice make sense if I were to substitute the unknown word with it?

- If there are no clues, then I will have to substitute the unknown word with each of the answer choices to figure out which one makes the most sense in context.

Application:

A. Write what you think the following words mean in the context of your reading. Then use the dictionary to check if you were right in your summation:

ingenious, reverting, counterpart, proposition, facilitate, deduce, elementary, imply, impervious

B. Based on your comprehension of the material you have just read, answer the following questions:

1. Give examples from your experience in everyday life of when you recall using the three types of context clues to make sense of unfamiliar words. These examples could be taken from verbal or written communication or a combination of both.

2. Tell about three things that you learned from this chapter.

3. What was confusing? What would you like to know more about from this chapter?

4. Look at the word "inadvertently" (in bold in the chapter) and describe in writing the mental reasoning that you used to determine what it meant within the context it was used.

Get to the Point! Main Ideas, Implied Main Ideas, and Supporting Details

(Do not forget to check titles and subtitles in this reading material and to predict what the reading material is going to be about. Bring to mind all that you know about the topic and all that you would want to know so that you begin reading as an active reader.)

Write your prediction based on topic and background knowledge:

What do you hope to gain from this reading material?

Subject-Specific Vocabulary:

narrative: something that is told or written like a story

Main Ideas and Implied Main Ideas

1   Have you had difficulty identifying a main idea sentence or coming up with one when the text does not have a main idea statement? You are not alone. The good news, however, is that you probably do find the main idea most times, but you may have difficulty when it is in material that is difficult to read. Your difficulty is either because of the **cumbersome** style of the written text and/or because you have limited knowledge of the vocabulary used. When you have listened to a lecture, a song, or a story, are you not able to tell in one sentence what that was all about? You probably can.

Movies

2   How many times have you tried to convince a friend to watch a movie that you thought was **sensational** and worth watching? Your friend asks what the movie is about. You tell your friend what the movie was about in one sentence. It is a very general sentence because you want her to watch the movie, and do not want to provide her with all the exciting details. However, in your zeal to encourage her to watch the movie, you forget your good **intentions**, and you begin to add details of selected parts of the movie that you were impressed with. Your friend, whose interest you have **piqued**, stops you short by suggesting that you are ruining the movie for her by providing all the details. In other words, you should have stopped after the one general statement that answered her question, "What was the movie about?"

Conversations and Class Lectures

3   Similarly, you may have been conversing with a group of friends. One friend begins to complain about her boyfriend's abusive behavior. She explains how on numerous occasions, her boyfriend shoved her, threw objects at her, and yelled at her. She tells you that she has had enough of his abusive behavior and she plans to leave him. At this point in the "narrative," someone reminds you all that the next class is about to start, so you split up and go your separate ways. However, another friend who was not present during this conversation joins you and asks what the group was talking about. You have your handle on the door to your class. You do not want to be late. In one general sentence, what would you say that the conversation was about? Think about this for a minute and then see if what you would say would be similar to the following:

She complained about her boyfriend's abusive behavior, and that she was going to leave him.

4   If you said something similar, you were on the right track. After class, if your friend pressed you further, you might share the details (for example, the behaviors described). If you notice, when we speak with someone, we rarely start off by stating that we are going to talk about this or that. We simply talk to communicate. The listener can then tell what the general idea is. In the **preceding** example, the friend did not start out the conversation by stating, "Now I am going to inform you of my boyfriend's abusive behavior, and that I am going to leave him," and then provide details. We **seldom** speak like that. Now, in a lecture situation in class, an instructor may start off by stating, "Today I am going to present Maslow's Hierarchy of Needs with examples." If your absent friend asked you later what the lecture was about, you probably would have repeated or paraphrased (put in your own words) the instructor's statement.

5   In the examples of the movie and the friend with the abusive relationship, a "main idea" was not provided. You had to figure it out. Similarly, *when you are asked for an implied main idea, you are asked for an unstated main idea.* This means that only the details are provided, and you have to figure out what the reading was about in one general statement. We do this subconsciously while we listen. Therefore, when we read, we should be able to do the same.

6   When someone is talking to us, our brain is constantly adapting its general notion of what is being stated because as the person continues talking, the brain adjusts this general, "What is she talking about?" statement to include most or all of the information the person is giving. Do you recall a time when someone was speaking to you, and you thought that he was talking about one thing, and he digressed and talked about something entirely different that had no connection to what you thought he was talking about in the first place? Did this not leave you somewhat confused? This is because you were paying attention to what was being said (active listening), and you were **formulating** an "implied main idea." However, after new information was added that appeared to have no connection to the topic, you had difficulty balancing your implied main idea. This is why sometimes you may even state to the speaker, "I am confused. Why don't you stay on topic?" or "What are you talking about?" How did you figure out the topic? Did the speaker state a topic? Chances are that he did not. Most times though, when people stay on topic, and we are actively listening, our implied main idea evolves to become generally inclusive of most of what was said.

7   We figure out implied main ideas in real life situations all the time. The TV comedies (sitcoms) you watch do not show titles or topics. If your wife missed an episode and asks you about it, you may tell her in one general statement.

Main Ideas/Implied Main Ideas in Reading

8   We do likewise as we read. However, fortunately many times reading passages provide enough information in a topic or title, and this gives us some insight to predict what the selection may be about even before we begin to read and **formulate** an implied main idea. Sometimes, a topic provides enough information to even predict a main idea before reading any of the main text. Moreover, a reading passage allows us to read and reread. Therefore, it is important not to jinx yourself by negative thoughts such as, "I cannot do this." Statements such as these will only serve to discourage you, and a negative attitude is not **conducive** to learning.

9   It makes sense for us, therefore, to let a topic—if one is provided—guide us to predict a main idea even before we begin to read. Some main ideas from titles/topics are easily predictable. Look at the examples below:

Insects of the Amazon; Stages of Grieving; Tips for College Success

10   If you are actively engaged (an active reader) with the passage, you will first bring to mind any background knowledge you have on these topics before you begin to read. You may even predict a main idea. So what if you are wrong? If upon further reading, you find out that your main idea needed to be adjusted, so what? You adjust your notion of the

main idea to fit the new information you have received by way of reading. Communication is a process that constantly evolves. However, we should keep in mind that a main idea is a general idea, and that it is stated as a complete thought.

11   Therefore, based on our prediction that the first passage (*Insects of the Amazon*) might be a listing, description, or both, of insects of the Amazon, we could possibly say, "There are many insects in the Amazon." For the second topic (*Stages of Grieving*), we would bring to mind all our background knowledge about grieving. We have either personally experienced or witnessed another's grief. We notice that the word "Stages" is used, which we know implies more than one stage. We could therefore state, "There are several stages of grieving." Now, you try the last topic: *Tips for College Success*.

12   Did you come up with something like, "There are several tips for college success"? If you did, was that very difficult? If you did not, do not worry too much; you will get a handle on main ideas soon. Recall what I said before: You do this most of the time when listening to people or watching television. Similarly, we formulate what something is even if we only use our sense of touch. For example, do you recall reaching into a drawer to look for something and instead, touched something else? Without actually seeing this object, your mind immediately thought about what it could be. You searched in your mind for a match with any previous experiences so that you could identify this object. The more sensations (details) you received from touching that object, the more thoroughly you were able to identify the object. This is also true of our experiences with sounds or with visual input. Our brain is designed to make sense of sensory input.

Too Broad? Too Narrow?

13   Notice how the words "many" and "several" are used to show generality in a main idea sentence? However, you must remember that a main idea or implied main idea has to fit the passage just right—just like your shoes must fit you just right in order to make walking comfortable. Your shoes cannot be too big (The main idea cannot be too broad or too general.) or too small (The main idea cannot be too narrow or too specific.).

Too Broad

14   What do we mean by the main idea being too broad? Let us look at the main idea: "There are many insects in the Amazon." Suppose that after reading the passage, we find that our prediction was correct in that the passage was indeed about the many insects of the Amazon. However, you realized that the only insects that were listed and described were carnivores (meat eaters). Your main idea is somewhat broad because it is suggestive of all sorts of insects of the Amazon. Could you adjust your main idea statement to be general but specific enough to "fit" the passage? Sure you can, and with very little difficulty! Could you not state, "There are many carnivorous insects in the Amazon"? Now, the main idea fits just right!

Too Narrow

15   If you used a detail as a main idea, it would be considered too narrow because it is not general enough to apply to all or most of the information in the passage. For example, if the passage about insects discussed some that were **camouflaged** and some that were not, and you decide that your main idea is "There are many camouflaged carnivorous insects in the Amazon," you will be excluding the insects that are not camouflaged. Therefore, this main idea would be too narrow (like shoes too small for your feet).

16   The reason I say "all" or "most" while discussing main ideas is because sometimes, in a passage, a writer may deviate from the main thrust of the message. **Subsequently**, in attempting to include all the information from the passage, we might have a main idea that is rather **awkward** and makes little sense. For example, suppose you are required to provide the central point (main idea of a long selection) of a chapter with the topic "School." After you read the chapter, you realize that it is about a child's (Molly) experiences at school. You want to state the central point as "Molly had many interesting experiences at school." However, in that long chapter, there is a paragraph in which the author **digresses** to talk about Molly helping her mother with her chores. Because you want to include everything, you change your central point to "Molly had many interesting experiences at school and she helped her mother with her chores." Do you see how awkward this statement is? If the author did not emphasize Molly's assistance with the chores, neither should you.

17   If you make it a habit to engage with your reading by continuing to predict as you receive new information, do the following: formulate a main idea, adapt, and **amend** it as you read, and you will find that if the main idea is stated in

the passage, it will look similar to what you had in mind. And, if it is not stated (implied main idea), your formulated implied main idea will look similar to one of the choices you may have on a multiple-choice test. I suspect we store all information in our memory as general ideas and that when we have to retrieve this information from memory, we first retrieve the information as a general idea followed by its details. What I am trying to impress on you is that getting a general idea from many details is something we all do on a daily basis whether we are attending a reading class or not, or whether we are educated or not!

18   Remember that in real-life situations, we are used to subconsciously creating main ideas from the information we receive. If you want to put this idea to the test, try the following: After you have watched a sitcom with two or more people, ask them to write down what the sitcom was about in one sentence. You do the same. Then, compare these statements, and you will be surprised how similar your statements are! Because the reasoning we use to answer reading comprehension questions is so similar to the kind of thinking we do in real life, we are fortunate that we find so many ways in which to practice our critical thinking in real, everyday situations. Are you still worried about not identifying the main idea and/or figuring out implied main idea?

19   Although I know that by now you are confident that you can identify main ideas, I must inform you that if you find the reading passage difficult to comprehend, finding the main idea and especially creating an implied main idea may not be an easy proposition. There are several reasons for this. One, there may be too many words that you do not know (vocabulary). Second, you may not have the necessary background knowledge to make sense of the written material. Last, you may not be engaged with the material because you are stressed. In a testing situation, you cannot do much about the first two reasons, but the last is in your control. You can try to de-stress and reread.

Use the Topic to Guide

20   However, all is not lost even if you are confused with the reading. Take time to look at the topic, if there is one. Remember that the reading has to be about the topic, and therefore a main idea statement should have all or most of the important words from the topic. Of course, the important words probably will be repeated in more than one sentence. For example, if the topic is "Environmental Issues in Florida," you can expect to see the words "environmental," "issues," and "Florida" in more than one sentence since these words are important. So, then, how do you decide which sentence is the main idea?

21   Well, there are some clues that may help you in making that decision. One such clue is the inclusion of some sort of general words or phrases, for example, *many ways, several reasons for,* and *a number of issues.* As you can tell, these words imply a sort of generalization. Avoid selecting sentences that begin with words such as *first, next, last, subsequently,* and *moreover* as the main idea. As you can tell, these words are going to tell about a more specific idea. For example, a sentence that begins with *"next"* does not cover information that was stated before; therefore, it cannot be the main idea sentence. It has to be a supporting detail. Recall that a main idea covers most or all of the important information in a written passage.

22   However, clue words may be misleading. For example, if you are asked for the main idea of a particular paragraph in a passage, what is being asked of you is the topic sentence (A topic sentence is usually expected of you when you are first learning to write a paragraph.). It is the main idea of the paragraph, and it may have the same clue words as those I mentioned in the preceding paragraph like *several reasons for* and *many ways;* however, it is not the main idea of the entire selection.   Therefore, understand what is being asked – main idea of paragraph or main idea of the selection? Also, it is important to note that a sentence that begins with "next" cannot be a main idea of a selection but could certainly be the topic sentence of a paragraph. By now you realize that main idea and topic sentence are sometimes used interchangeably when referring to paragraphs. The following relationships may help with your understanding of this discussion:

main idea of passage = central point, controlling idea, thesis, main idea
main idea of paragraph = main idea, topic sentence

23   Therefore, you could be asked the main idea of a passage (In the case of a research paper or an essay, this may be referred to as a "thesis statement"; in larger selections this may be referred to as a "central point"; and sometimes in English courses main idea may be referred to as the "controlling idea") and you could be asked for the main idea of a paragraph (topic sentence in writing terms). Both would probably have some general clue words. These clue words are the same for the main idea of a passage or for the main idea of a paragraph. Therefore, it is important to understand the question asked. Please keep in mind that just as a passage may not have a stated main idea—you may be required to write one—all

paragraphs may not have stated main ideas (topic sentences). If you are required to write the main idea for a paragraph, you will use the same sort of reasoning as you would for a passage. Also, keep in mind that topic sentences may begin with transitions like *first, second,* and *last.* However, you know that main ideas do not begin with such transitions. What is important to know is that although a main idea of a reading selection is not going to begin with transitions such as *first* and *last,* the main idea of a paragraph (topic sentence) or paragraphs within a selection sometimes do.

24   I am often quoted as saying, "There is no substitute for thinking." Therefore, I encourage you not to rely solely on clue words. They do not always lead you in the right direction and may even serve to confuse you at times. Use them only when you run into comprehension difficulty like when you **encounter** a particularly difficult reading passage. Understand that clue words such as *first, next, last, subsequently,* and *moreover* that appear at the beginning of a sentence do not indicate a main idea of a passage, but they could represent the main idea (topic sentence) of a single paragraph within a passage.

25   Refer to the following self-questioning technique that you can use to facilitate your understanding of a main idea and an implied main idea when you run into difficulty.

Self-Questioning Technique

Get to the Point!

- What is the topic? Who or what is the author talking about?
- What is the sentence with all the important words from topic and/or repeated words?
- Does this sentence cover all or most of the information given?
- Are there any clue words (for example: a number of, a series of, various causes, etc.) that generally introduce a main idea?
- Does all or most of the information fall under this main idea umbrella?
- If it does not, look for another sentence in the answer choices that fits better.
- Verify all the alternatives in the answer choices.

Implied Main Ideas

- Can I make a sentence with all the important words from the topic and/or repeated words?
- What are the major supporting details?
- What is the overall idea that would cover all of the major supporting details?
- Is there a similar idea listed among the response choices? If so, this would probably be the implied main idea.
- Have all of the responses been checked to look for the best fit?
- Choose the option that all or most of the passage's details support or explain.

Application:

A. Write what you think the following words mean in the context of your reading. Then use the dictionary to check if you were right in your summation:

cumbersome, sensational, intentions, piqued, preceding, digresses, formulating, evolving, formulate, conducive, subsequently, awkward, camouflaged, amend, encounter

B. Based on your comprehension of the material you have just read, answer the following questions:

1. Tell what was most helpful in this segment and why.

2. What was confusing? What would you like to know more about?

3. Give an example from real-life in which you determined the main idea.

4. What is the difference between main idea and implied main idea? Which of the two do you think is more difficult to answer in a multiple-choice question? Why?

The Devil Is in the Details! Supporting Details (Major and Minor)

26   So, then, what are supporting details? You got it! Most of the rest of the reading material that is not a main idea are the supporting details. That is easy enough; however, what may take some getting used to is **honing** your ability to be able to differentiate the major supporting details from the minor supporting details. In my opinion, this takes a little more skill than finding main ideas.

27   But first, why is it even important to be able to identify the two types of details? Is it not sufficient to simply know that these are details? It is important to differentiate between the major and minor details when you have to determine an implied main idea (recall that an implied main idea is not stated). By analyzing major supporting details, you could figure out a general idea that would be your main idea. This process becomes more crucial when reading a long passage. There may be so much information to deal with that coming up with a general sentence would be challenging. There may be details that are vying for your attention because you found them interesting. These are called **seductive** details because they "seduce" you away from the important ideas. However, these kinds of details are seldom major details. They are usually found as minor details. Sometimes you will find that a minor detail that caught your interest is the one that you focused on and then incorrectly presented as your implied main idea. Therefore, focusing in on only major details makes it so much easier to infer a main idea when one is not stated. Remember that in order to do well in reading comprehension tests, we have to carefully think through our answers.

28   What are major supporting details, and how do we find them? First, we have to know that major details are the ones that are less general than the main idea but more general than minor details. Therefore, we can say that major details are more specific than the main idea, but that minor details are even more specific than the major details. In other words, major details back up (support) the main idea directly, and the minor details back up (support) the major details directly. Minor details are not as closely related to main ideas as they are to major supporting details whereas major supporting details are related directly to the main idea as well as to their minor supporting details. Major details serve as the go-between for the main idea and minor details. Figure 7 should make the relationship clear. In Figure 7, the roof of the house represents the main idea or implied main idea. The roof of a house usually covers everything under it like the main idea (or implied main idea) is a sentence general enough to cover all or most of the information from the passage. The **vertical** lines connected to the roof represent pillars that hold up (support) the roof. These pillars are the major supporting details. The beams that support the pillars are the minor supporting details.

29   In Figure 8, for the sake of simplicity, only phrases and words are used to represent sentences. However, recall that the main idea is always stated as a complete thought. If you only had the topic *(Tips for College Success)* and major details like "time management," "attendance," "study," and "completion of assignments," would you not be able to determine a main idea (such as, *There are several tips for college success.*)? Of course you would! And, making this determination would be simpler by just considering the major details because once you consider the major details, it is assumed that you have also included the major details' supporting beams (minor details).

30   Refer to Figure 8 again. Each major supporting detail pillar serves as the main idea for its section of minor supporting detail beams. A section is the paragraph(s) in the **vicinity** of the major supporting detail. In other words, each major detail pillar serves as a main idea for the beams that support it. For example, the "time management" pillar is the main idea (topic sentence) for the "make to-do list," "prioritize," and "follow-through" beams that support it. The "attendance" pillar serves as the main idea for the "on-time daily," "If absent - study-partner," and the "check with instructor" beams that support it. You will use similar reasoning to understand the "study" and "completion of assignments" pillars.

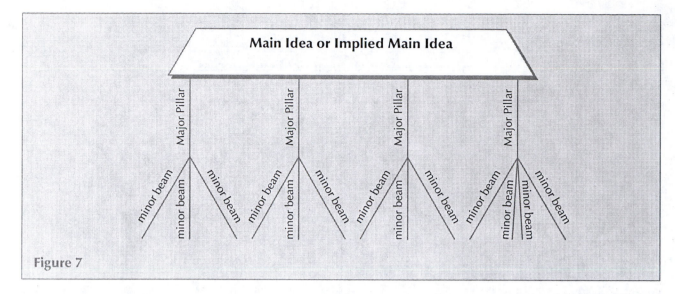

Figure 7

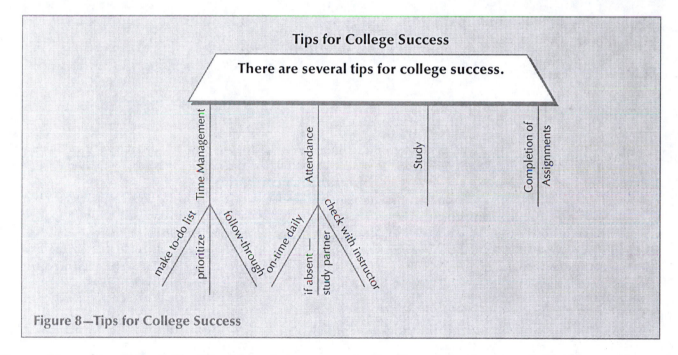

Figure 8—Tips for College Success

31   Now refer to Figure 9. The "Place" beam (minor supporting detail) represents the sentence, "Find a quiet place to study." Furthermore, this sentence has its own little beam supporting it (a minor detail more specific than the minor detail that preceded it), which represents the sentence, "It may be in a little corner of the room." Now, suppose all you are given are two sentences. One sentence is "There are several tips for college success." (main idea) and the other "It may be in a little corner of the room." Would there be any way to figure out the relationship between these two thoughts? Not unless you are **psychic**! You must read the selection in its entirety. However, if you were given "Find a quiet place to study." and "It may be in a little corner of the room.", you would surely be able to make sense of the connection between these thoughts. Therefore, understand that the further your beams (minor details) are from the roof (main idea), the less related they are to the roof (main idea). The beams (minor supporting details) are related directly to the pillars (major supporting details) that they are attached to and so on. The pillars (major supporting details) are directly attached to the roof (main idea). Therefore, you can easily see the connection of the "You must study." pillar (major supporting detail) to the roof (main idea: "There are several tips for college success."). Also, remember that as the beams get farther away from the roof, the more specific the information is going to be, and this is where we find our most interesting and seductive details.

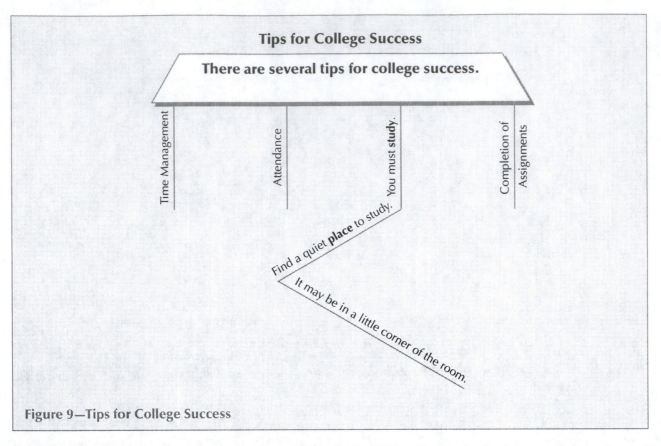

Figure 9—Tips for College Success

31   Again my favorite mantra: "There is no substitute for thinking." Therefore, understand that you will need to read the selection and separate the major from the minor details. Once you have the major details, you should be a pro at finding the implied main idea.

32   Recall that in my discussion of main idea, I had mentioned how clue words can be useful but also confusing if you do not know how and when to use them to assist you. Refer to this discussion earlier in this chapter. What if you were to write an essay using the figure of the house? Could you not make sentences using clue words (in this case transition words) such as *first, second, third,* and *last* to introduce each of your major details? You certainly could. But, understand that these clue words may also appear in beams even beyond the first level of minor detail beams. Refer to Figures 10a, 10b, and 10c to get a clearer understanding of what I mean.

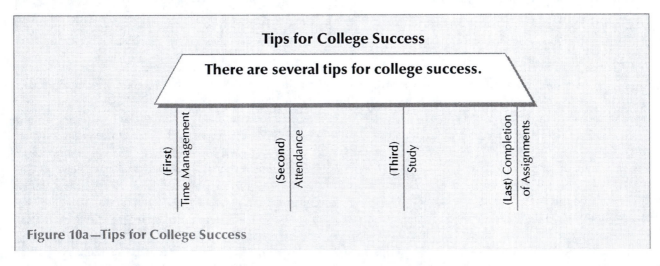

Figure 10a—Tips for College Success

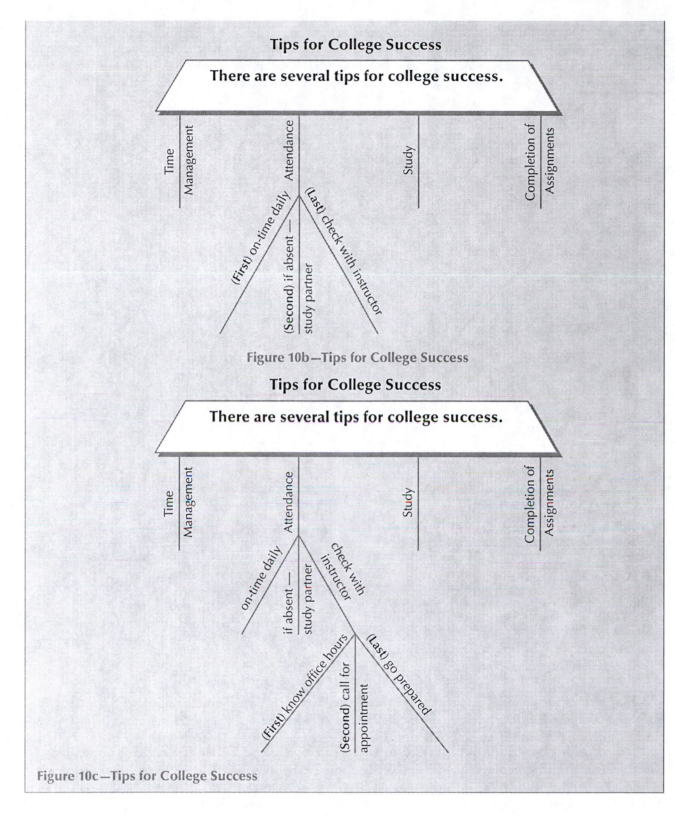

Figure 10b—Tips for College Success

Figure 10c—Tips for College Success

Outline

33   Now, we should have an even deeper understanding of the intimate relationship between reading and writing. If you excel at one, there is no reason for you not to excel at the other. Outlines for writing or for material read are similar to the house except that you will not use any form of illustration. An outline may look like the following:

Tips for College Success

There are several tips for college success.

- ✦ time management
  1. make to-do list
  2. prioritize
  3. follow-through
- ✦ attendance
  1. on time daily
  2. if absent – study partner
  3. check with instructor
     - know office hours
     - call for appointment
     - go prepared
- ✦ study
  1. find a quiet place to study
     - corner of room
  2. *(use your imagination and put an idea in here)*
  3. *(use your imagination and put an idea in here)*
- ✦ completion of assignments
  1. *(use your imagination and put an idea in here)*
  2. *(use your imagination and put an idea in here)*
  3. *(use your imagination and put an idea in here)*
  4. *(use your imagination and put an idea in here)*

34   The "Table of Contents" section of a textbook is often an example of an outline, is it not? What about the section of this book that provides chapter titles and subtopics? Did you preview this section prior to reading the chapters? If you did, how did doing that help with your comprehension?

35   I prefer graphic representations like that of the house illustration instead of outlines. You can come up with your own illustration to depict information in graphic form. These come in handy particularly when you have to study **copious** amounts of information. Keep in mind, however, that if you are required to write a summary, you are to provide a main idea and major supporting details only, and that these have to be presented in your own words.

36   A reminder: you may be asked for a central point. A central point is the same as a main idea, and the term is usually used when the reading selection is long. Also, keep in mind that for a research paper, a main idea is called a thesis statement. College essays also use thesis statements.

37　Please note: Although when you first learned to write an essay, you might have been taught that you must have a clearly stated main idea, you have now come to understand that sometimes good writing does not contain a stated main idea, and you have to infer it. You may have also been told that a main idea is usually the first sentence. A main idea can be located at the beginning of a paragraph, in the middle of a paragraph or even at the end of a paragraph. This does not make identifying a main idea easy. Therefore, we must rely on our own powers of reasoning to identify the main idea. What is important, however, is that we can identify it wherever it is located in the text, and that we can infer a main idea if it is not stated at all.

38　Refer to the following self-questioning technique that you can use to facilitate your understanding of major and minor supporting details when you run into difficulty.

Self-Questioning Technique

The Devil Is in the Details! Supporting Details (Major and Minor)

- What is the overall idea (main idea)?
- What directly backs up the overall idea? These would be the major supporting details. They could be reasons or examples.
- What indirectly backs up the main idea but directly backs up my major supporting details? These would be the minor supporting details.
- If I cannot figure this out, are there any clue words (for example: "for one thing," "another," "moreover") that generally introduce major supporting details? (These words can also introduce minor supporting details.)
- Minor supporting details are generally more specific than the major supporting details.
- The further away the idea is from being related to the main idea, the more likely it is that it is a minor supporting detail.
- Usually the most interesting or specific details are the minor supporting details.

Application:

A. Write what you think the following words mean in the context of your reading. Then use the dictionary to check if you were right in your summation:

honing, seductive, seldom, vertical, vicinity, psychic, copious

B. Based on your comprehension of the material you have just read, answer the following questions:

1. Depict the information from this section on supporting details as an illustration.
2. What was the central point of this section? State it as a complete thought.

Ideas Getting Hitched: Relationships Between/Within Sentences and Patterns of Organization

(Do not forget to check titles and subtitles in this reading material and to predict what the reading material is going to be about. Bring to mind all that you know about the topic and all that you would want to know so that you begin reading as an active reader.)

Your prediction based on topic and background knowledge:

What do you hope to gain from this reading material?

Subject-Specific Vocabulary:

transitions: in reading and writing these are words like *and, but,* and *then* that show the connection between one thought and another

1   "Getting hitched" in the context of this chapter implies a connection between and within sentences. So what are sentences? They are complete thoughts in written form. Therefore, a relationship between sentences must imply a connection between thoughts. How do we connect sentences in written text? We do so by using what we call transition words (for example: "also," "however," "subsequently"). *Transition* means to connect from one to the next. Therefore, we could say that a transition word serves as a bridge from one thought to the next so that the reader knows how the thoughts are related to each other. It makes the message easier for the reader to follow so that he does not have to guess. However, do not expect to rely on transition words alone to clue you in about relationships within and between sentences.

2   Sometimes, when you think there ought to be transition words, the writer has not used any. You must therefore read and analyze. Remember what I have said again and again: *There is no substitute for thinking.* In real life "speaking" situations, we are accustomed to not being clued in with transition words because colloquially using many transitions seems awkward. Therefore, in speaking we do not use transitions as often as we do when we are writing. One reason for this may be because we usually know our audience (listener), and the listener can ask questions if she is confused. In reading a written passage, we cannot ask questions of the author, and often, although we write with a particular audience in mind (I am writing for and to college students.), there is no way of knowing who will be reading our material.

Addition and Time Relationships

Read the examples below:

A simple example (1): *The woman sang. She danced.*   (no transition)

_____ *The woman sang. Also, she danced.*   (transition between sentences)

_____ *The woman sang, and she danced.*   (transition within a sentence)

A simple example (2): *The woman sang. She danced.*   (no transition)

_____ *The woman sang. Then, she danced.*   (transition between sentences)

_____ *The woman sang, and then she danced*   (transition within a sentence)

3   As you can tell, the basic sentences "The woman sang. She danced." do not give you, the reader, any specific indication of how the two thoughts are connected. Once I added the transition word "also," you knew that I am "adding" one thought to the previous thought; therefore, this is a relationship of "addition." Keep in mind however, that it makes sense to say that in order for written text (or speech) to be understandable, most, if not all, of the sentences (thoughts/ideas) in that text are connected by "addition" to the previous sentences (thoughts/ideas). After all, we 'piggy-back' on preceding ideas to make sense and therefore, we are adding on to previous thought. However, as in the previous example (2), when I added the transition word "then," you realized that I wanted to inform you that the woman danced after she sang. What was done first and what was done next was important for me to tell you. Therefore, these two sentences were related to each other by "time."

What Are Patterns of Organization?

4   Let us now pause to talk about **patterns of organization**. What are they? Simply put, patterns of organization are how most sentences are related in a given paragraph or passage. When we are discussing the connection between two sentences (thoughts) or two thoughts within one sentence, we are asked for the relationship between or within those thoughts. However, when we are discussing the connection among more than two thoughts, then we are being asked for the pattern of organization of thoughts (sentences). Stop to think about what a pattern is. We know that it is a graphic or other design that repeats itself, much like the patterns on wallpaper or fabric. This idea of repetition is what is implied by pattern of organization.

List of Items and Time Order

5   Look back at previous paragraphs. Can you identify any kind of relationships that repeat like a pattern? Are these patterns that of **time order** or a **list of items** (repeated time relationships are known as a pattern of *time order;* repeated addition relationships are known as a pattern of a *list of items*)?

6   Suppose you ask your 4-year-old nephew what he did yesterday. He might begin by telling you the following:

"Let's see. I got up and had cereal. Then, I went out to play with Ben, my best friend. Then, mommy took me to Judo class. Then, I went to McDonald's and ate a Happy Meal. Then, I watched TV. Then ..."

7   You get the picture? This child wants you to know what he did chronologically. The pattern you see repeating here is that of time relationship between sentences. But, because this monologue involved more than two sentences (two thought processes), you are asked for the pattern of how this child organized his thoughts. Hence, pattern of organization. The pattern of organization is that of **time order**. Think back to the time that you told someone about a movie you watched or about an accident that you were involved in. You were likely to have told them about it in chronological order. You did not spend any conscious time thinking about how you were going to organize your thoughts. Your brain organized it all for you! All you had to do was tell what happened. And, did you notice that if you left out an important

event, you went back and told the listener to "insert" it here or there? This is because our brains are designed to make sense of things.

8   Now, as you know, we listen to people all the time, and they automatically organize information in a way that is easy for us, the listener, to follow. We do this, too, when we are conversing with others. If our brains subconsciously organize thoughts in lightning speed before we begin to speak, and even while we give information, why would a writer not do the same? In fact, it is crucial for a writer to organize his thought patterns in a way that the reader can understand. The next time you listen to someone relay information to you verbally, ask yourself what pattern of organization he is using. Also, I am sure that you have some of your written assignments around. Look through them. What pattern of organization have you used? Have you used more than one?

9   Now, let's say that you found out that your sister had taken your four-year-old nephew to the mall to shop for school-related items, and you asked him what she had bought him. He might begin by telling you the following:

"Let's see … Oh yes, Mommy bought me shoes. And she got me clothes. And pencils … and crayons … and a book bag. Oh! I forgot. She also got me some bubblegum …"

10   What is the pattern of organization here? Yes, you see the thoughts related by addition and, the repeated use of the word "and," so it makes sense to infer that this is a pattern of organization called "addition." However, this pattern is called a **list of items**. If you think of it, it is the same as addition. I would personally have preferred for it to have been called an 'addition' pattern of organization so that it could be in keeping with all the other relationship and corresponding patterns of organizations that you are going to learn about—as these are referred to in the same terms—but **list of items** is a term already coined in reading comprehension, and I am afraid I cannot change it. It is suffice for you to know that it means the same as repeated addition relationships. It is like a list that you make when you go to the grocery store. You are simply listing your thoughts and adding one to the other. If you noticed, when the child informed you what his mother purchased for him at the mall, you could not tell what he got first or second or last. He did not tell you chronologically. He simply added one item to the next item and so on.

11   Of course, there are many words (transition words) that could clue the reader about relationships between and within sentences. You are more familiar with the English language and are, therefore, not limited to using just "then" or "and" or "also" like your 4-year-old nephew. You know that words such as *subsequently, next, first, while,* and *finally* can clue the reader to the relationships between thoughts (that of "time"). Similarly, words such as *additionally, moreover, another,* and *furthermore* can clue the reader to the relationships of "addition."

Different Relationships in One Pattern

12   As we proceed with this discussion, it is important for you to remember that unlike a pattern in fabric, a pattern of organization of written thoughts is usually not found in a pure state. What I mean is that if you analyze the relationships in a 10-sentence paragraph, for example, you may find that the pattern of organization may be that of **time order** because information is being presented chronologically. It would not make sense to present the information in any other form of organization, yet there are two sentences that are related by "addition." This is okay. You will find that not all sentences are related the same way ("time"). However, most of them will be ("time"), and that will be your pattern of organization (**time order**).

13   Sometimes in a comprehension test, you may be asked the pattern of organization of a reading selection, and you will be able to identify one definite pattern. However, you may then be asked the relationship between two sentences within that selection. You may be tempted to select the same type of relationship as what you selected for the pattern of organization, but you may find that your answer is incorrect. What I mean is that you may have determined after reading a selection, that the pattern of organization is that of **time order** and therefore, the relationship between two sentences is that of time, but the relationship between the two sentences presented to you may be that of "addition." Therefore, you must pay attention to what is being asked and analyze the sentences. Remember that they do not have to correspond with the pattern of organization although most sentences in that selection would.

14   Sometimes, you may find that a passage almost equally represents two patterns of organization, and this is common when a passage is long. For example, in a real life scenario, it is quite common when someone is talking to you for a long time about a complicated matter that she may use more than one pattern of organization. She may do this to help you, the listener, understand the flow of her thoughts. Similarly, a writer may do the same.

Main Idea Correspondence to Pattern of Organization

15   Also understand that a main idea generally corresponds with a pattern of organization. What do I mean? Well, consider that you have predicted from the title "Tips for College Success" that the main idea may be "There are several tips for college success." Could you not, therefore, infer that the pattern of organization will be that of a "list of items" before you even begin reading, or while you are formulating your implied main idea? Does it not make sense that the author will address one "tip" after another? If someone had asked you to tell him about the things you like about college, would that person not be predicting that you would be talking about these things one after another as in a **list of items**? However, if someone asked you how your first day in college went, that person would probably have expected you to tell him chronologically what had happened that day (**time order**).

16   What if you are wrong with your prediction of the main idea and, therefore, also wrong with your subsequent prediction of pattern of organization? Do you foresee dire consequences for incorrect predictions? Predicting keeps you engaged and active in your reading comprehension. Adjusting and making "corrections" is not only normal but is also necessary in the comprehension process.

17   The larger point here is that the main idea or the implied main idea usually corresponds with a pattern of organization. The next time your instructor tells you that she is going to talk about something, predict how she is going to organize the material to be presented based on the topic. Look at your high school or college textbooks. How would you expect your history textbook to be organized? What about your psychology textbook? On a more personal note, what about a summary or synopsis of a movie you watched? Or a summary of your personal diary entries?

18   If I informed you that I would be telling you about the steps involved in baking a cake, would you not realize that I would be telling you these steps in chronological order (time order)? It would not make sense to tell you in any other way, would it? But, what if I tell you that I am going to inform you about the ingredients that you need to bake a cake? Would you not predict that I will tell you this as a list of items? Keep in mind that sometimes a passage can be identified as both time order as well as a list of items. For example, if I discussed not only how to bake a cake but I also informed you of the ingredients needed to bake the cake, the pattern could be both time order as well as a list of items. However, in short reading excerpts as in small paragraphs the overall pattern is usually one or the other. Keep in mind that all reading material does not have to have only one discernable pattern of organization. The pattern could be a combination—especially when it is a lengthy reading—of two or more patterns of organization. I think by now you have a good idea of what I am talking about. However, we still have more relationships and patterns to discover.

Definition and Example, and Illustration

19   Another relationship between sentences is that of **definition and example**. Closely related to this is the relationship of **illustration**. Refer to the following examples:

Communism is a repressive form of government. China is a communist country.

Dyslexia is a form of learning disability that affects reading. Pablo Picasso was dyslexic.

20   If you analyze the two examples above, you will notice that for each example the first sentence defines a term (communism, dyslexia), and the second sentence is an example of it. In my opinion, a relationship of **definition and example** is the easiest to identify. Now, read the following examples:

China is a communist country. There is no freedom of speech, religion, or press, and it is run by a dictator.

Pablo Picasso was dyslexic. He had difficulty with processing language.

21   Upon analysis of the above sentences, you will have realized that illustration is not so different from definition and example. After all, what does the word illustration mean? Does it not mean to make something so clear in your mind that it is almost as though someone drew a picture? When we define and give examples, we also illustrate—make clear. The only difference between the first and second set of sentences is that in the second set of sentences there are no definitions. Only descriptions of behaviors are given following a term (communist, dyslexic) from which we deduce the meaning of the terms. Either way, I restate to emphasize: Whether the relationship is that of **definition and example** or **illustration**, in my opinion, these are the simplest relationships to identify.

22   Similarly, a **definition and example** pattern of organization (or **illustration**) may present itself, for example, in a chapter in your social science textbook under the topic of Communism. You may find that communism is defined at great length. Following this definition may be a discussion of some communist countries. When defining communism at such length, the author will illustrate this concept for the reader. Therefore, whether it be a pattern of **illustration** or **definition and example** is a matter of semantics (a good opportunity to look up this word). Also, realize that some of the "clue" words for illustration as well as for definition and example are usually the same: *for example, such as,* and *to illustrate.* But, by now, we are not going to be dependent on these so-called "clue" words, are we? We are thinking critically for ourselves!

23   I am going to take a shortcut and use creative license to henceforth refer to Pattern of Organization as PO (POs for plural).

Cause and Effect

24   On to the next relationship and PO! **Cause and effect** is another term you will have to get accustomed to. But, first, we must understand that *cause* is what makes something else happen (the reason), and *effect* is what happens (the result). Read the sentence below:

> *I came late because I was in a traffic jam.* (Understand that there are two thoughts expressed in this sentence: *I came late and I was in a traffic jam.)*

25   In the above sentence, the traffic jam (the reason) is what made me come in late. Therefore, coming in late was the effect (the result). Keep in mind that the sentence could also have been written as: *The traffic jam caused me to be late.* Either sentence portrays the same message. The cause and effect do not change. Knowing how the clue word *because* is used to signify this causal relationship is important. There are other examples of such clue words: "consequently," "reason," "since," and "due to."

26   How might we encounter a **cause and effect** pattern of organization? What if my main idea was: *The traffic jam today caused me many inconveniences.* You would expect me to tell you about the inconveniences. These inconveniences would be the results of the traffic jam (the cause). So, the one cause (traffic jam) resulted in many effects (for example: late to class, less time on tests, parking problems). Alternatively, more than one cause can result in one effect. For example, what if my main idea was: "Several factors have caused the number of abortion clinics to decrease"? If, for example, this main idea was followed by an explanation of the factors (for example, fewer abortions, threats of violence) that resulted in this decline of abortion clinics (one effect) this would also be classified as a **cause and effect** PO.

Comparison and Contrast

27   My very favorite PO is **comparison and contrast**. First, we need to know what these words mean in this context. Comparison means how ideas are similar. Contrast means how things are different. From experience I have noticed that although these are simple enough concepts, my students would often confuse "comparison" with "differences." Upon reflecting on possible reasons for these misconceptions, I found that this is probably the case because in real-life situations when someone says that he is comparing you to so-and-so, you are usually expecting to find how you are different from that person. That is why if your parents commented, "Why can't you be like your big brother?" you might have felt hurt and complained to your friends stating, "I am tired of my parents comparing me to how well my big brother did in college." Of course in this context, your parents were referring to differences between you and your brother. Perhaps because we have learned from experiences such as these that our parents are in actuality contrasting us with someone else, we think that *comparison* in reading also means differences. Therefore, it would help to make a mental note that in the context of this reading comprehension chapter, *comparison* means how things are similar. *Contrast* means how things are dissimilar or different. Therefore, some examples of comparison clue words are: "similarly," "in like manner," "likewise," and "both." On the other hand, contrast clue words are: "on the other hand," "however," "although," and "despite." Let us see how a comparison relationship will look like by reading the following sentences:

> *You know that words such as "additionally," "moreover," "another," and "furthermore" can clue the reader to the relationships between your thoughts (that of addition). Similarly, words such as "subsequently," "next," "first," "while," and "finally" can clue the reader that the relationships between your thoughts are that of time.*

28   If you think that you are having a déjà vu moment, I am happy to inform you that you have been actively reading because you read these sentences earlier on in this chapter. Did you notice how these sentences are telling you how addition words clue you to an addition relationship just like time words clue you to a time relationship? Since you are being shown similarities between the ideas, this is a relationship of comparison. Now read the following sentences:

She is thrifty. However, her husband is a spendthrift.

29   A difference is being stated in her spending habits and his. Therefore, this is an example of a "contrast" relationship.

30   For **comparison and contrast** PO examples, think of how you would answer the following questions:

1. *How are Dwayne Wade and Michael Jordan similar on the basketball court?*

2. *Contrast Dwayne Wade's and Michael Jordan's moves on the basketball court.*

31   We are going to infer that you have enough background knowledge on these two basketball players to answer these questions. If your answer had to show at least four similarities (for question 1) and four differences (for question 2), you would notice that the pattern of organization for answer 1 would be that of comparison (similarities) and for answer 2 would be that of contrast (differences). Now, what if you had to answer this following question?

Tell how Dwayne Wade and Michael Jordan are similar and different on the basketball court.

32   Now, your answer would be similar to a **comparison and contrast** PO. Perhaps while answering this question, you decided that first you would talk about similarities in one paragraph, and then in the second paragraph, you would talk about the differences. If you looked back at your own written work and were asked to identify the PO (Your written work becomes the reading selection.), you would rightly say "comparison and contrast."

33   However, if you were asked only to identify the PO of the first paragraph, you would have to say "comparison" because you addressed similarities in the first paragraph. And, of course if you were asked to identify the PO of the second paragraph, you would have to say "……….." (I know that you have got it!).

34   I am particularly partial to comparison and contrast POs. Take a look at Figure 11.

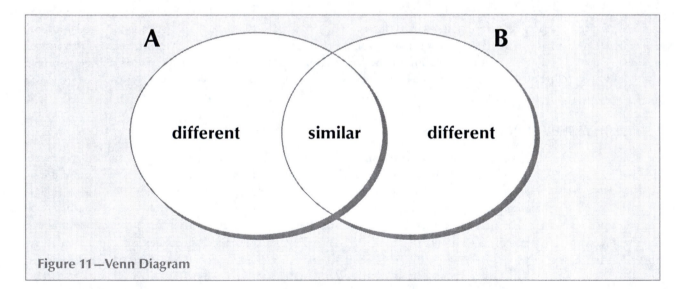

Figure 11—Venn Diagram

35   Some of you probably remember this diagram from when you learned sets and subsets in mathematics. I have found it a particularly useful tool for planning for writing and for study purposes. If I need to study the circulatory and the respiratory systems for my biology class and I know that my instructor requires me not only to know how these systems are different, but also how they are similar, I could represent/illustrate that information graphically in a Venn diagram and use that as a study tool. Similarly, if I needed to write an essay about the similarities and differences between these systems, I could use this Venn diagram to plan out what I am going to write. For me, it is better than an outline. If you are a visual learner, the diagram might appeal to you.

Other Relationships and Patterns of Organization

36   There are other types of relationships that you may use in writing and may encounter in reading comprehension tests. For example, "spatial" relationship is like a description that shows location or position: how close an object is in relation to another (for example: facing, next to); how distant (for example: far, beyond); or in what direction (for example: right, left, up, down). Read the following examples to recognize this type of relationship, and then think of similar examples that you might have encountered in your everyday life:

> The cottage was far. It was located just beyond the winding road.

> The car was in the driveway facing the street, and the driver had gone around the back to the fence on the right.

37   When might you encounter a **spatial** PO? It makes sense, does it not, that you may find such a pattern when there is a description of locations on a map or directions to your home for a holiday party?

Another type of relationship is that of a **restatement** of an idea. For example, how often have I used the words "in other words" in this textbook? Why have I done that? Is it not to repeat the same thought in a different way so that you may better understand? A *restatement,* therefore, expresses the same thought but differently. Often, it is preceded by "in other words" or "to put it simply." We have also heard these words during our conversations with people. If more than one thought is being restated, you probably will have a **restatement** PO although I do not see this as being a common PO.

38   What about a **problem and solution** PO? What would that look like? Of course it makes sense that in this organization there will be a stated or implied problem, and a solution to that problem. For example, a patient may have a medical problem, and how the problem was solved would make for a problem-solution PO. Think of how you would express a "problem and solution" situation in your own life.

39   Whatever the situation, it would help to keep in mind that in English, there are no absolutes. English is a living language, and language evolves when it is used and tried out in many ways. Therefore, this chapter is not all-inclusive. Know that you may encounter relationships and POs with synonymous or even new names. For example, a **list of items** PO may very well be called an **addition** PO. What about a **classification** PO in which ideas are grouped into subcategories. It resembles a list of items PO and has the same transition clues usually followed by words such as "type," "group," and "kind" (for example: "another type" and "last kind"). You may find a **description** PO listed as one of the answer options but instead be looking for an **illustration** PO. However, you do not find the illustration PO in your options of multiple-choice answers. You must ask yourself: Is not illustrating a concept very much like describing it? Remember that there is no substitute for thinking!

40   Refer to the following self-questioning technique that you can use to facilitate your understanding of relationships and patterns of organization when you run into difficulty.

Self-Questioning Technique

Ideas Getting Hitched! Relationships and Patterns of Organization

To answer a question on relationships (addition and time):

- Does the idea in the second sentence add to the idea in the first sentence: I bought a shirt. I also bought a jacket. If it does, then the relationship between the two sentences is that of *addition*.

- Are there familiar clue words (transition words) such as "also," "moreover," and "additionally" that may introduce an *addition* relationship?

- Is the first idea showing a chronological connection to the second idea (e.g., I bought a shirt. Then, I bought a jacket.)? If it is, then the relationship between the two sentences is that of *time*.

- Are there familiar clue words (transition words) such as "first," "second," "then," and "during" that may introduce a time relationship?

To answer a question on pattern of organization (list of items and time order):

- Do I recognize any clue words (transition words) such as "one," "another," and "furthermore" that introduce *addition*? Or "first," "next," "finally," "then," which may introduce time? If most of the transitions are those of addition, then it is usually a *list of items* pattern of organization. If most of the transitions are those of *time*, then it is usually a *time* pattern of organization.

- Read, or if I have already read, skim the passage and look for a pattern.

- Has most of what the author is saying been put in chronological order? If yes, then it is a *time* pattern of organization. The transitions are similar to those seen in time relationships between sentences.

- Would most of the ideas listed in the passage make sense regardless of the order of the written ideas? If yes, then this is probably a *list of items* pattern of organization. The transitions are similar to those seen in addition relationships between and within sentences.

Remember: Although a pattern of organization may be one type, relationships within or between sentences in the same reading selection could be a different type. For example: The pattern of organization of the passage may be time; however, two sentences within the passage may be related by addition.

Remember: The same transition words may be used to introduce different patterns of organizations (for example: "first," "second," "last" could be used for a list of items or a time pattern of organization).

To answer a question on relationships (definition and example/illustration, cause and effect, comparison and contrast):

- Does the idea in the second sentence explain the idea in the first sentence: She is schizophrenic. She talks to imaginary people and hears voices. If it does, then the relationship between the two sentences is probably that of illustration. If the relationship between the two sentences is that of definition and example, it may read: Communism is a repressive form of government (definition). China is a communist country (example).

- Are there familiar clue words (transition words) like "such as," "for example," "to illustrate" that will indicate a definition and example or an illustration relationship?

- Do the ideas in the sentence(s) show that something or things caused other thing(s) to happen (for example: I was late to class because my car broke down.)? If it does, then the relationship between or within the two sentences is that of cause and effect.

- Are there familiar clue words such as "because" or "as a result" that may introduce a cause and effect relationship?

- Do the ideas in the sentence(s) show that something or things caused other thing(s) to happen (for example: I was late to class because my car broke down.)? If it does, then the relationship between or within the two sentences is that of cause and effect.

- Are there familiar clue words such as "because" or "as a result" that may introduce a cause and effect relationship?

- Are the ideas in the sentence(s) being compared: My brother is intelligent. Likewise, my cousin is smart. Or contrasted: "My brother is educated. However, my cousin is illiterate." If it is both: "My brother and sister are both intelligent; however, my brother is good-looking while my sister is unattractive", then it is a relationship of comparison and contrast.

- Are there familiar clue words such as "alike," "likewise," and "similarly" that may introduce a comparison relationship? Are there words like "however," "on the other hand," and "nevertheless" that may introduce a contrast relationship?

  To answer a question on pattern of organization (definition and example/illustration, cause and effect, comparison, contrast, comparison and contrast):

- Do I recognize any clue words? Remember that I may recognize a few different types of clue words, but the pattern of organization will probably be whatever relationship is *most* used.

- If the passage has a definition followed by examples, it is probably a pattern of definition and example. If the passage explains a concept, it is probably a pattern of illustration.

- Read, or if you have already read, skim the passage and look for a pattern.

- The transitions are similar to those seen in relationships between and within sentences.

  Remember: Although a pattern of organization may be one type, relationships within/between sentences in the same reading selection could be a different type (for example: The pattern of organization of the passage may be "contrast"; however, two sentences within the passage may be related by addition.).

Application:

A. Write what you think the following words mean in the context of your reading. Then use the dictionary to check if you were right in your summation:

colloquially, monologue, chronological, suffice, accustomed, déjà vu, partial, preceded

B. Based on your comprehension of the material you have just read, answer the following questions:

1. Tell what was the most helpful in this segment and why.

2. What was confusing? What would you like to know more about?

3. Give an example from your life in which you determined a pattern of organization. It could be from a reading, lecture, conversation, or television.

4. Why would a relationship between two sentences not always correspond to the pattern of organization of that selection?

5. Give two examples of main ideas, explain how you would predict a pattern of organization, and give reasons why.

The Punch Line: Inferences

Chapter Six

Subject-Specific Vocabulary:

logic: a rational way to think about or understand something

(Do not forget to check titles and subtitles in this reading material and to predict what the reading material is going to be about. Bring to mind all that you know about the topic and all that you would want to know so that you begin reading as an active reader.)

Your prediction based on topic and background knowledge:

What do you hope to gain from this reading material?

1   Of all the chapters, I must admit that I like explaining inferences the best. Perhaps it is because we probably use the same mental processes to infer as a detective does to solve a case. *Inference* is drawing a conclusion or reading between the lines. We all draw conclusions every day at home, at our workplace, and everywhere that we exist in a conscious state of mind. In other words, we infer all the time—most times unknowingly. If inferring is a part of life, then you might think that you must already be an expert at it. Not necessarily. In order to infer, you must be able to use the right evidence to lead you to the right conclusion. Background knowledge is also a must.

2   Now, let's pretend that we all walked into a classroom this morning and found a man dead, lying in a pool of blood, with more than one gunshot wound to his head. There is a gun lying by his side. What will you infer from this scene? You will probably infer that the man is dead, and that the man was murdered. But how would you know—after all, the dying man did not use his blood to write on the floor or the wall that he had been murdered. (This may happen in the movies, but not likely in real life!) You will probably tell me that this is simple—he is dead because he is not breathing, he is stiff and cold, and he has more than one bullet in his head. Also, you would tell me that the bullet wounds are an indication that he must have been murdered.

3   Yes, this logic makes sense. We base our *inference* on the evidence before us. This is why we did not infer that the man committed suicide. How could he? He had more than one gunshot to his head! Now, once the police detective comes to look at this murder scene, she will draw other conclusions, such as in what direction the bullet entered the man (based on blood spatter pattern), and when the coroner comes in, he will be able to draw a reasonable conclusion as to the time of death. Now, we probably—unless we had knowledge of **forensic** science—would not have enough background knowledge to draw all of the additional inferences that were made based on expert background knowledge even though the same evidence was in front of us. So, you see how much you already know about something does help with drawing conclusions.

Inferences in Jokes and Cartoons

4   The importance of background knowledge cannot be overstated. For example, if you try to analyze a political cartoon that has limited or no written text and you have no idea of the current political climate, you may not be able to draw the conclusion the cartoonist intended.

5   A reason that I like the way inferences work is because I like to tell jokes and listen to them as well. Jokes draw on your ability to use the evidence (what is being relayed) and to draw the conclusion (inference) based on your background knowledge. Think about the last joke you heard, and why you laughed. You will probably realize that the part that was funny was the conclusion (the punch line). Did you notice that the funny part was implied? In other words, you had to figure it out based on the evidence provided in the joke. When you laughed, you were able to infer the funny part. This means that it was not stated—you figured it out based on what you were told in the joke.

6   Now you should know why when people do not get the punch line of a joke that they are not getting the inference, and that when you have to explain to them why the joke is funny, you are explaining the evidence that makes it funny. Therefore, jokes rely on your ability to infer in order for the joke to be funny.

7   The importance of background knowledge cannot be overstated. For example, if you are telling a joke involving the engines of a sports car, a sedan, and a luxury car to a person who is unaware of these cars' engines, he may not find the joke funny, would he? We can infer that this is because the person does not have sufficient background knowledge to use the evidence to draw a conclusion which is needed to make the joke funny. Remember what I had stated before: vocabulary is also a component of background knowledge. Therefore, if a person does not know the meanings of certain key words in a joke and is unable to look for connecting evidence, a joke will have lost its humor.

8   While we are on the subject of jokes, keep in mind that when you translate jokes from the original language into another, some jokes may no longer be funny. Although you may understand the words, your background knowledge may not include knowledge of the culture in which the joke originated. Therefore some jokes are humorous only when told in their original contexts. All this goes to show is that words and the way we use language are strongly tied to the culture of the language. Thanks to Karen Taghi Zoghi, who has provided you with jokes and puns in Part Four for your reading pleasure. As you find yourself smiling or laughing, remind yourself that drawing inferences is causing you to smile or laugh. And, for good measure, you can then analyze your reaction by asking yourself what specific information was provided in the joke that made you draw the conclusion. Did your background knowledge on the subject help?

9   Once again, how much you know about a topic will also determine whether you "get it." Therefore, it is vital to use what is said or written as your evidence to back up your conclusion(s).

Answering Inference Questions

10   In reading selections, just like when you are listening to people, you will need to draw reasonable conclusions. Therefore, it is important that you pay close attention to what you are reading so that you can make the right inferences. This requires you to think critically—as a doctor makes a diagnosis based on symptoms. This is how you will be required to infer certain ideas from reading texts and other written material; therefore, get used to inferring!

11   When answering a question based on inference, you must ask yourself whether you can justify your response with evidence in the reading selection. Reading comprehension tests are all about your logical backed-by-evidence-type of responses. You are not asked for your opinions or your feelings about reading material. Sometimes you will read material that may be particularly harsh to your **psyche**. For example, what if you had to read about the philosophy of the Klu Klux Klan? You cannot let emotion override your analysis of the written material; instead, you will be required to draw conclusions based only on what is written and of course your background knowledge. Therefore, you may draw an inference that is offensive to you. As long as it is based on the evidence in the text, and your background knowledge, it is the correct inference. Selecting a response that may be harsh does not imply that you are in compliance with the author's viewpoints. It simply means that you can draw a reasonable conclusion based on the evidence in the written material.

12   Another important aspect of inferences is that you can draw more than one conclusion based on a given situation or reading selection. How many conclusions you can draw will depend on your background knowledge. Just like in the case of the murdered man, we could draw only one conclusion; however, the detective and coroner—with the same evidence—could draw more based on their expert background knowledge.

Inferences and Implied Main Ideas

13   Sometimes an implied main idea and an inference may be confusing. One similarity between the two is that neither are stated in the reading material. Although implied main idea is like an inference, these terms are not used interchangeably. An implied main idea refers to one overall general statement that covers all or most of the information from the passage and answers the question, "What is this reading about?" The reader concludes what this main idea is based on the major supporting details. On the other hand, an inference is a conclusion that the writer implies, and the reader himself must infer solely based on some or all the ideas in the selection. An inference will not, however, answer the question "What is this reading about?" Also, a reader can often draw more than one inference from a reading selection; however, this same selection will have only one implied main idea. Keep in mind that if in a test you are given a statement taken from the passage, it cannot be an inference or an implied main idea since neither of these is actually stated (written) in the text itself.

14   Last—in my opinion—inference has a positive connotation (words are either positive, negative, or neutral) and an assumption (which is like an inference) has a negative connotation. This is why when you have inferred wrongly, people will be quick to correct you by stating something like, "You have assumed wrong." Very seldom will people say, "You have inferred wrong." Therefore, the next time you are talking with someone, you may want to add to your conclusion, "Have I inferred correctly that ..." This gives a much more positive spin on the dialogue and often avoids misunderstandings.

Inferences from Graphs and Charts

15   Sometimes you may have to analyze graphs and charts. These are visual representations of information. For example, you may have seen a line graph displayed at work showing the profits made by the company over the last five years. We draw inferences from graphs and charts just like we do from cartoons. These visual representations are intended for you to analyze, evaluate, and draw conclusions from limited written text. The following are three examples of such graphs and charts. Each one is followed by inference statements.

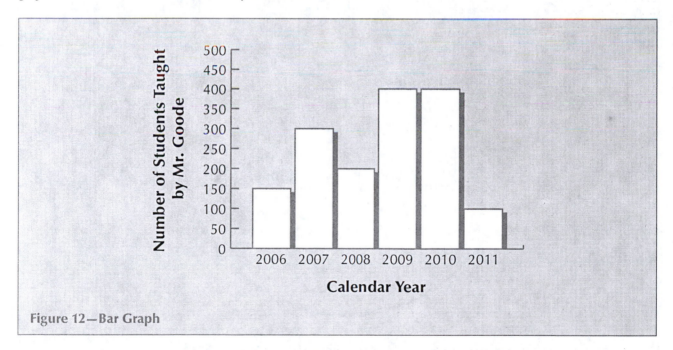

Figure 12—Bar Graph

16   Inferences: In 2009 and 2010, Mr. Goode taught the same number of students; For the years **spanning** from 2006 to 2011, Mr. Goode taught the fewest number of students in 2011; Mr. Goode taught more students in 2007 than he did in 2006, 2008, and 2011, but he taught fewer students in 2007 than he did in 2009 and 2010.

17   Now, it is your turn to draw a conclusion.

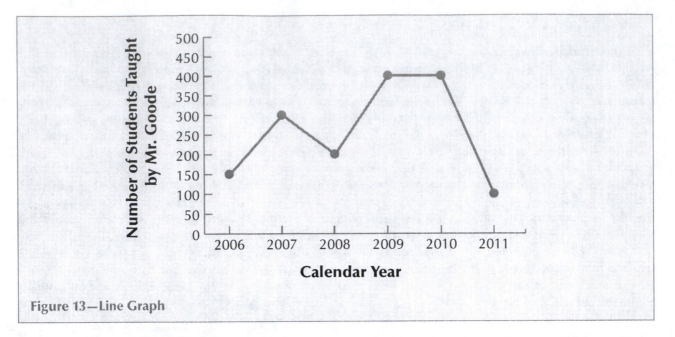

Figure 13—Line Graph

18   A line graph is similar to a bar graph in that it usually shows how something changes over time. Businesses like to use it to emphasize trends in profits and things of that nature. I have used the same data from the bar graph to represent in the line graph. You would draw the same conclusions because the evidence (information represented in the graphs) is the same.

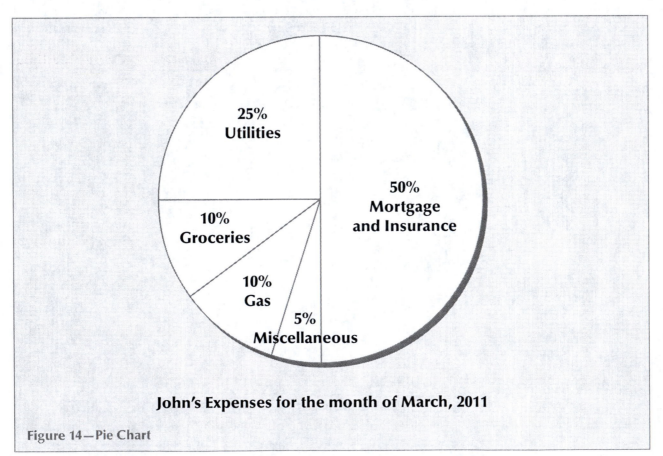

Figure 14—Pie Chart

19   Keep in mind that in the pie chart above, the whole circle (pie) represents 100 percent. Suppose this is a visual representation of your friend's budget. What kind of inferences would you make? These are the conclusions I drew: John spends half of his earnings on mortgage and insurance; John spends the same amount of money on groceries as he does for gas (10 percent and 10 percent); John spends the least amount of money on miscellaneous expenses (5 percent). I am sure you can figure out the rest.

20   Refer to the following self-questioning technique that you can use to facilitate your understanding of inferences when you run into difficulty.

Self-Questioning Technique

The Punch Line: Inferences

- What does inference mean?
- What background knowledge do I have about this topic or passage I have read?
- What conclusions do I remember drawing while I was reading?
- Is there a response like mine in the answer choices?
- Is there evidence in the passage to back up that inference?
- If there is no evidence, then I must read the other choices and ask the same questions until I have exhausted all alternatives and choose the one that has the most evidence to back it up.

Application:

A. Write what you think the following words mean in the context of your reading. Then use the dictionary to check if you were right in your summation:

forensic, psyche, spanning

B. Based on your comprehension of the material you have just read, answer the following questions:

1. Tell what was the most helpful in this chapter and why.

2. What was confusing? What would you like to know more about?

3. Give an example from real-life in which you were able to infer correctly.

4. How is implied main idea similar to and different from inference? What was the importance of background knowledge in the example that you provided when answering question 3? What evidence did you use to draw your conclusion?

How Gullible Are We? Fact, Opinion, and Bias

(Do not forget to check titles and subtitles in this reading material and to predict what the reading material is going to be about. Bring to mind all that you know about the topic and all that you would want to know so that you begin reading as an active reader.)

Your prediction based on topic and background knowledge:

What do you hope to gain from this reading material?

1   I know you must be thinking that finally you have a chapter on a skill that you are familiar with. Almost every time I ask my students what facts and opinions are, someone will respond that a fact is a statement that is true and an opinion is what we think about something. In reading comprehension, a fact is a statement that can be proven right or wrong by **objective** means. How can something that you know as false be accepted as a fact? Look at the following sentences:

The earth is flat.

Two percent of women in the USA had breast cancer in 2009.

Fact

2   Now, you definitely know that the earth is not flat, and no one can make you believe that—at least I hope not! And, you can pretty much be assured—unfortunately—that 2 percent is too small a number to be accurate about the breast cancer rate of women in the U.S. However, I do know with certainty that there is no one single human being who has knowledge about everything, and even if someone is an expert in a particular field, information changes from day to day, and this is particularly true in this age of technology. The **authenticity** of information changes in microseconds. If I am taking a reading comprehension exam, I cannot possibly know what percent of women had breast cancer in 2009 unless I had that background knowledge. Reading selections in reading comprehension tests could be on any subject or topic, and I cannot possibly be expected to know the truth about the facts and figures contained in all possible reading selections. Moreover, facts and figures and knowledge are continually evolving and changing, and therefore, what is true today may not be true tomorrow.

Subject-Specific Vocabulary:

bias: showing subjectivity

3   A testing situation like the one you are going to find yourself in is not like a *Who Wants to Be a Millionaire?* television program where **participants** are permitted lifelines to call experts or ask the audience to help them determine the correct answer. Neither are you permitted to go to a computer and do research to figure out if something is true. Therefore, you have to rely on asking yourself just one question: Can I objectively prove whether this statement is true or false? If you can prove the authenticity of the statement, provided you go to the right sources, then all you can do is select "Fact.".. Therefore, the two above examples of sentences in reading comprehension would be considered statements of fact.

4   An important point to keep in mind as you go through college is the difference between fact and opinion questions in reading comprehension and true and false questions in content area (like science and geography) tests. I have already explained fact and opinion—you are not being tested on your knowledge of content. For true and false questions, you are being tested on your recall and understanding of content taught. For example, for a science test on the circulatory system, you might have this item: The heart has four chambers. You will be asked to circle "true" or "false." The purpose of this type of question is to determine whether you know your content.

Opinion

5   Now, the opinion part is easy. Yes, you are right! It is my opinion that opinion is easy to identify! Opinions are what we think about anything. There is no right or wrong answer, and there is no way of proving the statement true or false as in a fact statement. Value or judgmental words (for example, "wonderful," "gorgeous," "nasty," "ignorant") often signal opinion statements. Just because someone states that, "It is a fact that Muhammed Ali is the greatest boxer of all times," does not mean that this statement is a fact although you might agree with this statement. This statement still shows **subjectivity** (it is not objective). There is no objective way to prove this statement true or false. However, suppose I gave a survey in my classroom and asked students to write down the name of a boxer who they thought was the greatest boxer of all times, and suppose that all the students wrote "Muhammed Ali," and I wrote a statement: "According to a survey in Dr. Noronha-Nimmo's class, Muhammed Ali is the greatest boxer of all times." Is this a statement of fact, opinion, or perhaps both fact and opinion? What do you think?

More on Fact and Opinion

6   If you selected "fact," you would be correct. Although the statement had a value word "greatest," and although the students gave their opinions, you could still verify the authenticity of their statements, could you not? For example, you could look at that survey and see the proof for yourself that this survey was indeed given, and that these were actually the students' opinions about the greatest boxer. Therefore, the statement is fact. Similarly, if you were given a statement: "According to the author, the mayor is doing a good job." Of course this statement is the author's opinion. However, it is a factual statement in that it is the author's opinion of the mayor because you can go into the reading selection and show where he stated his opinion. By checking off this statement as a fact, you are not implying that the author's opinion is a fact—because this cannot be proven—but what you are indeed saying is that this is the author's opinion as per the evidence in his own written words ("I think that the mayor is doing a good job.").

7   I had mentioned judgmental words as signaling opinions. It is important for me to mention that many times words such as "ought to," "should," "should not," and "must" signal opinions. Sometimes because we agree with these strong statements about what we must or must not do, and we value the ideas represented in these sentences as universal truths, we have a tendency to think that these statements are facts instead of opinions. For example, suppose that you are reading a selection about tolerance of varying religious beliefs, and after some discussion about tolerance, you read a statement: "People should not **desecrate** other people's religious books." Can you think of any one in your social circles who may disagree? Probably not! Would you be tempted, therefore, to check this statement off as fact? I hope not because it is still only an opinion! There is no way of objectively proving this statement.

8   I have mentioned this before, and this is just a reminder: Keep in mind that questions on reading comprehension tests do not take into account how you feel about a statement or the reading material. Therefore, always analyze statements without injecting feeling into them, and you will be able to differentiate between fact and opinion more easily. You could be reading a passage written by a **bigot** and a racist, for example, and there may be statements written as facts.

These "facts" may be **offensive** to you, but as long as you know that these "fact" statements can be proven right or wrong, you must check that statement off as "fact."

9   Please also understand that statements could be a mixture of fact and opinion as evidenced in the following statement:

The movie *For Colored Girls* stars Janet Jackson; it was superb.

10   Yes, you are right! The first part of the statement can be proven. Even if you did not watch the movie, you can find out whether there was such a movie, and whether it starred Janet Jackson. Therefore, this part is a fact. However, the second part of this statement is the author's opinion of the movie. It is purely subjective. There is no way to prove whether the movie is superb or not, even if you may think so.

Bias

11   As your reading journey takes you through many paths, you will begin to notice more clearly when something is written as an objective or a subjective piece. When you listen to people talk, you can also tell, if you engaged in that sort of analysis, whether the speaker is presenting material in a factual manner or as his perspective (point of view). For example, how often have you listened to sports commentators during and after a sports event and wondered if the commentators had watched the same game you did? You have probably found that while one commentator may have used more favorable terms (subjective) while describing the game or the players, another may have been more critical (subjective) whereas another commentator may have spoken in neutral terms (objective). It would seem to you that instead of reporting the game objectively, the two sports commentators injected their own perspectives and subjective views (bias) into their comments while the third showed no bias.

12   Because sometimes we have strong personal views about something or someone, we also have a tendency to be biased (subjective). It is human nature. Can you tell that I am biased in favor of reading? Did you notice this during your earlier readings of this book? What gave me away? Do you agree that remaining totally objective about everything and everyone in life would make for a **humdrum** existence? However, there are many instances when bias is unacceptable, whether it is considered a part of human nature or not. For example, in job hiring practices, you would not want to be interviewed by someone who is partial to hiring members of his own ethnic group, regardless of the applicant's **credentials**, would you? What about an instructor you have had in the past or currently have who shows favoritism toward male students and scores their assignments higher than female students? Could you say that the scoring of these assignments is subjective instead of objective, as it should be? This is why multiple-choice-type tests are considered objective forms of grading because either your answers are right or wrong. However, the grading of essay assignments can, by their very nature, cause some subjectivity. Perhaps you scored higher on your essay than your classmate did because the topic that you chose was one that the instructor found personally interesting. Therefore, instructors who grade written work try to be as objective as possible by providing students with exact criteria by which they will be evaluated. This helps with being objective.

13   Another area where bias is unacceptable is in journalism or news reporting. Consider the following:

At approximately 10:00 p.m., police were called to the scene of a domestic dispute. By the time the officers arrived at the house, the man had stabbed his wife to death. (1)

*At approximately 10:00 p.m., police were called to the scene of a horrific domestic dispute. By the time the officers arrived at the **dilapidated** house in a seedy part of town, the crazy man had stabbed his beautiful wife to death. (2)*

14   Now I know that you can tell that (1) contained no opinion statements. These sentences reported events objectively; however (2) contained some opinions. Refer to the words judging the dispute (*horrific*), house (*dilapidated*), man (*crazy*), town (*seedy*), and wife (*beautiful*). Because the reporter injected her own opinions into these statements, this report would be considered biased. There is no place for bias in journalistic reports. Therefore, if you plan to receive your degree in journalism, you have to be particularly sensitive to biased material. You have to learn to report without injecting your bias or opinion even if you are sensitive about the topic. For example, you may be the victim of domestic violence yourself, but you cannot cover a story on domestic violence and inject your bias. You have to report the story objectively.

15   This does not mean, however, that journalists do not write opinionated pieces. They do, but these are clearly presented as such. In the newspaper, you should expect to see no statements of opinions with headline news-type of reports. Similarly, research papers and articles are also expected to be objective. Once you can identify even one opinion statement, the written piece is suspect of bias.

16   I am not stating that the entire newspaper is devoid of bias. If you read the *Letters to the Editor* section, you will mostly find writing that is very subjective (opinionated) because people write in how they feel about different issues. Being able to tell when bias exists—especially when it is **subtle**—is a higher form of analysis. You will have to think critically. Quite often you must have heard on the radio and/or the television opposite views on how a sports team is performing. Most times you will notice that sports analysts cannot keep their personal bias from showing. Whom are you to believe? It helps if your analysis takes you into processing this type of information even more deeply by asking yourself, "What important information has been left out that should have been included?" or "Why has the analyst presented so many positives and expressed only a few negatives about the team?" Similarly, you might ask yourself why one major newspaper decided to cover a major world crisis (for example, the tsunami in Japan) on its front pages whereas another decided to cover a sports event on its front pages. The chapter discussing argument in reading will help you better understand this type of reasoning.

17   Asking yourself these types of **intriguing** questions as you read assists you in engaging with the written material. It is almost like getting into a person's head beyond the words she is using and figuring out her agenda based on her spoken or written words. Analysis of language, whether written or spoken, can be enjoyable and challenging. The next time you hear a commentary about the President, try to guess whether the person speaking is a Republican, a Democrat, or an Independent, and then ask yourself how you came to that conclusion.

18   Refer to the following self-questioning technique that you can use to facilitate your understanding of fact, opinion, and bias when you run into difficulty.

Self-Questioning Technique

How Gullible Are We? Fact, Opinion, and Bias

- Does the statement contain value words such as "terrible," "wonderful," "disgusting," or "best"? If it does, it probably represents an opinion.

- Can the information in the statement be proven true or false by objective means? In other words, would you be able to quantify it or locate it? If yes, then it is a fact although you may know that you can prove it to be incorrect. If the statement cannot be proven, then it is an opinion.

- Often "should" or "ought to" represent an opinion. Other value words that introduce judgment (for example: "exceptional," "wonderful") are indicative that a statement is an opinion.

  For questions on bias:

- Does the author have a view that is subjective—either positive or negative—about the topic? If he/she does, then the written passage is biased.

- If the selection is neutral—or objective—then the passage is not biased.

Application:

A. Write what you think the following words mean in the context of your reading. Then use the dictionary to check if you were right in your summation:

deviate, ludicrous, authenticity, participants, subjectivity, objective, desecrate, bigot, humdrum, credentials, dilapidated, subtle, intriguing, offensive

B. Based on your comprehension of the material you have just read, answer the following questions:

1. Tell what was the most helpful in this chapter and why.

2. What was confusing? What would you like to know more about?

3. Give two examples each from other readings of facts and opinions.

4. Why is determining bias so important? How will knowing about it affect the way you view the world?

The Why and the How: Author's Purpose and Tone

(Do not forget to check titles and subtitles in this reading material and to predict what the reading material is going to be about. Bring to mind all that you know about the topic and all that you would want to know so that you begin reading as an active reader.)

Your prediction based on topic and background knowledge:

What do you hope to gain from this reading material?

1   First, I know that you know what *purpose* means. Of course it means the reason for something. What is important to understand is that in this particular context, we are going to discuss the reason why the author writes, and not why you have chosen to read. (Your reason for reading was discussed in an earlier chapter.)

Tone

2   You also know what *tone* means. How many times has someone told you to watch the tone of your speech because it is upsetting him? You have also heard someone say, "It is not what you said, but how you said it that bothered me." In speech, this usually means not only how something sounds but also the words chosen to make the listener feel the attitude of the speaker toward the listener, toward the topic, or both. Of course in speech, we do have the additional clues of actually hearing the tone and observing the body language, besides analyzing the words. In writing, we only have the author's words to determine his tone, and therefore if an author wants the reader to know that he feels a certain way, he must portray that by the type of words he strings together.

3   Not so long ago, we talked about being objective and subjective. These are tones in writing. If an author is objective, he wants us to know that he is **neutral** about a topic. He does not feel one way or the other, and he is not going to take sides. If a writer wants you to buy a certain product, he will have a **persuasive** or convincing tone, and he will be subjective. When you purchase a card for your spouse on Valentine's Day, do you not purchase it based on the sentiments expressed in the card because you want to project a certain tone? Have you or do you know someone who received a letter from the phone company threatening to turn off the phone service because the company has not received payment? That was a different tone.

Subject-Specific Vocabulary:

irony: the use of words that mean the opposite of what you really think, especially in order to be funny; a situation that is strange or funny because things happen in a way that seem to be the opposite of what you expected

sarcasm: the use of words that mean the opposite of what you really want to say especially in order to insult someone, to show irritation, or to be funny

4   Knowing what tone means in this context is easy enough. What is problematic is that the sky is the limit when it involves words that describe tone. In other words, how strong your vocabulary is will determine whether you can correctly answer a multiple-choice question on tone. In a multiple-choice question, you may read a particularly "sad" selection and state that it has a sad tone, and you will be right. However, in a multiple choice question, words describing tone will be given to you, and "sad" may not be one of the choices. Instead, "mournful" may be the synonym used. If you do not know what "mournful" means and also do not know the meanings of all or some of the other choices, you could only, at best, guess the answer. If you look up the synonyms for "sad" in a dictionary, you will probably find more words than you bargained for. This is another reason why knowledge of vocabulary is so important in reading comprehension, and it is the common thread that binds all of these skills together. I would go so far as to say that learning vocabulary alone could probably help you get through a reading comprehension test!

Some Tone Words

5   Since there are many tone words, what words should you focus on? I do not know the answer to that. All I can tell you is that from my experience with teaching reading, there are some words that I have encountered more often than others. You have, too. You probably know some of these: *pessimistic, optimistic, **ironic**, **sarcastic**, **nostalgic**, objective, subjective, neutral, **inspirational**, **humorous**, apologetic, threatening, persuasive, sympathetic.* If you are interested in learning the unfamiliar words, look them up, and make them your own. You know how to do that by now.

6   Think about my tone thus far. I am certain that my tone has not remained the same. In some places, I have used a motivational tone (to inspire), in others, a matter-of-fact tone (to convey information). Think about the last time someone accused you of being sarcastic. Were you really sarcastic (saying one thing but meaning quite the opposite with the intent of hurting someone's feelings), or did the other party misjudge your tone? Sometimes our use of sarcasm may not be intended to be hurtful but instead to be witty. Sarcasm is a form of irony.

7   In *verbal* irony what is said and what is meant are opposites. In literary circles, this *verbal* irony may be referred to as *rhetorical* irony. In *situational* irony you expect one outcome, but an entirely unexpected and opposite outcome takes place. For example, I love telling jokes, but I do not like watching comedies. Is that not ironic? Would you not expect—given my **propensity** (If you do not know this word, look it up!) for jokes—that I would enjoy watching comedies? Instead, if I had the time to watch movies, I would rather watch a psychological thriller. Research "dramatic irony" and learn more about the ones I have already mentioned here. Have fun while learning about all these different flavors of irony!

Author's Purpose

8   Now, let's get back to the discussion on *purpose*. Okay, what are the common reasons that a writer writes?

9   One reason is **to inform**. Textbooks are a classic example of this purpose. What do you think my purpose for writing this text is? Yes, to impart knowledge about reading, and therefore my purpose is to inform you, the reader. Some other examples of this type of purpose are: *The National Geographic, Newsweek, Time,* and major newspapers. The overall purpose for my writing this book is indeed to inform you, but there are sections of this book which hope to inspire you, or to convince you that reading is a terrific idea!

10   Another purpose for writing is **to entertain**. This means that the author writes for your reading pleasure. Examples of this type of purpose are: novels (fiction), feature magazines, and joke books. It is important to note that often we associate the word "entertain" with humor or comical situations; however, in this context, entertain covers more than writing that contains humor. For example, you may read a horror story that keeps you awake at nights, but you still choose to continue to read it because it pleases you to do so. You are frightened out of your **wits**, and there is nothing funny about blood, guts, and **gore**. However, you know that it is just a story, and that you enjoy a good horror plot. Similarly, you may read a romance novel that depicts the **plight**, and then at the end, the sad **demise** of the young couple. This story may have you weeping at times, but you choose to read it because you like to read such romantic novels. You do not find the plot funny, but it connects with your hunger for a romantic story. I think by now I have made the point.

11   Yet another purpose for writing is **to persuade** the reader. *Persuade* is another word for *convince*. How many times have you persuaded your parents to lend you some money so that you could purchase something you wanted? You knew exactly what to say to which parent so that he/she would give in easily. We learn early on how to **manipulate** our parents

into giving us what we need. A baby persuades his parent to pick him up by crying, and crying longer and harder if he is initially ignored. Oh! The power of persuasion! When we try to get the reader to think as we do in writing, we are in **essence** using our powers of persuasion. An example of this would be the note you wrote your boyfriend or girlfriend telling him/her that you are truly apologetic about the argument you had, and that you are really worthy of a second chance. Or, what about that note you passed in high school – or perhaps even in your class now – to that lovely young lady or that handsome young man, convincing him/her that he/she would not regret going on a date with you? So, now you know that when your English instructor asks you to write a persuasive argument for or against an issue, that you are writing for the purpose of convincing the reader (In this case, it will be your instructor who will be grading you.) about agreeing with your point of view on an issue.

12   Although I have listed only three purposes here, my list is not all-inclusive. You may be able to pinpoint more specific purposes like: **to inspire** (for example, a daily inspirational book) or **to incite** (for example, flyers with **inflammatory** language inciting people to engage in violent acts against an ethnic group). Therefore, expect to see purposes for writing described in other words and in other ways. Also, if it is easier for you to think of these purposes in terms of real-life situations that you are almost sure to be engaged in, then think of what you watch and hear on television. The purposes of sitcoms; movies, whether funny, horrific, or sorrowful; and soap operas can be compared to the writing purpose of **to entertain**. The purposes of news programs, such as local news, *20/20, Dateline,* and Discovery Channel programs can be compared to the writing purpose of **to inform**. What specifically can you compare on television to the writing purpose of **to persuade**? If you answered "commercials," you were right! After all, the sole purpose of most commercials is to convince the viewer that he needs to buy the product.

13   Keep in mind that it is the author's purpose for writing that we have addressed and not your purpose for reading. Why do I make this careful **distinction**? My response is simple. What if you love to read books on zoology, and you pick up textbooks on zoology and read them much like your friend may read a romance novel. Has the author written the zoology textbook for entertainment purposes or for informational purposes? The answer is clear. The author's purpose is to provide information although your purpose for reading the textbook may be purely for your reading pleasure. Just because you like to read that sort of material in your free time does not make the author's purpose **to inform** change to that of **to entertain**. Also, remember that an author could write information in an entertaining manner with lots of humor. You could say that his tone was entertaining and humorous; however, you still need to realize that the text was written to inform.

14   Refer to the following self-questioning technique that you can use to facilitate your understanding of an author's purpose and tone when you run into difficulty.

Self-Questioning Technique

The Why and the How: Author's Purpose and Tone

For questions on Purpose:

- What is the reason for the author's writing?

- If the author is giving information, it is probably to inform.

- If the author is trying to convince the reader about something, then it is probably to persuade.

- If the author has written to appeal to the imagination, or to amuse, it is probably to entertain.

For questions on Tone:

- How do I think the author felt toward his/her topic?

- Is there any evidence (words the author used or how he/she used them) that made me draw that conclusion?

- If I do not have support in the passage to back up the attitude I think the author has, I must reread or skim and look for evidence to make a proper determination of tone.

Application:

A. Write what you think the following words mean in the context of your reading. Then use the dictionary to check if you were right in your summation:

ironic, sarcastic, nostalgic, neutral, inspirational, humorous, persuasive, propensity, wits, gore, plight, demise, manipulate, essence, incite, inflammatory, distinction

B. Based on your comprehension of the material you have just read, answer the following questions:

1. Tell what was the most helpful in this chapter and why.

2. What was confusing, and what would you like to know more about?

3. Indicate which sections of the newspaper would you find examples of the three purposes for writing: to inform, to persuade, and to entertain?

4. Define tone in reading in your own words. Tell why the role of vocabulary development is so crucial in answering multiple-choice questions about tone.

Choosing Between the Devil and the Deep Blue Sea! Argument in Reading

(Do not forget to check titles and subtitles in this reading material and to predict what the reading material is going to be about. Bring to mind all that you know about the topic and all that you would want to know so that you begin reading as an active reader.)

Your prediction based on topic and background knowledge:

What do you hope to gain from this reading material?

1   Is there ever a good reason to argue? Well, in reading and writing there is! First, let us discuss what connotation (Do you recall this word?) the word *argument* has. In real-life situations, when we are having an argument, the connotation is usually negative because the "discussion" is usually not going anywhere. Most times there are a lot of **allegations hurled**, feelings hurt, and no **resolution**. It seems to me that most people do not get into verbal **altercations** intentionally. People usually start a discussion in good faith only to have it **railroaded** by someone who either changes the subject, or who makes unfair and/or **unsubstantiated** statements. After that turning point, it appears that the "discussion" devolves into an all-out battle to gain control. However, sometimes in everyday conversations, people do have discussions and debate various issues informally. These debates are also considered arguments (without the negative association)—very much like in writing.

2   The good news is that in reading and writing contexts, the word *argument* does not have a negative connotation. It is a neutral word. All it does is explain the type of writing. It closely resembles a debate in real life. The word *debate* is also neutral In a real life debate situation—provided of course that people know the rules of a debate—persons present their points of view and then support (back up) their points by providing relevant evidence so that the listener can be influenced on the strength of the support provided. If you have listened to a debate in high school, or better still, been a part of a debate team, you would know how participants present their points and support them. "Argument" in writing (*rhetoric*) also works in this way.

3   In the context of speech and writing, *rhetoric* means the art of being able to use language in a manner that makes for a good persuasive argument. But, understand that you might encounter the word *rhetoric* and infer a different meaning. For

Subject-Specific Vocabulary:

propaganda: the spreading of ideas, information, or rumor for the purpose of helping or injuring an institution, a cause, or a person

fallacy: a false or mistaken idea (argument)

example, when someone says "I got nothing out of it. It was just rhetoric" (empty talk) or "I cannot stand the rhetoric!" (pretentious words), it means that what was being said had no intellectual merit. And, then there are rhetorical questions that are asked, but the person who asks does not expect a response or already knows the answer. Again, I cannot emphasize enough the importance of understanding a word in its context.

Relevant Support

4   For you to determine if someone gave sufficient and relevant support in a debate situation, you would have had to listen carefully and weigh each support (piece of evidence) to determine if it was relevant or not. This is where your analytical skills need to be particularly acute because if the support (evidence) is not directly related to the point the speaker is making, it is irrelevant to the point, and therefore, not debatable. Similarly, in writing, an author makes a point and backs it up with relevant support. It is up to you, the reader, to determine if the argument is well supported and logical. In other words, has the author given enough support to back up his point (adequate), and, more importantly, has this support indeed backed-up the point (relevant)?

5   Of course, by this time you also realize that how much background knowledge you have on the subject will go a long way toward determining whether support is relevant. When reading, all you have to do is to analyze the information presented. In writing, you will be asked to make an argument for or against a topic (usually controversial). When you write, it would **behoove** you to first figure out what background information you have on the topic, and then determine if you have sufficient and relevant support to back your assertion. You will, of course, have to keep in mind that the reader is going to also use similar reasoning about your writing to determine the very same things.

Main Ideas and Points of Arguments

6   I am pleased that sometimes students bring their background knowledge about *main ideas* to this discussion on **argument**. Are you reflecting on any connections between these concepts? It is simple really. The point in an argument is very much like a main idea. The *relevant supports* you identify for an argument are like the *major* and *minor supporting details* that support a main idea. In other words, in arguments, points serve as main ideas for their relevant supports. And, when the writer just provides support and not the point, you are bound to ask yourself, "So what is your point?" When you analyze a possible point, you have determined the implied main idea (implied point) for that support now, have you not? However, keep in mind that although points of arguments are like main ideas, not all main ideas are points of arguments. Read the statements below to understand what I mean:

> *The health policy legislation is criminal.* (point - like main idea)

> *There are several sections in the health policy legislation.* (main idea; not a point of an argument)

Adequate Support

7   Students usually understand what is meant by the "relevant" part of an argument. However, sometimes students will ask me how much support is considered adequate. I usually tell them that there is no magic answer. Usually, how much support an author has to provide to back up a point depends on the importance of the point she is making. For example, if it was important for you to persuade—whether it be verbally or in writing—the school board members that corporal punishment should be banned, you would probably have to provide much evidence to support your argument. You would be trying to change the school board members' long-standing perspective of how they view consequences in school.

8   On the other hand, if all you had to do was to support the point, "Alda's restaurant has the best home-cooked meals in town," not much support is probably required because this is not as important an issue as the previous example. Therefore, the importance of the topic to the audience (the listener or the reader) and the gravity of the topic usually determine how much support a writer (or speaker) may have to provide.

9   As a reader, keep in mind that jumping to hasty conclusions (making generalizations) based on insufficient support even if that insufficient support is relevant, can cause you to make assumptions about people and things. This would

make you appear to be easy to succumb to persuasion with very little support, especially on important topics. This is essential to understand because realize that if the topic is an important one, it may have a serious consequence. Think about the debates that probably take place in the jury room. Do you think that when a person's life is on the line that a decision based on insufficient support would not have negative consequences? This falls in the realm of common sense although someone had once told me that common sense was not all too common! (Pause for thought!)

More on Relevant Support

10   Now, let us get back to relevant support. Read the sentences below and analyze them to determine whether the support is relevant or not.

Vote for Denise Ward. Our families have voted for her party for generations. Besides, she is a woman, and we women need to band together. You will be a traitor to the women's movement if you vote otherwise.

11   You might already have had personal experience debating politics or religion and found out that these types of "discussions" can get quite hairy quickly! Therefore, you must have "all your ducks in a row," or you will risk sounding illogical. In other words, you must have relevant support. In the example I provided, the support was irrelevant. Who you vote for should not be determined by your family's party affiliations, by the candidate's gender, or by your fear of being rejected. Instead, if you are selecting a candidate, your vote should be cast based on the issues the candidate stands for, and whether she is best qualified to run for that position.

Fallacies

12   In reading, when you correctly assess the relevancy and/or the adequacy of a written argument and find the argument has no merit, you have found a fallacy (error) in the author's reasoning that could have resulted in your drawing a wrong conclusion had you not been **vigilant**. These errors fall under several categories of ***fallacies*** such as *personal attack, begging the question, false cause,* and *either-or*. In the example I provided earlier in favor of Denise Ward, the author personally put the reader in an *either-or* position by stating that the reader's choice for candidate could have been motivated by only two considerations: to be loyal to women's causes or to be a "traitor." The author was **exploiting** a social relationship by suggesting that because there is an **affiliation** due to one's gender, the reader should be convinced. The reader's consideration (or counter-argument—the reasoning that is taking place in your head) should be that "loyalty" or "disloyalty" has nothing to do with the selection of a candidate.

13   The particular names or terms that are given for the type of errors in reasoning are not important to the discussion here. These can probably be found in an English handbook. It is enough to suggest that the more carefully you look at the reasons why a point is being presented (usually to persuade the reader), and whether the author is making supports logically and adequately to back the point, the more you are in the position to determine whether the argument has merit or not. This takes practice. Knowing an author's prior perspective toward a topic may keep you, the reader, alert for errors in reasoning. For example, if you know that someone is biased in favor of one political party, and that someone wants to make an argument for why you should change your own party affiliation, you are more likely to read that selection carefully to make sure that the support given is relevant. After all, you know from personal experience that when someone is strongly biased for or against a topic, and he is trying to persuade you otherwise, he may sometimes revert to presenting irrelevant and/or inadequate support in the hope that you will agree with him without your realizing that the argument has no merit. I think that some of us have been guilty on occasion of masking our supports for an argument and presenting them as pure logic, hoping that the other person will not apply logic to expose the "holes" or fallacies in our argument! And, sometimes we just do not realize that our argument is unsound.

14   As you are surely able to tell, being able to analyze and determine whether an author's argument has merit is a **discerning** process. Being able to inform someone that his argument has **flaws** and to tell him why makes you feel like the intellectual that you are. You need real analytical and evaluative **prowess** to do this well, and I have no doubts that you can and will. This is a process that takes time. You will be pleased to know that even those of us whom you see as experts sometimes get sucked into illogical arguments that are so expertly **manipulated** by the author (or speaker) that unless the errors in reasoning are pointed out to us, we too may miss them! Please read the following example:

15   *Ann is running for office. Jill the opposing candidate has made many statements about Ann on national television. One such statement about the senator is that Ann is not of good moral standing because she is a divorcee. This puts Ann's party on the defensive and her top advisers spend valuable time, money, and energy **refuting** this claim by stating that Ann is not a divorced woman as her one-day marriage had resulted in an annulment. The response from Ann's party is just as **outrageous** as Jill's statement. Instead of asking what significance a candidate's marital status has to running for the office of the mayor, Ann's advisers continue an all-out campaign to refute this claim. There is obviously an error in the reasoning that Jill's party forwarded for why constituents should not vote for Ann, but Ann's party does not recognize the error, and instead engages in a back-and-forth with the opposing party. It is later that both the media and Ann's party catch on and begin to question the merit of the argument.*

16   You may remember the last election in your county or state. If you do not, do not worry. You will have plenty of election experiences to begin to analyze the merit of political advertisements that try to convince you to either vote for or against a candidate or a proposition. **Suffice** to say that you will notice that often the support given for the point (for example, that one candidate is best qualified for office) is purposefully misleading, inadequate, and many times outright irrelevant.

Propaganda

17   According to the Merriam-Webster Dictionary, *propaganda* is described as "the spreading of ideas, information, or rumor for the purpose of helping or injuring an institution, a cause, or a person" and "ideas, facts, or allegations spread deliberately to further one's cause or to damage an opposing cause; *also:* a public action having such an effect." Because the intent of propaganda is to persuade whether it be for "helping or injuring," it is used in much the same way as an argument (intent to persuade). Although propaganda may present relevant support, which may be true or false and/or may be adequate or inadequate, it is recognized because of its purpose as a tool to change views for political or personal gain.

18   Most times "propaganda" is used in a negative connotation. It is sometimes used as a political ploy to **incite** people's emotions and imaginations and often serves as a **smokescreen** to **detract** from real issues. In other words, the argument set forth is usually flawed and is intended to exploit people's emotions. Before long, misunderstandings amongst communities and ethnic groups, take place. Stand-ins, riots, demonstrations, and walk-outs become center stage, and many times even the demonstrators have no idea about the issues that they are advocating for. They will usually tell you that they heard this or that which **enraged** them enough to take a **stance**. The **authenticity** of where that information/argument originated or whether it is sound or even the agenda of the persons presenting the argument sometimes fall on deaf ears. **Repressive** governments often use propaganda to keep citizens in a state of ignorance, confusion, and sometimes even fear. This does not mean that free societies do not use propaganda. They do, too; however, the more informed and educated a citizenry is, the more difficult it is to be successful with propaganda techniques.

Propaganda Techniques

19   Propaganda techniques come in varying forms. In order to get a better understanding, you can research the many propaganda techniques. Like most concepts, there are many terms for the various forms of propaganda. I have provided a few examples below:

20   **Name Calling:** This technique employs negative words to attach to a person or an idea to elicit negative feelings from the reader. The reader's feelings then override the type of logical analysis of the argument that should take place. Think of examples of this technique used in our everyday lives. In my opinion we have all probably been subjected to this type of propaganda technique.

21   **Plain Folks:** This technique employs the use of "I am one of you" type of **hype**. The person presenting the message is depicted as sharing the values of the audience he is trying to seduce into either voting for him, buying his products, or accepting his ideas. The audience believes the message has merit regardless of the relevancy or adequacy of the support of the argument. This is why oftentimes you may see a politician whom you have never seen dressed in anything but a suit and tie come to your working-class neighborhood in a regular shirt with the long sleeves rolled-up. He wants your vote by playing on your feelings portraying himself as your neighbor. You are more likely to be positively inclined toward the message instead of analyzing it for what it really is.

22   **Card Stacking:** This technique is when information is provided that is selectively positive or negative depending on the writer's or speaker's motivation. If the speaker wants the listener to agree to some idea, he will present mostly the pros with very few—if any—cons and vice versa.

23   **Testimonial:** Prominent people or celebrities serve as endorsements for a product, idea, or person. It is important to ask yourself questions like "Whose interest do these endorsements serve?," "Do the endorsers know this product, idea, or person well?," and "What was the endorser's motivation to endorse?"

24   **Glittering Generalities:** This technique is the opposite of the "name calling" technique. In this case, positive words are associated with a person, cause, or idea. These general claims are not backed up with evidence. For example, portraying someone as virtuous (for example: "honest" and "patriotic"), or an item for sale as "best."

25   **Bandwagon:** You may have heard the expression "Jump on the bandwagon!" What this means is that without checking its merits, do something just because everyone else seems to be doing it. You will find many examples of this technique when you are bombarded with salespeople, commercials, and such suggesting that you should do something because everyone else is doing it, and that if you do not, you will be left out.

26   There are other propaganda techniques. You can research those on your own. I have presented some that you will probably encounter in your everyday situations. By this time, you must have realized how language can be used in ways to **provoke**, incite, **pacify**, or seduce people. When you create language, as in writing and speaking, do you also use—perhaps **inadvertently**—such propaganda techniques to convince your listener/reader of the **veracity** of your argument?

27   At the beginning, I told you that an argument is like a debate with opposing points of view, usually on a controversial topic. When someone decides to speak or write persuasively for or against any idea, he or she is usually coming from a certain perspective. Regardless of perspective, a good argument calls for taking a position and relying on logic for support. If an argument includes statements of opinion, that argument is not likely to be sound. What is my perspective on reading as I make an argument in favor of reading?

Point of View

28   How many times have you been in a situation where all your friends wanted to give you their points of view even if you did not want their advice? Young women will probably connect to the example I am going to provide. For example: If a young woman is having difficulty with her boyfriend, and her friends know about it, I would say this woman's friends are going to volunteer their advice based on their perspectives, background knowledge, and experience. Do you not think that the young woman would know what points of view her friends are putting forward? Do you not think that you could listen to or read and be able to tell what position the person who is writing or speaking is coming from? Of course you can, and you do. Read the following two statements on the subject of homework:

There is much too much homework given.

There is entirely not enough homework given.

29   If I told you that one statement was made by a student and the other by an instructor, do you think that you could predict which statement was made by whom? You know that you can. This is because you know from background knowledge and experience that most students are likely to complain about too much homework while instructors are likely to complain that there is not enough homework given. These are definite points of view!

30   You may want to read *Wicked: The Life and Times of the Wicked Witch of the West*, authored by Gregory MaGuire. His books are stories written from a different character's perspective. For example, *"Wicked"* is written from the witch's point of view. The witch is a character in *The Wizard of Oz* (by Lyman Frank Baum) story that was written from Dorothy's perspective. Similarly, there is another book, *Confessions of an Ugly Stepsister* also by Gregory MaGuire. It was written from the perspective of the stepsister from the *Cinderella* story (The Brother's Grimm). Reading books like these gives us an appreciation for varying points of views.

31   You might recall a section on "point of view" (POV) in the chapter "Real Versus Imaginary: Nonfiction Versus Fiction" in Part One of this text where POV was discussed as an element of fiction used in literary analysis. However, in this chapter on argument, POV is addressed as a perspective. Therefore, this POV may be in a sense thought of as an element of an argument. After all, the perspective and the motivations of the person presenting an argument are important. Is he a reliable source? Is she an expert on the topic? What does he personally have to gain from making this persuasive argument?

32   Think of my point of view about reading. Is it different from yours? How so? What about our views of the English language? Are they the same? Have I made a solid argument in favor of reading? Has my perspective been that of an expert in reading? What are my motivations?

33   Refer to the following self-questioning technique that you can use to facilitate your understanding of argument in reading when you run into difficulty.

Self-Questioning Technique

Choosing Between the Devil and the Deep Blue Sea! Argument in Reading

- Is there a point—like a main idea—the author is trying to state in the selection? This point is the author taking a stand for or against something or someone for the purpose of persuading the reader.

- Does the selection have logical (relevant) support to back up that point? (These are like major supporting details)

- Where did I locate this evidence?

- Does the selection have a sufficient (adequate) amount of evidence to back up the point?

- Has the author presented some support for the point that has no connection to the point? This support would be considered irrelevant.

Application:

A. Write what you think the following words mean in the context of your reading. Then use the dictionary to check if you were right in your summation:

allegations, hurled, resolution, altercations, railroaded, unsubstantiated, behoove, ultimately, vigilant, exploiting, affiliation, discerning, flaws, prowess, manipulated, allegations, perpetuated, refuting, outrageous, suffice, smokescreen, detract, enraged, stance, authenticity, perpetuating, myth, repressive, hype, provoke, incite, pacify, inadvertently, veracity

B. Based on your comprehension of the material you have just read, answer the following questions:

1. Tell what was the most helpful in this chapter and why.

2. What was confusing? What would you like to know more about?

3. Research two other errors in reasoning (For example, like the *either-or*) that I have not presented in this chapter. Tell what they are and give an example of each.

4. Make an argument for or against taking this course. Write the point and then provide at least four supports to back up your point. Have fun while you are writing!

It Is Just the Beginning!

Chapter Ten

Application:

Based on your comprehension of the material you have read in this book, answer the following questions:

1. Describe my overall tone in this book and tell why I took that tone. Did my tone change based on some topics?

2. Write a central point for each chapter. Remember that this has to be stated as a complete thought.

3. Find, identify, and write one example to represent each type of relationship (definition and example/illustration, addition, time, cause and effect, compare, contrast, compare and contrast, and spatial).

4. What chapter was the most helpful? What chapter was the least helpful to you? Why?

5. Find, identify, and write one example of fact and one of opinion. Explain each.

6. Write three inferences from "Let Me Introduce Myself ..." For each, give evidence to support your answers.

7. Use any paragraph in this book to give an example of a major supporting detail and one minor detail. Tell how you decided on these. (When answering this question identify the page number and paragraph number)

8. A. Identify any paragraph in this book as having bias and one that has no bias.
   B. Which chapter, in your opinion was the most biased?
   Explain each selection. When answering questions A & B identify the page number, paragraph number, and chapter.

9. Can you identify any paragraph in this book in which I have made an argument for or against something or someone? Find one such paragraph, and explain why and how you came to decide on this. Remember that an argument has to be both relevant and adequate. When answering this question identify the page number and paragraph number.

10. Did I present a good argument in favor of learning new vocabulary? Why? Give support for your answer.

11. List at least three specific connections you have discovered between reading and writing skills (for example: relationship concepts in reading are similar to transitions in writing).

12. What purpose did I have for writing this book? Explain.

Subject-Specific Vocabulary:

survey: to ask (many people) a question or a series of questions in order to gather information about what most people do or think about something

13. What have you learned about yourself as a reader after you completed your reading surveys from Parts One and Two? Did you compare the results of the two surveys? (Note: You will need to come back to this question, after you complete the surveys in this chapter.)

1   Wow! We have come a long way on this journey. Even if you read this book under duress—meaning that your instructor pressured you to—I hope that you are none the worse for it! I trust that you realize that there is no end to this journey of discovery of self as a reader. Just like your journey in life continually evolves as a man, woman, father, mother, employee, and such, so, also, you evolve as a reader. What I mean is that if you were asked to explain who you were as a student when you were in high school and then again who you are as a student in college, you will probably be describing two different persons! This is because with your continual encounters with education, your perspective of self as an educated person changes. And it is this way with reading. You may want to read about the many ways that you can apply reading skills to everyday type of activities in *Read Your World* in Part Four.

2   I hope that you will continue to evolve as a reader and realize that we all have the ability to read and grow, but that we do this in our own time and in our own way. I hope that I have made the way a little easier and helped make you a little more interested in reading. Perhaps you will start a library at home. All you need is a small bookshelf that you will fill with books you want to read and your favorites that you want to reread. Perhaps you will read to someone else or inspire others to read (You may want to check my *Romance a Book* list of book titles in Part Four.). Perhaps you will consider ordering magazines such as *Time, Newsweek,* or *Reader's Digest* (my favorite!). And, then perhaps, you will make frequent trips to the library and bookstores because the experiences found there are a balm to your hectic life. I dream that you will find it to be so! Whatever you do, I sincerely hope that you will feel the same joy I do when I read.

3   Please take some time to complete the survey below. Then compare it to your survey in Part One of the book ("Your Attitude Counts") and reflect on whether your attitude toward reading has changed. Also, write to me at the e-mail I have provided in the "Let Me Introduce Myself ..." section. Let me know what you liked, what was difficult, and what you thought should be included or excluded as you navigated this book.

Complete the following survey:

Rate from 1–42 (with 42 being the highest score) the importance of reading to your life goals _____

Post-Reading Survey (Part A)

Please circle the response that best describes you.

1. I like it when someone reads to me	Most of the time	Sometimes	Never
2. I enjoy reading in my native language.	Most of the time	Sometimes	Never
3. My experiences with high school and/or college textbooks have been good.	Most of the time	Sometimes	Never
4. I like class assignments that require me to read a book/ novel.	Most of the time	Sometimes	Never
5. I read even when I am not required to.	Most of the time	Sometimes	Never
6. I would consider reading during my leisure time.	Most of the time	Sometimes	Never
7. I know that reading can be fun.	Most of the time	Sometimes	Never
8. I open a textbook expecting it to be interesting.	Most of the time	Sometimes	Never
9. I preview textbooks before the course begins.	Most of the time	Sometimes	Never

10. This reading course was a good use of my time.	Most of the time	Sometimes	Never
11. I have read at least one book/novel in the last three months (not required for any class).	Yes	No	
12. I have encouraged someone else to read.	Yes	No	
13. I have discussed book(s) with my friend(s).	Yes	No	
14. I am likely to discuss this textbook with my friend(s).	Yes	No	

Analyze your responses: (Most of the time = 3; Sometimes = 2; Never = 1; Yes = 3; No = 1). For questions 1 through 14, add your scores based on your responses. The highest score is a 42 and the lowest score is a 14. The higher your score, the more likely that your attitude toward reading is positive and vice versa. Now look at the number you put for the importance of reading to your life goals. If that number is 42 or close to 42, you are saying that you know reading is going to be a part of your life. Now, reflect on the survey score you received. If your total survey score is high—which means that you have a positive attitude toward reading—then, you are neck-to-neck with your life goals.

If your score on the total reading survey is low, and your "life goals" score is high, this means that you will have to work on improving your attitude so that your attitude can facilitate your learning and your appreciation of reading, which in turn will keep up with your life goals. This makes reading and learning so much more enjoyable!

4   Did completing this survey give you a déjà vu experience? It should have if you completed the first reading survey at the beginning of this book. It is almost identical. Look at your scores for the survey you took in the section "Your Attitude Counts" and see if there is a difference. I hope that your attitude toward reading has changed for the better. Is the score that you put in for "life goals" similar to your first survey, or do you have a higher score now? I hope that the score in this area did not go down! Does your total reading survey score now correspond to your "life goals" score?

5   You are not done! You have one other survey to complete. Please take the time to complete it. It may shed some light on your overall understanding of reading in general.

Post-Reading Survey (Part B)

Please circle the response that best describes you.

1. Reading books can be fun.	Most of the time	Sometimes	Never
2. Reading textbooks can be enjoyable.	Most of the time	Sometimes	Never
3. Reading is more than identifying mainideas, fact and opinion, and learning vocabulary.	Most of the time	Sometimes	Never
4. Reading courses are useful for success in college.	Most of the time	Sometimes	Never
5. Reading comprehension and writing are interrelated.	Most of the time	Sometimes	Never
6. Reading comprehension and listening are interrelated.	Most of the time	Sometimes	Never
7. Reading comprehension and speaking are interrelated.	Most of the time	Sometimes	Never

8.	Reading comprehension is similar to the thinking done to solve everyday problems.	Most of the time Sometimes Never
9.	Vocabulary is vital to understanding language.	Most of the time Sometimes Never
10.	Reading comprehension is not all that complicated.	Most of the time Sometimes Never

Analyze your responses: (Most of the time = 3; Sometimes = 2; Never = 1). For questions 1 through 10, add your scores based on your responses. The highest score is a 30 and the lowest score is a 10. The higher your overall score, the more likely you have understood how life experiences prepare us for reading and how reading prepares us for life. Need I say more?

6   I take this opportunity to thank you for sharing this journey of discovery of self-as-reader. I encourage you to continue to read. Also, please accept my gratitude for your contribution to the Felix Noronha Education Endowment fund (Refer to "Let Me Introduce Myself ..." section). My father would be pleased to know that his legacy is realized through the promotion of education.

7   I know that you will be bombarded with textbooks, but I want you to give them a chance to "talk" to you (*personification!*) and to allow yourself to discover their many secrets. Let your imagination create that unique and intimate bond that can only exist between a reader and a writer. I wish you well with your educational endeavors. Now, go break a leg!

Reason to Reason

Part Three (A)

Foreword

Dear Student:

1   Part Three has been divided into subsections A and B. Part Three (A) focuses on excerpts from textbooks currently used in college for subjects ranging from College Survival Skills to Criminal Justice. (Information for section B is addressed in the *Foreword* for that section.) Reading material for section A has been selected based on several considerations, such as reader interest, the cost of "purchasing" this material for inclusion in this book, readability (fairly easy to difficult), and diversity of content. All these selections have been taken verbatim from content-area textbooks. However, since I have not used any material in this section from English and/or literature textbooks, you are not likely to engage in the sort of critical thinking that is usually typical in those courses while analyzing figurative language, connotation of words, and such. For an understanding of what I mean, you may want to refer to the chapter on "Say What? The Nuances of English" (Part Two).

2   Each selection begins with pre-reading questions to engage you before you begin to read. It also includes some post-reading questions following the reading and the skills-based questions. One question you'll answer before you get started relates to the time you begin to read the excerpt. Another question requires you to predict a main idea from the topic. Additionally, based on your predicted main idea, you'll also be asked to predict a pattern of organization and the author's purpose.

3   As you'll notice, these pre- and post-reading questions don't relate to the typical comprehension questions on application of skills (such as main idea, tone, and bias) that follow these types of reading selections in reading comprehension exercises. Those questions are addressed later. Instead, these pre- and post-reading questions are designed to have you both engage with the reading material and to provide you with knowledge of self-as-reader.

4   You will record the time after you have read the selection and have completed the specific skills comprehension questions. Also, you will rate (by circling) whether you found the excerpt good, fair, or poor. When you rate the selection, you'll probably take into consideration such factors as vocabulary, background knowledge, interest level, and length of the reading selection.

5   Another question refers to a title/topic. You will answer whether the topic is one for which you could easily predict an implied main idea. Additionally, you will predict what kind of course requires this type of reading material and whether you have sufficient background knowledge to facilitate your reading comprehension. You will answer whether you are familiar with most, some, or none of the subject-specific vocabulary. Similarly, you will answer if you are familiar with most, some, or none of the nonsubject-specific vocabulary.

6   You'll be asked to answer whether you find the text reader-friendly or not reader-friendly. What I mean by reader-friendly is whether the material is conveniently labeled with subtitles that allow you, the reader, to know that the author is going to discuss another subtopic within the larger discussion, thereby facilitating predictions. Also, do most or all the paragraphs have identifiable topic sentences and transitions that allow you to easily follow the flow of the author's thoughts? What about the length of the sentences? Are all or most of the sentences long and complex? As a result, did you have to reread many of these sentences to make sense of more than one idea? Are concepts or ideas easily defined? (You will use similar reasoning to determine reader-friendly text in poems and plays in section B.)

7   Last, if you are able to check answers to the skills questions, you can record the percentage you earned. If you have 10 specific skill comprehension questions, each question is worth 10 points. Therefore, you'll deduct 10 points for each incorrect answer out of 100, and this will be your percentage earned. You'll also be able to write in how many questions you answered incorrectly and in what category. Refer to Figure 4 in "The Chemistry of Reading" (Part Two) that shows what reading skills fall under what categories (literal, inferential, critical). This gives you an idea of what areas you are having difficulty with. As you continue with the reading selections, you may notice a pattern emerging. In other words, are you having difficulty mostly in the skills in the "inferential" category (for example, main ideas and relationships)? This means that you'll need to practice applying these skills them to various reading contexts.

8   Keep in mind that comparisons of scores among these exercises are not easy to make. One exercise may contain more questions—or no questions—on one skill than another exercise. Also, you may find one reading passage more reader-friendly and shorter than another. All these factors make it difficult to compare all these exercises. However, categorizing your errors should provide you with insight on "skill areas" you may need to focus on. We all make mistakes while learning. Look on a mistake as an opportunity to learn. In other words, we must allow our errors to work for us by providing us with insight into what we need to address so we don't repeat the mistake.

9   You may ask what purpose this information serves. Remember that when we read critically, we are also being reflective. We learn about our reading behaviors and under what conditions we read best by analyzing why we did well on one reading comprehension activity and not another. Having prior knowledge, for example, that a reading selection does not "look" reader-friendly may prompt us to purposefully be more focused and to be vigilant for when we are "zoning out." Hopefully, this type of knowledge will make our reading experience more successful. Perhaps prior knowledge of difficult text material will help you plan to read that text when you are most likely to be alert. Similarly, prior knowledge of difficult text that is also lengthy will help you plan to read the material not only when you are most likely to be alert but also to read in smaller chunks with breaks in between, especially if you are prone to a short attention span. You may understand that based on the topic, you can sometimes predict main idea, purpose, and pattern of organization with some accuracy.

10   Recording your starting and ending times focuses you to reflect on why it might have taken you longer to read and answer questions on a short excerpt as opposed to a longer one. Could it perhaps have been because the short excerpt was difficult to process? Or perhaps the excerpt was interesting, and therefore, you spent more time processing it in depth? What if you took longer to process the 10 comprehension questions in one selection than in another? Could it be that the questions were more difficult? After you've read and processed most or all of these reading selections and their corresponding questions, you'll have a better understanding of the possible reasons for doing well, or vice versa, on reading comprehension tests. Your instructor may point out other ways in which to use these questions—or add new ones—to help you analyze your scores, your strengths, and your weaknesses.

11   When you grade your 10 specific skill comprehension questions, you may be able to check to see if the rating you gave the material (good, fair, poor) corresponds with a higher or lower score. Similarly, you could check whether your rating as reader-friendly or not reader-friendly corresponds with your rating of good, fair, or poor, and/or your score. I often state that you can't really study for a reading comprehension test. Factors such as the ones you are going to be reflecting on by answering the pre- and post-reading questions affect your score. Remember that you aren't tested on memory of content but on your comprehension of content. Furthermore, if you factor in knowledge of vocabulary and background knowledge, that are crucial to your success, you'll realize that comprehension questions are anything but memorization of content since you could be given reading excerpts or passages from any content area!

12   In Part Four you will find a listing of websites that have exercises on specific reading skills such as main idea, inferences, and tone. I hope that you will take advantage of these additional opportunities to apply your reading skills. Keep in mind, however, that some websites may close down. Therefore, if you cannot access any of the sites listed, look for other credible websites.

13   You'll also find that statements of opinions are seldom found in the reading excerpts in this section. This is because the author is not likely to present his opinions but rather state verifiable information. As you ponder these issues, you'll understand why it was difficult for me to provide you with multiple choice comprehension questions in certain skill areas such as inference, argument, and author's purpose (in texts the author's purpose is almost always to inform). These selections were not conducive to these types of questions. You may ask, Why did I not provide you with other selections from which such questions could be gleaned? The answer is simple. I wanted you to encounter the type of reading you are likely to find in college content textbooks. In Section B you'll find reading material that includes those 'other' skills because most of that material is considered literary text (often found in English Literature textbooks), and you'll be able to apply skills such as inference and tone.

Much Regards,

2011

What If Cultural Relativism Is True?

Judith A. Boss

Pre-Reading Questions

1. What background knowledge do I have on this topic/title?

2. What subject-specific words do I know on this topic/title?

3. Based on the topic/title, I think that I will not find opportunities to apply the following skills. (Hint: for example, in a Biology text excerpt, you are not likely to find an opinion):

4. What implied main idea can I predict from the topic/title?

5. Based on the predicted implied main idea, what pattern of organization do I expect to find in this excerpt?

6. Based on the predicted implied main idea, what author's purpose and tone do I expect?

time started:

What If Cultural Relativism Is True?

1   Further analysis of cultural relativism reveals that, like ethical subjectivism, it is fraught with problems and contradictions.

2   *Cultural relativism offers no criteria for distinguishing between reformers, such as Martin Luther King Jr. and Susan B. Anthony, who may break the law as an act of conscience, and common criminals.* Both the social reformer and the criminal break cultural norms; both, therefore, are immoral. Identifying what is moral with what is legal is problematic, since some laws—such as laws supporting slavery or prohibiting women from voting—are clearly unjust and reasonable people believe they should be changed.

3   *Because it identifies morality with maintaining the status quo, cultural relativism cannot explain moral progress.* Yet most people believe that the abolition of slavery in the United States, the civil rights movement, and granting women full rights of citizenship all represented moral progress. Similarly, cultural relativism cannot account for the fact that most people believe that there are ways in which their own society can be improved. Not only does cultural relativism prevent criticism of other cultures, it also rules out the possibility of engaging in a rational critique of one's own cultural customs.

4   *Cultural relativism encourages blind conformity to cultural norms rather than rational analysis of moral issues.* Rather than using dialogue, we resolve a moral issue simply by taking a poll or calling a lawyer. But surely this is not an accurate description of how we make moral decisions or resolve moral issues. Legalizing abortion and capital punishment did not stop moral debate over those two issues. Futhermore, the fact that most Americans eat meat is irrelevant to someone who is struggling with the morality of meat-eating.

5   *Cultural relativism does not work in pluralistic cultures.* Although it may have been possible a century ago for anthropologists to identify the cultural norms of relatively isolated and static cultures, in the rapidly changing modern world it is becoming more and more difficult to draw sharp distinctions between cultures or even to figure out what our own cultural norms are. Most of us are members of several cultures or subcultures. We may be members of a Catholic, Cambodian, Native American, African American, or homosexual subculture whose values may conflict with those of the wider culture. Indeed, the so-called dominant cultural values are sometimes simply the values held by a small group of people who happen to hold the power in that culture.

6   We also cannot assume that simply because the majority holds a certain value that it is desirable. In his essay *On Liberty,* John Stuart Mill (1806–1873) argues that basing public policy on the will of the people can result in the "tyranny of the majority." Suppression of freedom of speech and religion, censorship of the press, and discrimination against minorities have all, at some time, had the blessing of the majority.

7   *The belief that there are no shared universal moral values can lead to suspicion and mistrust of people from other cultures or subcultures, rather than tolerance and a sense of community.* We may feel that "they" do not share our respect for life; that people from other cultures may even have dangerous values. Because cultural relativism rules out the possibility of rational discussion when cross-cultural values come into conflict and persuasion fails, groups may resort to either apathy and isolationism when the values of other cultures are not a threat, or to violence when another culture's values or actions create a threat to one's own way of life. We can see this in the current conflict involving the United States and Iraq and other Middle Eastern countries.

8   This being said, even though relativist moral theories may not stand up under the scrutiny of critical analysis, they contain at least a grain of truth. Cultural relativism reminds us that culture and history are important in the moral life. Our traditions, our religious values, and our political and social institutions all shape the way in which we apply moral values. Although culture may not be the source of fundamental moral principles and values, it influences how they are interpreted and prioritized. In their concern to disavow ethical relativism, too many philosophers have divorced morality from the actual historical and cultural settings in which we make our moral decisions, but cultural relativism takes this observation too far. Although the application of specific moral principles is relative to cultures, this does not imply that these moral principles are the creation of cultures.

9   Global ethicists reject the reduction of morality to cultural customs and the uncritical defense of traditional knowledge and local customs—particularly oppressive customs. Cultural relativism is a reminder of how easily we can confuse custom and tradition with morality. Because of this, we need to be able to critically analyze not just issues that are controversial but also customs that society accepts as perfectly moral.

Specific Skill Comprehension Questions

1. The main idea for the sub-topic *What If Cultural Relativism Is True?* is that:

   a. cultural relativism works sometimes.

   b. further analysis of cultural relativism reveals that, like ethical subjectivism, it is fraught with problems and contradictions.

   c. because it identifies morality with maintaining the status quo, cultural relativism cannot explain moral progress.

   d. we can see this in the current conflict involving the United States and Iraq and other Middle Eastern countries.

2. Which of the following is a minor supporting detail?

   a. Cultural relativism does not work in pluralistic cultures.

   b. Because it identifies morality with maintaining the status quo, cultural relativism cannot explain moral progress.

   c. Cultural relativism encourages blind conformity to cultural norms rather than rational analysis of moral issues.

   d. We can see this in the current conflict involving the United States and Iraq and other Middle Eastern countries.

3. The word ***prohibiting*** as used in paragraph two which begins with *Cultural relativism offers* ... means:

   a. forbidding.

   b. permitting.

   c. allowing.

   d. exhibiting.

4. The word ***static*** as used in paragraph five which begins with *Cultural relativism does not work* ... means:

   a. showing little or no change.

   b. electrical current.

   c. friendly.

   d. hospitable.

5. The word ***apathy*** as used in paragraph seven which begins with *The belief that there are no* ... means:

   a. emotion.

   b. indifference.

   c. violence.

   d. nonaggressive methods.

6. What is the relationship between the two sentences below:

Most of us are members of several cultures or sub-cultures. We may be members of a Catholic, Cambodian, Native American, African American, or homosexual subculture whose values may conflict with those of the wider culture.

   a. illustration

   b. compare

   c. contrast

   d. cause and effect

7. The pattern of organization of this selection can best be described as:

   a. spatial.

   b. cause and effect.

   c. compare and contrast.

   d. list of items.

8. What is the relationship within the following sentence:

Because it identifies morality with maintaining the status quo, cultural relativism cannot explain moral progress.

   a. definition and example

   b. compare and contrast

   c. cause and effect

   d. illustration

9. What is the relationship between the following sentences:

Because it identifies morality with maintaining the status quo, cultural relativism cannot explain moral progress. Yet most people believe that the abolition of slavery in the United States, the civil rights movement, and granting women full rights of citizenship all represented moral progress.

   a. cause and effect

   b. compare and contrast

   c. contrast

   d. definition and example

10. *In their concern to disavow ethical relativism, too many philosophers have divorced morality from the actual historical and cultural settings in which we make our moral decision, but cultural relativism takes this observation too far.*

   The above statement is:

   a. fact.

   b. opinion.

   c. fact and opinion.

   d. none of the above.

Time (after reading selection and completing all specific skill comprehension questions):

Post-Reading Questions

1. The text was (underline your selection):

    • reader-friendly   • not reader-friendly

2. Did the topic/title provide me with enough information to predict a main idea? Did I have enough background knowledge on the subject that facilitated my reading?

3. a. This excerpt came from a college textbook. The college course I think this excerpt corresponds with is:

    Underline your selection for both b and c below.

    b. I was familiar with **most/some/none** of the subject-specific vocabulary.

    c. I was familiar with **most/some/none** of the nonsubject-specific vocabulary.

4. I think that the readability of this excerpt was on my (underline one): **Independent (comfort) level, learning level, frustration level**. (For information about readability levels, refer to "Sink or Swim! English Language Learner and Reading Strategies," Part One.)

    Score based on percentage of the number correct:

    Rating of reading material (circle your selection):   good   fair   poor

    Rating of reading material (circle your selection):   reader-friendly   not reader-friendly

    Number of incorrect answers: Literal ___   Inferential ___   Critical ___

    (**Literal:** phonics, vocabulary; **Inferential:** main idea, implied main idea, supporting details, relationship between and within sentences, patterns of organization, inferences; **Critical:** author's purpose, tone, fact and opinion, bias, argument, figurative language)

Follow-Up Exercises

1. Write an outline for this selection.

2. Paraphrase paragraph five in no more than five sentences. The paragraph begins *"Cultural relativism does not work …"*.

Why Punish?

Cassia Spohn

Pre-Reading Questions

1. What background knowledge do I have on this topic/title?

2. What subject-specific words do I know on this topic/title?

3. Based on the topic/title, I think that I will not find opportunities to apply the following skills. (Hint: for example, in a Biology text excerpt, you are not likely to find an opinion):

4. What implied main idea can I predict from the topic/title?

5. Based on the predicted implied main idea, what pattern of organization do I expect to find in this excerpt?

6. Based on the predicted implied main idea, what author's purpose and tone do I expect?

time started:

Why Punish?

1   In *The Brothel Boy*, Norval Morris (1992a) tells the story of District Officer Eric Blair, a young and inexperienced Burmese magistrate who must decide the fate of a young man who has been charged with the rape and murder of a 12-year-old girl. The "brothel boy," perhaps mimicking the behavior of adults in the brothel where he worked, offered the girl money to have sex with him. She refused, they struggled, and she fell, hitting her head on a sharp rock. Several days later, she died. District Officer Blair wonders whether this unfortunate young man—who is described as "illiterate," "stupid," and "quite retarded"—should be punished at all and, if so, what his punishment should be. While acknowledging that the brothel boy should be blamed for what he did, the magistrate questions whether he is guilty of the crimes with which he is charged. "The boy meant no harm, no evil," he states. "The more I thought about him and his crime, the less wicked it seemed, though the injury to the girl and her family was obviously extreme; but it was a tragedy, not a sin" (Morris 1992a: 16).

2   As he attempts to understand the accused and his crime, Officer Blair discusses the case with Dr. Veraswami, a Burmese physician. Unlike Blair, Veraswami has no doubts about "what should be done with him." "He will be hanged, of course," Veraswami tells Blair. Officer Blair argues that the brothel boy "meant no harm insofar as he understood what was happening" and therefore is "less worthy of being hanged than most murderers" (Morris 1992a:16). Dr. Veraswami disagrees:

> He was conscious of what he was doing. And being conscious, backward and confused though he is, mistreated and bewildered though he was, he must be held responsible. You must convict him, punish him, hang him ... you must treat him as a responsible adult and punish him. (p. 19)

3   When Officer Blair asks the doctor whether there is no room under the law for mercy, for clemency, the doctor replies, "Justice, Mr. Blair, is your job. Justice, not mercy" (p. 21). Eventually, of course, the brothel boy is hanged.

4   According to Dr. Veraswami, justice requires that the brothel boy be punished. But why is this so? Why is punishment, rather than forgiveness or revenge, the appropriate response to his offense? What purpose does punishment serve in this case?

5   As noted earlier, questions such as these have long intrigued philosophers and legal scholars. In the sections that follow, we define punishment and discuss the justifications for its imposition.

The Concept of Punishment

6   Before we can answer the question, "Why punish?" we must explain what is meant by *punishment*. According to H. L. A. Hart (1968:1), an English philosopher, there are five necessary elements of punishment:

- It must involve pain or other consequences normally considered unpleasant.

- It must be for an offense against legal rules.

- It must be of an actual or supposed offender for his or her offense.

- It must be intentionally administered by human beings other than the offender.

- It must be imposed and administered by an authority constituted by a legal system against which the offense is committed.

7   Stated more simply, punishment involves infliction by the state of consequences that are considered to be unpleasant on a person who has been convicted of a crime. According to this definition, the judge who sentences a man convicted of murder to 30 years in prison is imposing a punishment on him. The prison sentence is an "unpleasant consequence," the penalty is imposed on a man found guilty of murder, which is an offense against the legal rules, and the penalty is intentionally imposed by a judge who has the legal authority to order and implement it.

8   It may be easier to illustrate the concept of punishment by explaining what punishment is not rather than what it is. According to Hart's definition, individual and group acts of vengeance do not constitute punishment. Neither the

man who avenges his sister's rape by physically assaulting her alleged attacker nor the mob that snatches the condemned man from the local jail and lynches him is imposing punishment. Although both cases involve "pain or other consequences normally considered unpleasant," neither incorporates all the necessary elements of punishment. In the case of the man who avenges his sister's rape, the person attacked may not actually have committed the crime, and the brother does not have the legal authority to administer the consequences. And even if we assume that the condemned man has been found guilty of a crime, the lynching mob does not have the authority to seize him and put him to death.

9   In these two scenarios, the unpleasant consequences do not constitute punishment because they are not administered by someone with the authority to do so. But not all government-administered consequences, no matter how painful or unpleasant, are punishment. Consider the forced relocation of more than 100,000 Japanese Americans living in California during World War II. Although the order was issued by the president of the United States and the consequences—internment in relocation camps and, in some cases, loss of property—were certainly unpleasant, the Japanese Americans were not guilty of an offense against the legal rules. They were rounded up and forced to relocate because of a belief that they constituted a threat to national security, but they had committed no crime. Another example would be a government-ordered quarantine of people with an infectious disease. In this case, the government legitimately confines these people to their homes not because of any crime they have committed but because doing so will control the spread of the disease. In both of these situations, there was no crime, and therefore there can be no punishment.

10   Some scholars add a sixth essential feature to Hart's five-part definition of punishment. They contend that the person ordering or administering the unpleasant consequences must have a "justification" for doing so (see Packer 1968; Walker 1991). As Walker notes, "A justification is called for because what is involved is the imposition of something unpleasant regardless of the wishes of the person on whom it is imposed" (Walker 1991:2). It is to this issue—the justification of punishment—that we now turn.

The Justification of Punishment

11   Consider the following hypothetical situation. A federal district court judge sentences Jason Miller, a first-time offender who has been convicted of selling 5 grams of crack cocaine to an undercover narcotics officer, to 5 years in prison. When asked why she imposed the sentence she did, the judge replies, "Five years is the mandatory sentence under the federal sentencing guidelines; it is the sentence prescribed by the law." Is this a sufficient justification for the punishment imposed? It is certainly true that the judge has the legal authority to impose the prescribed penalty. However, this does not explain why this punishment—indeed any punishment at all—is justified in this case. The judge's response tells us nothing about the purpose for which the punishment is imposed.

12   Why do we punish those who violate the law? Although the answers to this question vary widely, they can be classified into two distinct categories: *retributive* (desert-based) justifications and *utilitarian* (result-based) justifications. According to retributive theory, offenders are punished because they have done something wrong, something blameworthy, and therefore deserve to be punished (Hospers 1977; Moore 1968; von Hirsch 1976). In other words, retributive justifications of punishment "rest on the idea that it is right for the wicked to be punished; because man is responsible for his actions, he ought to receive his just deserts" (Packer 1968:37). In contrast, utilitarian justifications of punishment emphasize the prevention of crimes in the future. Punishment is seen as a means of deterring offenders from reoffending or discouraging others from following their examples (deterrence) or preventing offenders from committing additional crimes by locking them up (incapacitation) or reforming them (rehabilitation). Whereas retributivists equate punishment with desert, utilitarians justify punishment by the results it is designed to achieve.

Specific Skill Comprehension Questions

1. The implied main idea of the first five paragraphs (up to *The Concept of Punishment*) is:

   a. Dr. Veraswami believes that the brothel boy should be hanged.

   b. The girl's death was an accident.

   c. The brothel boy was hanged for the accidental death of the girl.

   d. A magistrate and a doctor debated about appropriate punishment for a boy charged with rape and murder.

2. The implied main idea of the section under *The Justification of Punishment* is:

   a. The justification to punish violators is classified into two distinct categories.

   b. The judge imposed the sentence she did based on the mandatory sentence under the federal sentencing guidelines.

   c. Utilitarian justifications of punishment emphasize the prevention of crimes in the future.

   d. Retributive justifications of punishment emphasize the idea that the wicked deserve to be punished.

3. The pattern of organization of paragraph one under *Why Punish?* is that of:

   a. list of items.

   b. compare.

   c. compare and contrast.

   d. time order.

4. The pattern of organization of the entire section under *The Concept of Punishment* is that of:

   a. definition and example.

   b. cause and effect.

   c. list of items.

   d. time order.

5. What is the relationship within the sentence below:

   In these two scenarios, the unpleasant consequences do not constitute punishment because they are not administered by someone with the authority to do so.

   a. addition

   b. compare and contrast

   c. cause and effect

   d. definition and example

6. In the story about the brothel boy under section on *Why Punish?* it can be inferred that the magistrate:

   a. did not want the brothel boy to hang for the death of the girl.

   b. probably knew the brothel boy.

   c. did not want the brothel boy to be punished at all.

   d. is inefficient at his job.

7. *But not all government-administered consequences, no matter how painful or unpleasant, are punishment.*

   The above statement is:

   a. fact.

   b. opinion.

   c. fact and opinion.

   d. none of the above.

8. The author's primary purpose for the section under *The Concept of Punishment* is:

   a. to convince.

   b. to explain.

   c. to inspire.

   d. to entertain.

9. The author's tone for the section under *The Justification of Punishment* is:

   a. biased.

   b. ironic.

   c. detached.

   d. instructive.

10. *As noted earlier, questions such as these have long **intrigued** philosophers and legal scholars.*

   The word **intrigued** as used in the above sentence means:

   a. bothered.

   b. upset.

   c. interested.

   d. excited.

Time (after reading selection and completing all specific skill comprehension questions):

Post-Reading Questions

1. The text was (underline your selection):

   • reader-friendly   • not reader-friendly

2. Did the topic/title provide me with enough information to predict a main idea? Did I have enough background knowledge on the subject that facilitated my reading?

3. a. This excerpt came from a college textbook. The college course I think this excerpt corresponds with is:

   Underline your selection for both b and c below.

   b. I was familiar with **most/some/none** of the subject-specific vocabulary.

   c. I was familiar with **most/some/none** of the nonsubject-specific vocabulary.

4. I think that the readability of this excerpt was on my (underline one): **Independent (comfort) level**, **learning level**, **frustration level**. (For information about readability levels, refer to "Sink or Swim! English Language Learner and Reading Strategies," Part One.)

Score based on percentage of the number correct:

Rating of reading material (circle your selection):   good   fair   poor

Rating of reading material (circle your selection):   reader-friendly   not reader-friendly

Number of incorrect answers: Literal ___   Inferential ___   Critical ___

(**Literal:** phonics, vocabulary; **Inferential:** main idea, implied main idea, supporting details, relationship between and within sentences, patterns of organization, inferences; **Critical:** author's purpose, tone, fact and opinion, bias, argument, figurative language)

Follow-Up Exercises

1. Write a summary of this reading material of no more than five sentences.

2. Paraphrase the seventh paragraph under subtopic *The Concept of Punishment* (begins *Stated more simply, …*).

Drug Use, Abuse, and Addiction

Howard Abadinsky

Pre-Reading Questions

1. What background knowledge do I have on this topic/title?

2. What subject-specific words do I know on this topic/title?

3. Based on the topic/title, I think that I will not find opportunities to apply the following skills. (Hint: for example, in a Biology text excerpt, you are not likely to find an opinion):

4. What implied main idea can I predict from the topic/title?

5. Based on the predicted implied main idea, what pattern of organization do I expect to find in this excerpt?

6. Based on the predicted implied main idea, what author's purpose and tone do I expect?

time started:

Drug Use, Abuse, and Addiction

(An excerpt from *Drug Use and Abuse: A Comprehensive Introduction*)

1   *Drug addiction* is defined by the National Institute on Drug Abuse as "a chronic, relapsing brain disease that is characterized by compulsive drug seeking and use, despite harmful consequences" (*Science of Addiction* 2007: 5). In contrast, *drug abuse* implies the misuse of certain substances; it is a moral, not a scientific, term: "An unstandardized, value-laden, and highly relative term used with a great deal of imprecision and confusion, generally implying drug use that is excessive, dangerous, or undesirable to the individual or community and that ought to be modified" (Nelson et al, 1982: 33). Drug abuse "implies willful, improper use due to an underlying disorder or a quest for hedonistic or immoral pleasure" (N. Miller 1995: 10). Numerous definitions of drug abuse reflect social values, not scientific insight: "One reason for the prevalence of definitions of drug abuse that are neither logical nor scientific is the strength of Puritan moralism in American culture which frowns on the pleasure and recreation provided by intoxicants" (Zinberg 1984: 33). Such definitions typically refer to:

1. the nonmedical use of a substance

2. to alter the mental state

3. in a manner that is detrimental to the individual or the community and/or

4. that is illegal.

2   For example, the American Social Health Association (1972: 1) defines drug abuse as the "use of mood modifying chemicals outside of medical supervision, and in a manner which is harmful to the person and the community." Other definitions, such as those offered by the World Health Organization and the American Medical Association, include references to physical and/or psychological dependency (Zinberg 1984).

3   The *Diagnostic and Statistical Manual of Mental Disorders, Fourth Edition* (DSM-IV), published by the American Psychiatric Association (1994: 182), refers to substance abuse as a "maladaptive pattern of substance use manifested by recurrent and significant adverse consequences related to the repeated use of substances. There may be repeated failure to fulfill major role obligations, repeated use in situations in which it is physically hazardous [such as driving while intoxicated], multiple legal problems, and recurrent social and interpersonal problems."

4   In fact drug abuse may be defined from a number of perspectives: "The legal definition equates drug use with the mere act of using a proscribed drug or using a drug under proscribed conditions. The moral definition is similar, but greater emphasis is placed on the motivation or purpose for which the drug is used. The medical model opposes unsupervised usage but emphasizes the physical and mental consequences for the user, and the social definition stresses social responsibility and adverse effects on others" (Balter 1974: 5).

DRUG USE CONTINUUM

5   The *use* of psychoactive chemicals, licit or illicit, can objectively be labeled drug *abuse* only when the user becomes dysfunctional as a consequence, for example, is unable to maintain employment, has impaired social relationships, exhibits dangerous—reckless or aggressive—behavior, and/or significantly endangers his or her health Thus, drug *use*, as opposed to drug *abuse*, can be viewed as a continuum. At one end is the nonuser who has never used prohibited or abused lawful psychoactive drugs. Along the continuum are experimental use and culturally endorsed use, which includes the use of drugs—wine or peyote, for example—in religious ceremonies, and recreational use. "Regardless of the duration of use, such people tend not to escalate their use to uncontrollable amounts." For example, "long-term cocaine users have found that recreational patterns can be maintained for a decade or more without loss of control. Such use tends to occur in weekly or biweekly episodes and users perceive that the effects facilitate social functioning" (Siegel 1989: 222–223). In the United Kingdom (UK), for example, "of the 11 million people in the UK (27 percent of the

population aged 16–74) who have ever used illicit drugs at some point in their life, probably no more than 300,000 (1 percent) are drug dependent" (Frisher and Beckett 2006: 127). At the far end of the drug use continuum is the drug-dependent, the compulsive user whose life often revolves around obtaining, maintaining, and using a supply of drugs. For the compulsive user, failure to ingest an adequate supply of the desired drug results in psychological stress and discomfort, and there may also be physical **withdrawal** symptoms.

6   Understanding the use of psychoactive substances as a continuum allows the issue of drugs to be placed in its proper perspective: There is nothing inherently evil or virtuous about the use of psychoactive substances. For some—actually many—people, they make life more enjoyable; hence the widespread use of **caffeine, tobacco,** and alcohol without serious unpleasant effects. For others, drugs become a burden as dependence brings dysfunction. In between these two extremes are a variety of drug *users*, such as the underage adolescent using tobacco or alcohol on occasion, as is very common in our society. Adults may experiment with illegal drugs—marijuana and cocaine, for example—without moving up to more frequent, that is, recreational use. The recreational user enjoys some beer or cocktails on a regular basis or ingests cocaine or heroin just before or at social events, during which the drug eases social interaction for this actor. Outside of this specific social setting, the recreational user abstains and thereby is in control of his or her use of drugs. Thus, even for cocaine, a very addictive drug, only 15–16 percent of people become addicted within ten years of first use (T. Robinson and Berridge 2003). For some, recreational use crosses into compulsive use marked by a preoccupation with securing and using drugs in the face of negative consequences, losing a job, severe disruption of social relationships, and/or involvement with the criminal justice system.

7   "The more spectacular consequences of cocaine abuse are not typical of the drug's effects as it is normally used any more than the phenomena associated with alcoholism are typical of the ordinary consumption of that drug" (Grinspoon and Bakalar 1976: 119). "Acknowledging potentially healthy relationships with drugs allows us to better identify unhealthy ones." Although this may sound heretical to those who readily categorize all illicit drug *use* as *abuse*, "the refusal to recognize healthy relationships with stigmatized drugs hinders our understanding of drug-related problems and healthy relationships with them" (Whiteacre and Pepinsky 2002: 27).

8   What we know about those who use psychoactive drugs is skewed toward compulsive users, particularly with respect to illegal drugs: Noncompulsive users have received very little research attention because they are hard to find: "Much data on users are gathered from treatment, law enforcement, and correctional institutions, and from other institutions allied with them. Naturally these data sources provide a highly selected sample of users: those who have encountered significant personal, medical, social, or legal problems in conjunction with their drug use, and thus represent the pathological end of the using spectrum" (Zinberg et al. 1978: 13). Such data "cannot be used to support a causal interpretation because of the absence of information on individuals who may have ingested a drug but had minimal or no negative consequences" (Newcomb and Bentler 1988: 13), such as the recreational user.

ADDICTION

9   *Addiction* is from the Latin verb *addicere,* meaning "to bind a person to one thing or another." Often used interchangeably with the term *dependence,* addiction denotes a complex illness characterized by repeated, compulsive, at times uncontrollable behavior that persists even in the face of adverse social, psychological, and/or physical consequences. For many people addiction becomes chronic, with relapse possible even after years of abstinence. The elements are the same no matter whether the addiction is to alcohol, tobacco, controlled substances, or sex: compulsion and continuation despite adverse consequences. Norman Miller (1995) avoids use of the term *drug abuse* and opts instead for **addiction** characterized by:

1. *Preoccupation:* The addict assigns a high priority to acquiring drugs. Social relationships and employment are jeopardized in the quest for drugs and the consequences of use.

2. *Compulsion:* The addict continues to use drugs despite serious adverse consequences. He or she will often deny the connection between the adverse consequences and the use of drugs.

3. *Relapse:* In the face of adverse consequences, addicts discontinue drugs but subsequently return to abnormal use.

10   In sum, "drug addiction is defined as having lost control over drug taking, even in the face of adverse physical, personal, or social consequences" (Society for Neuroscience 2002: 33).

11   Dennis Donovan (1988: 6) conceives of addiction as a "complex, progressive behavior pattern having biological, psychological, sociological, and behavioral components. What sets this behavior apart from others is the individual's overwhelmingly pathological involvement in or attachment to it, subjective compulsion to continue it, and reduced ability to exert personal control over it. ... The behavior pattern continues despite its negative impact on the physical, psychological, and social function of the individual."

DEFINITION DETERMINES RESPONSE

12   A variety of lawful substances are addicting and have been abused by any number: of "respectable persons," including top government officials, not to mention people in sports, entertainment, and the popular media. Social expectations and definitions determine what kind of drug-taking is appropriate and the social situations that are approved and disapproved for drug use. The use of drugs is neither inherently bad nor inherently good—these are socially determined values (Goode 1989). Thus, Mormons and Christian Scientists consider use of tea and coffee "abusive," while Moslems and some Protestant denominations have the same view of alcohol, although they permit tobacco smoking. The National Commission on Marijuana and Drug Abuse (1973: 13) argues that the term *drug abuse* "must be deleted from official pronouncements and public policy dialogue" because the "term has no functional utility and has become no more than an arbitrary codeword for that drug use which is presently considered wrong." Moderate use of a drug will be defined as *abuse* (and illegal) or it will be considered socially acceptable (and lawful) as society determines, regardless of the actual relative danger inherent in the substance. In other words, how society *defines* drug abuse determines how society *responds* to drug use.

PSYCHOACTIVE DRUGS

13   Later we will examine psychoactive drugs in each of three categories according to their primary effect on the central nervous system (CNS): depressants, stimulants, and hallucinogens. (Some chemicals, such as cannabis and MDMA, also known as ecstasy, have a combination of these characteristics.) A drug can have at least three different names: chemical, generic, and trade; and drugs that have a legitimate medical use may be marketed under a variety of trade names. Trade names begin with a capital letter, while chemical or generic names are in lowercase.

DEPRESSANTS

14   Depressants depress the CNS and can reduce pain. The most frequently used drug in this category is alcohol; the most frequently used illegal drug is the **opiate** derivative **heroin**. Other depressants, all of which have some medical use, include morphine, codeine, **methadone, OxyContin, barbiturates,** and **tranquilizers**. These substances can cause physical and psychological dependence—a craving—and withdrawal results in physical and psychological stress. Opiate derivatives (heroin, morphine, and codeine) and opiumlike drugs such as methadone and OxyContin are often referred to as **narcotics**.

STIMULANTS

15   **Stimulants** elevate mood—produce feelings of well-being—by stimulating the CNS. The most frequently used drugs in this category are caffeine and **nicotine**; the most frequently used illegal stimulant is cocaine that, along with **amphetamines**, has some limited medical use.

HALLUCINOGENS, "CLUB DRUGS," MARIJUANA/CANNABIS, INHALANTS, AND PRESCRIPTION DRUGS

16   **Hallucinogens** alter perceptual functions. The term *hallucinogen* rather than, for example, *psychoactive* or *psychedelic*, is a value-laden one. The most frequently used hallucinogens are **LSD** (lysergic acid diethylamide) and **PCP (phencyclidine)**; both are produced chemically, and neither has any legitimate medical use. There are also organic hallucinogens, such as mescaline, which is found in the peyote cactus. The lawful use of peyote is limited to the religious ceremonies of the Native American Church, which some, but not all, states exempt from their controlled substances statutes.

17   **Club drugs** is a term used to characterize psychoactive substances associated with dance parties or raves, in particular **MDMA**, known as ecstasy.

18   **Cannabis**, frequently used in the form of marijuana, exhibits some of the characteristics of hallucinogens, depressants, and even stimulants. Its lawful use (in the liquid form of **tetrahydrocannabinol**, or **THC**, its psychoactive ingredient) is limited to the treatment of glaucoma and to reduce some of the side effects of cancer chemotherapy.

19   **Inhalants** include a variety of readily available products routinely kept in the home, such as glue, paint thinner, hair spray, and nail polish remover. They produce vapors that, when inhaled, can cause a psychoactive response.

20   **Prescription drugs** are available lawfully only with a doctor's prescription and include opiates such as codeine and morphine as well as drugs used to treat depression and other disorders.

Specific Skill Comprehension Questions

1. *For many people addiction becomes chronic, with relapse possible even after years of **abstinence**.*

   The word **abstinence** as used in the above sentence means:

   a. doing without something that is wanted.

   b. enjoying something.

   c. being sick.

   d. being hospitalized.

2. *There is nothing **inherently** evil or virtuous about the use of psychoactive substances.*

   The word **inherently** as used in the above sentence means:

   a. terribly.

   b. essentially.

   c. absolutely.

   d. greatly.

3. The implied main idea of the section under *Drug Use Continuum* is:

   a. the drug addict and his/her habits are problematic.

   b. drug use can be viewed as a continuum.

   c. psychoactive substances can be viewed as a continuum.

   d. at the far end of the continuum is the drug-dependent.

4. An inference that can be made from the paragraph 6 under *Drug Use Continuum* is that:

   a. caffeine and tobacco are psychoactive substances.

   b. there is nothing inherently evil or virtuous about the use of psychoactive substances.

   c. for cocaine, only 15–16 percent of people become addicted within 10 years of first use.

   d. it is okay to experiment with drugs.

5. The pattern of organization for the section under *Addiction* is:

   a. spatial.

   b. list of items.

   c. cause and effect.

   d. definition and illustration.

6. What is the relationship within the sentence below:

The moral definition is similar, but greater emphasis is placed on the motivation or purpose for which the drug is used.

   a. compare

   b. contrast

   c. addition

   d. illustration

7. What is the relationship within the sentence below:

Outside of this specific social setting, the recreational user abstains and thereby is in control of his or her use of drugs.

   a. addition

   b. illustration

   c. cause and effect

   d. compare and contrast

8. The author shows:

   a. bias against drug use.

   b. bias in favor of drug use.

   c. bias in favor of some drug use.

   d. no bias.

9. The author's tone can best be described as:

   a. nostalgic.

   b. objective.

   c. informal.

   d. concerned.

10. The author's purpose can best be described as:

   a. to persuade

   b. to inform

   c. to entertain

   d. to inspire

Time (after reading selection and completing all specific skill comprehension questions): _____

Post-Reading Questions

1. The text was (underline your selection):

   • reader-friendly   • not reader-friendly

2. Did the topic/title provide me with enough information to predict a main idea? Did I have enough background knowledge on the subject that facilitated my reading?

3. a. This excerpt came from a college textbook. The college course I think this excerpt corresponds with is:

   Underline your selection for both b and c below.

   b. I was familiar with **most/some/none** of the subject-specific vocabulary.

   c. I was familiar with **most/some/none** of the nonsubject-specific vocabulary.

4. I think that the readability of this excerpt was on my (underline one): **Independent (comfort) level, learning level, frustration level**. (For information about readability levels, refer to "Sink or Swim! English Language Learner and Reading Strategies," Part One.)

   Score based on percentage of the number correct:

   Rating of reading material (circle your selection):   good   fair   poor

   Rating of reading material (circle your selection):   reader-friendly   not reader-friendly

   Number of incorrect answers: Literal ___   Inferential ___   Critical ___

   (**Literal:** phonics, vocabulary; **Inferential:** main idea, implied main idea, supporting details, relationship between and within sentences, patterns of organization, inferences; **Critical:** author's purpose, tone, fact and opinion, bias, argument, figurative language)

Follow-Up Exercises

1. Write a summary of this reading material of no more than five sentences.

2. Paraphrase paragraph 6 under subtopic *Drug Use Continuum* (begins *Understanding the use of …*).

Racial Discrimination and Global Justice

Judith A. Boss

Pre-Reading Questions

1. What background knowledge do I have on this topic/title?

2. What subject-specific words do I know on this topic/title?

3. Based on the topic/title, I think that I will not find opportunities to apply the following skills. (Hint: for example, in a Biology text excerpt, you are not likely to find an opinion):

4. What implied main idea can I predict from the topic/title?

5. Based on the predicted implied main idea, what pattern of organization do I expect to find in this excerpt?

6. Based on the predicted implied main idea, what author's purpose and tone do I expect?

time started:

Racial Discrimination and Global Justice

1   In January 2009 Barack Obama made history when he became the first African American president of the United States. His election was celebrated as evidence of progress in race relations in the United States. If an African American can become president, then racism must not be as much of a barrier as we previously thought, or so the reasoning goes. However, does Obama's election show that we are now living in a postracial America, as some claim? Mark Potak, director of the Southern Poverty Law Center's Intelligence Project, which monitors hate groups, says "no." Already, racial slurs and hate crimes have been reported in response to Obama's bid for the presidency and his election. Potak worries that this may just be the beginning. "Historically," he says, "a major advance is followed by a backlash."

2   Sadly, racism is still a harsh reality for many African Americans. Racial segregation in schools is back to levels of the late 1960s. African Americans earn only two-thirds of what European Americans earn, and the unemployment rate is about twice as high. In addition, black men are seven times more likely than white men to end up in jail. In this chapter we'll be looking at some of these issues involving racism, both in the United States and globally.

DEFINING THE KEY TERMS

3   **Race** is a loose classification of groups of people based on physical characteristics. Race is more than just a set of physical characteristics, however; it is how people define themselves and others. As such, race is also a social construct. For example, although Jews were singled out as a distinct, inferior race in Nazi Germany, in the United States Jews are generally regarded as white. Hispanics, on the other hand, despite their physical and cultural diversity, are sometimes classified as a race in the United States.

4   **Racism** is an ideology or worldview that makes race one of the key defining characteristics of a person. Two fundamental premises of racism are (1) humans can be divided into distinct biological groups and (2) some of these groups are morally inferior to others. The Nazi worldview of Aryan superiority was based on an elaborate pseudoscientific description of Jewish biological inferiority. Slavery was also bolstered by scientific theories of biological inferiority. Dr. W. H. Holcombe of Virginia wrote in 1861: "The Negro is not a white man with a black skin, but of a different species, ... the hopeless physical and mental inferior [of the white, and] organically constituted to be an agricultural laborer in tropical climates—a strong animal machine."

5   Because racial groups are seen as inherently different, racism leads to an "us/other" mentality, thereby justifying granting privileges to certain groups while denigrating others. The "other" is seen as contaminated and to be avoided. The "one drop" of blood criterion, which designates anyone as black who has even one black ancestor, and the scrutinizing of the pasts of Germans for Jewish ancestry illustrate this fear of racial contamination.

6   Racism implies prejudice. **Prejudice** is based on negative feelings and stereotypes rather than reason. Racist stereotypes can also be used to justify war and police action, as in the stereotype of the Arab terrorist and the violent young black man. Globally, racism manifests itself in the way affluent nations treat nations whose people are predominantly of non-European descent.

7   **Discrimination** occurs when we treat people differently based on their group membership. Unjust discrimination occurs when we base our actions on prejudices rather than relevant differences. Racial discrimination can take many forms, including hate speech, the use of Asian and Latin American mail-order bride services by middle-aged American men who blame their problems with women on feminism, and our lack of response to genocide and the suffering of refugees in the Sudan.

8   Racism occurs on two levels—the personal and the institutional. Multiculturalists believe that racism is based primarily on individual ignorance and that education is the solution. Critical race theorists, such as Charles R. Lawrence III, emphasize the political and social aspects of racism that privilege certain interpretations of history everyday experience. According to Lawrence, to dismantle racism we need to confront the dominant societal and institutional structures—such as the family and religion, economic, and legal systems—that maintain it.

From *Analyzing Moral Issues*, 5th Edition, by Judith A. Boss. Copyright © 2010 by The McGraw-Hill Companies, Inc. Reprinted by permission of The McGraw-Hill Companies, Inc.

9   **Institutional racism** occurs when the law or a social system is set up to provide advantages to one group of people at the expense of another. Institutional racism exists because of the actions of individuals who either have the power to make and carry out discriminatory policies, or allow them to continue. Slavery and Jim Crow laws are two obvious examples of institutional racism. Schools also act as agents in perpetuating racism. The myth that schools promote upward mobility among immigrant minority groups is directly contradicted by the finding that the social mobility of second- and third-generation Hispanics is downward.

10   Institutional racism affects foreign as well as domestic policy. The use of people in Third World nations, as well as nonwhite immigrants in this country, as sources of cheap labor reflects institutional racism. Indeed, the very term Third World reflects the Western belief in the inferiority of non-Western countries.

11   Sometimes institutional racism is indirect. For example, the funding of schools with local, rather than state or federal, taxes means that children from poorer neighborhoods, which may be predominantly black, receive an inferior education. Patterns of environmental use, such as the destruction of American Indian lands by mining companies and the placement of toxic waste sites near minority communities, also reflect institutional racism.

12   Institutional racism is perpetuated by the media as well as by legal and religious institutions. The 1915 film The Birth of a Nation, based on the best-selling book The Clansman, degraded blacks and glorified the Ku Klux Klan. The movie was an instant hit, at least with white people.

13   Like sexism, racism is embedded in our everyday language. The term *American* is assumed to mean white, usually white male. Other groups of Americans are distinguished from "real" Americans by the use of qualifying terms, as in *African American, Asian American, Arab American,* or *Native American.* In contrast, one rarely hears the term *European American.*

Specific Skill Comprehension Questions

1. The word **bolstered** as used in paragraph four which begins with *Racism is an ideology or worldview ...* means:

   a. updated.

   b. supported.

   c. popular.

   d. inferior.

2. The word **denigrating** as used in paragraph five which begins with *Because racial groups are seen ...* means:

   a. applauding.

   b. acclaiming.

   c. defaming.

   d. assuring.

3. The implied main idea of this selection is:

   a. Racism is an ideology or worldview that makes race one of the key defining characteristics of a person.

   b. Racism implies prejudice.

   c. Racism occurs on two levels: the personal and the institutional.

   d. Racism, discrimination, and institutional racism are key terms that need to be defined for a discussion on racial discrimination and global justice.

4. What is the relationship between the sentences below:

   Institutional racism exists because of the actions of individuals who either have the power to make and carry out discriminatory policies, or allow them to continue. Slavery and Jim Crow laws are two obvious examples of institutional racism.

   a. addition

   b. time order

   c. illustration

   d. contrast

5. The pattern of organization of this selection can best be described as that of:

   a. definition and example.

   b. cause and effect.

   c. time order.

   d. compare and contrast.

6. *The movie was an instant hit, at least with white people.*

   The above statement is:

   a. fact.

   b. opinion.

   c. fact and opinion.

   d. none of the above.

7. *For example, the funding of schools with local, rather than state or federal, taxes means that children from poorer neighborhoods, which may be predominantly black, receive an inferior education.*

   The above statement is:

   a. fact.

   b. opinion.

   c. fact and opinion.

   d. none of the above.

8. The author shows:

   a. no bias.

   b. bias is in favor of racism.

   c. bias against racism.

9. The author's tone can best be described as:

   a. straightforward.

   b. sarcastic.

   c. reverent.

   d. ironic.

10. The author's purpose can best be described as:

    a. to persuade.

    b. to inspire.

    c. to inform.

    d. to entertain.

Time (after reading selection and completing all specific skill comprehension questions):

Post-Reading Questions

1. The text was (underline your selection):

    • reader-friendly   • not reader-friendly

2. Did the topic/title provide me with enough information to predict a main idea? Did I have enough background knowledge on the subject that facilitated my reading?

3. a. This excerpt came from a college textbook. The college course I think this excerpt corresponds with is:

    Underline your selection for both b and c below.

    b. I was familiar with **most/some/none** of the subject-specific vocabulary.

    c. I was familiar with **most/some/none** of the nonsubject-specific vocabulary.

4. I think that the readability of this excerpt was on my (underline one): **Independent (comfort) level, learning level, frustration level**. (For information about readability levels, refer to "Sink or Swim! English Language Learner and Reading Strategies," Part One.)

    Score based on percentage of the number correct:

    Rating of reading material (circle your selection):   good   fair   poor

    Rating of reading material (circle your selection):   reader-friendly   not reader-friendly

    Number of incorrect answers: Literal ___   Inferential ___   Critical ___

    (**Literal:** phonics, vocabulary; **Inferential:** main idea, implied main idea, supporting details, relationship between and within sentences, patterns of organization, inferences; **Critical:** author's purpose, tone, fact and opinion, bias, argument, figurative language)

Follow-Up Exercises

1. Illustrate the key terms in this selection in graphic form.

2. Summarize the first two paragraphs of this selection in no more than three sentences.

Definition of Concepts: Matter and Energy

Elaine Nicpon Marieb

Pre-Reading Questions

1. What background knowledge do I have on this topic/title?

2. What subject-specific words do I know on this topic/title?

3. Based on the topic/title, I think that I will not find opportunities to apply the following skills. (Hint: for example, in a Biology text excerpt, you are not likely to find an opinion):

4. What implied main idea can I predict from the topic/title?

5. Based on the predicted implied main idea, what pattern of organization do I expect to find in this excerpt?

6. Based on the predicted implied main idea, what author's purpose and tone do I expect?

time started:

Definition of Concepts: Matter and Energy

Matter

1   Matter is the "stuff" of the universe. More precisely, **matter** is anything that occupies space and has mass. With some exceptions, it can be seen, smelled, and felt.

2   For all practical purposes, we can consider mass to be the same as weight. However, this usage is not quite accurate. The *mass* of an object is equal to the actual amount of matter in the object, and it remains constant wherever the object is. In contrast, weight varies with gravity. So while your mass is the same at sea level and on a mountaintop, you weigh just slightly less on that mountaintop. The science of chemistry studies the nature of matter, especially how its building blocks are put together and interact.

States of Matter

3   Matter exists in *solid, liquid,* and *gaseous states.* Examples of each state are found in the human body. Solids, like bones and teeth, have a definite shape and volume. Liquids such as blood plasma have a definite volume, but they conform to the shape of their container. Gases have neither a definite shape nor a definite volume. The air we breathe is a gas.

Energy

4   Compared with matter, energy is less tangible. It has no mass, does not take up space, and we can measure it only by its effects on matter. **Energy** is defined as the capacity to do work, or to put matter into motion. The greater the work done, the more energy is used doing it. A baseball player who has just hit the ball over the fence uses much more energy than a batter who bunts the ball back to the pitcher.

Kinetic versus Potential Energy

5   Energy exists in two forms, or work capacities, and each can be transformed to the other. **Kinetic energy** (ki-net′ik) is energy in action. We see evidence of kinetic energy in the constant movement of the tiniest particles of matter (atoms) as well as in larger objects (a bouncing ball). Kinetic energy does work by moving objects, which in turn can do work by moving or pushing on other objects. For example, a push on a swinging door sets it into motion.

6   **Potential energy** is stored energy, that is, inactive energy that has the *potential,* or capability, to do work but is not presently doing so. The batteries in an unused toy have potential energy, as does water confined behind a dam. Your leg muscles have potential energy when you sit still on the couch. When potential energy is released, it becomes kinetic energy and so is capable of doing work. For example, dammed water becomes a rushing torrent when the dam is opened, and that rushing torrent can move a turbine at a hydroelectric plant, or charge a battery.

7   Actually, energy is a topic of physics, but matter and energy are inseparable. Matter is the substance, and energy is the mover of the substance. All living things are composed of matter and they all require energy to grow and function. The release and use of energy by living systems gives us the elusive quality we call life. Now let's consider the forms of energy used by the body as it does its work.

Forms of Energy

- **Chemical energy** is the form stored in the bonds of chemical substances. When chemical reactions occur that rearrange the atoms of the chemicals in a certain way, the potential energy is unleashed and becomes kinetic energy, or energy in action.

For example, some of the energy in the foods you eat is eventually converted into the kinetic energy of your moving arm. However, food fuels cannot be used to energize body activities directly. Instead, some of the food energy is captured temporarily in the bonds of a chemical called *adenosine triphosphate (ATP)* (ah-den'o-sēn tri"fos'făt). Later, ATP's bonds are broken and the stored energy is released as needed to do cellular work. Chemical energy in the form of ATP is the most useful form of energy in living systems because it is used to run almost all functional processes.

- **Electrical energy** results from the movement of charged particles. In your home, electrical energy is found in the flow of electrons along the household wiring. In your body, electrical currents are generated when charged particles called *ions* move along or across cell membranes. The nervous system uses electrical currents, called *nerve impulses*, to transmit messages from one part of the body to another. Electrical currents traveling across the heart stimulate it to contract (beat) and pump blood. (This is why a strong electrical shock, which interferes with such currents, can cause death.)

- **Mechanical energy** is energy *directly* involved in moving matter. When you ride a bicycle, your legs provide the mechanical energy that moves the pedals.

- **Radiant energy,** or **electromagnetic energy** (e-lek"tro-mag-net'ik), is energy that travels in waves. These waves, which vary in length, are collectively called the *electromagnetic spectrum*. They include visible light, infrared waves, radio waves, ultraviolet waves, and X rays. Light energy, which stimulates the retinas of our eyes, is important in vision. Ultraviolet waves cause sunburn, but they also stimulate our body to make vitamin D.

Energy Form Conversions

8   With few exceptions, energy is easily converted from one form to another. For example, the chemical energy (in gasoline) that powers the motor of a speedboat is converted into the mechanical energy of the whirling propeller that makes the boat skim across the water.

9   Energy conversions are quite inefficient. Some of the initial energy supply is always "lost" to the environment as heat. (It is not really lost because energy cannot be created or destroyed, but that portion given off as heat is at least partly *unusable*.) It is easy to demonstrate this principle. Electrical energy is converted into light energy in a light bulb. But if you touch a lit bulb, you will soon discover that some of the electrical energy is producing heat instead.

10   Likewise, all energy conversions in the body liberate heat. This heat helps to maintain our relatively high body temperature, which influences body functioning. For example, when matter is heated, the kinetic energy of its particles increases and they begin to move more quickly. The higher the temperature, the faster the body's chemical reactions occur. We will learn more about this later.

Specific Skill Comprehension Questions

1. The implied main idea for the information under the subtopic *Forms of Energy* is:

   a. Legs provide mechanical energy when riding a bicycle.

   b. Energy is all around us.

   c. Electrical and mechanical energy are the same.

   d. There are four forms of energy.

2. In paragraph 3 under *States of Matter,* all the following are details **except**:

   a. Solids, like bones and teeth, have a definite shape and volume.

   b. Matter exists in *solid, liquid,* and *gaseous states.*

   c. The air we breathe is a gas.

   d. Liquids such as blood plasma have a definite volume, but they conform to the shape of their container.

3. What is the relationship between the two sentences below:

   For all practical purposes, we can consider mass to be the same as weight. However, this usage is not quite accurate.

   a. cause and effect

   b. spatial

   c. contrast

   d. addition

4. What is the relationship between the two sentences below:

   Energy conversions are quite inefficient. Some of the initial energy supply is always "lost" to the environment as heat.

   a. The second sentence explains the first one.

   b. The second sentence restates the first sentence.

   c. cause and effect

   d. compare and contrast

5. The author's primary purpose is to:

   a. inspire.

   b. persuade.

   c. inform.

   d. entertain.

6. The author's tone can best be described as:

   a. objective.

   b. subjective.

   c. pessimistic.

   d. nostalgic.

7. The author:

   a. shows bias in favor of chemistry.

   b. shows bias in favor of energy.

   c. does not show bias.

8. *The higher the temperature, the faster the body's chemical reactions occur.*

   The above statement is:

   a. fact and opinion.

   b. fact.

   c. opinion.

   d. none of the above

9. The pattern of organization for the information under the subtopic *Forms of Energy* is that of:

    a. compare and contrast.

    b. cause and effect.

    c. time order.

    d. list of items.

10. *Liquids such as blood plasma have a definite volume, but they* **conform** *to the shape of their container.*

    The word **conform** as used in the above sentence means:

    a. attach to.

    b. spill from.

    c. similar form.

    d. shapeless.

Time (after reading selection and completing all specific skill comprehension questions):

Post-Reading Questions

1. The text was (underline your selection):

    • reader-friendly   • not reader-friendly

2. Did the topic/title provide me with enough information to predict a main idea? Did I have enough background knowledge on the subject that facilitated my reading?

3. a. This excerpt came from a college textbook. The college course I think this excerpt corresponds with is:

    Underline your selection for both b and c below.

    b. I was familiar with **most/some/none** of the subject-specific vocabulary.

    c. I was familiar with **most/some/none** of the nonsubject-specific vocabulary.

4. I think that the readability of this excerpt was on my (underline one): **Independent (comfort) level, learning level, frustration level**. (For information about readability levels, refer to "Sink or Swim! English Language Learner and Reading Strategies," Part One.)

    Score based on percentage of the number correct:

    Rating of reading material (circle your selection): good   fair   poor

    Rating of reading material (circle your selection): reader-friendly   not reader-friendly

    Number of incorrect answers: Literal ___   Inferential ___   Critical ___

    (**Literal:** phonics, vocabulary; **Inferential:** main idea, implied main idea, supporting details, relationship between and within sentences, patterns of organization, inferences; **Critical:** author's purpose, tone, fact and opinion, bias, argument, figurative language)

Follow-Up Exercises

1. Write a summary of this reading material of no more than 10 sentences.

2. Paraphrase paragraph 9 under subtopic *Energy Form Conversions* (begins *Energy conversions* are …).

When Perceptions Vary

Steven A. Beebe, Susan J. Beebe, and Diana K. Ivy

Pre-Reading Questions

1. What background knowledge do I have on this topic/title?

2. What subject-specific words do I know on this topic/title?

3. Based on the topic/title, I think that I will not find opportunities to apply the following skills. (Hint: for example, in a Biology text excerpt, you are not likely to find an opinion):

4. What implied main idea can I predict from the topic/title?

5. Based on the predicted implied main idea, what pattern of organization do I expect to find in this excerpt?

6. Based on the predicted implied main idea, what author's purpose and tone do I expect?

time started:

When Perceptions Vary

1   George and Martha have been married for, well, forever; they know each other very well, and each knows how the other thinks. So you'd think that their perceptions of things, events, and people would line up, right? Wrong. George and Martha are driving home from a party, chatting about what happened at the event. George believes that everyone had a good time, that the house was filled with interesting, pleasant, relatively good-looking people, and that he received positive responses from everyone he talked to. Martha saw the party differently. She tells George that the reason people looked good was that most of them either had had plastic surgery to "hold back Father Time," were botoxed beyond all recognition, or were younger, "replacement" partners for all the divorcees who attended the party. Some of the women brought younger men as their dates (a process known as "cougaring"), and many people at the party disliked each other so intensely that they stayed on opposite sides of the room all night. Martha's interpretation of events isn't based on prior or external knowledge, but on her perceptions from observing and interacting with people at the party. And about George's perception that everyone at the party liked him? Martha says, "Think again." She tells George that as soon as he left one group of men in a conversation and walked away, they signaled to one another with their "body language" that they thought George was a doofus. What's going on here? Who's right, George or Martha?

2   In actuality, no one's right or both people are right, because what this example illustrates are differing perceptions of the same reality. There's no "truth" to be found, only different "takes" on the same people and set of events. Both sets of perceptions are correct and valid, even though they differ, because varying perceptions are the norm in life. You know this to be true in your own life experience—even people you're very similar to and know quite well can differ from you dramatically in their perceptions of people and events.

3   One explanation for why perceptions vary—no matter whether we're similar to or different from another person— has to do with experience and background. Everyone's history and life experiences are different. So while you may hold opinions, attitudes, and values similar to those of another person, you aren't a carbon copy of that person. Your life experiences, how you were raised, and how you developed contribute a great deal to how you perceive things, events, and people in your life. These elements create a filter through which you observe and process the world around you.

4   For example, let's say that you grew up with a loving grandmother whose house you always looked forward to visiting, mainly because of the wonderful aromas of grandma's cooking. Now, as an adult, when you walk into any bakery, those wonderful smells trigger fond memories of your grandmother, so the smells are positive stimuli for you. But for someone who had a stern, abusive grandmother who also had great smells in her house, those smells might trigger a different response when she or he encounters them later in life. You may be drawn to bakeries not just for the sweets, but because the stimulus evokes memories of your grandmother; for someone else, the memories of grandmother associated with the smells might trigger negative feelings of fear, possibly even anger. That person would likely want to go nowhere near a bakery. Similar experiences can trigger different meanings in people, so we shouldn't be surprised when different reactions occur.

5   In addition, people are divergent in what they key in on when perceiving events people. Research shows that the brains of men and women function differently in terms of how they process and interpret stimuli, leading to differences in how women and men respond verbally and nonverbally to others. In general, men tend to perceive more of the general sense of a situation or have more global perceptions about people In contrast, women tend to perceive more atomistically, finding meaning in detail These tendencies are particularly pronounced when it comes to processing nonverbal information.

6   The causes of these tendencies are complex and multifaceted: They include cognitive development, modeling (taking after the behaviors of, primarily, a same-sex parent), and socialization. Women and girls are socialized toward connection and congruence with other people; thus, they tend to display, perceive, and interpret emotional cues more readily and accurately than men and boys. For example, women tend to detect nuances in people's facial expressions and eye behavior, attend to subtle changes in vocal cues, and remember people's appearance. The sex differences are consistent across U.S. and non-U.S. subjects and across age groups.

7   Because of these differences, sometimes women can "miss the forest for the trees," while men may miss the fine points. You probably remember scenes in movies where a woman on a date covers the eyes of the man she's with and

asks him for details about her appearance and of the decor in the restaurant. When he can't do it, she's made her point about him "ignoring the little things." It's not that men intend to ignore small details, but that many men just tend to process stimuli more globally than women. But this difference is often bewildering, and it can become a sore spot for many heterosexual couples.

Specific Skill Comprehension Questions

1. What is the implied main idea of this selection?

   a. Men tend to ignore small details.

   b. Women tend to pay attention to small details.

   c. Perceptions vary among people and among men and women.

   d. One explanation why perceptions vary has to do with experience and with background.

2. What is the relationship within the sentence below:

   Some of the women brought younger men as their dates (a process known as "cougaring"), and many people at the party disliked each other so intensely that they stayed on opposite sides of the room all night.

   a. cause and effect

   b. definition and example

   c. addition

   d. time

3. *These tendencies are particularly **pronounced** when it comes to processing nonverbal information.*

   The word ***pronounced*** as used in the above sentence (in paragraph five) means:

   a. inconspicuous.

   b. unremarkable.

   c. interesting.

   d. strongly marked.

4. *For example, women tend to detect **nuances** in people's facial expressions and eye behavior, attend to subtle changes in vocal cues, and remember people's appearance.*

   The word ***nuances*** as used in the above sentence (in paragraph six) means:

   a. subtle differences.

   b. anger.

   c. depression.

   d. happiness.

5. What is the relationship within the sentence below:

   Research shows that the brains of men and women function differently in terms of how they process and interpret stimuli, leading to differences in how women and men respond verbally and nonverbally to others.

   a. compare and contrast

   b. cause and effect

   c. definition and example

   d. addition

6. *In addition, people are divergent in what they key in on when perceiving events and people.*

   The above statement is:

   a. fact.

   b. opinion.

   c. fact and opinion.

7. *There's no "truth" to be found, only different "takes" on the same people and set of events.*

   The above statement is:

   a. fact.

   b. opinion.

   c. fact and opinion.

8. The pattern of organization of paragraph five is mostly:

   a. compare.

   b. contrast.

   c. classification.

   d. spatial.

9. Paragraph four is an example of a/an:

   a. oxymoron.

   b. simile.

   c. metaphor.

   d. analogy.

10. Based on this reading, we can infer that:

   a. Men and women perceive the same reality differently.

   b. Men cannot be trusted to focus on details.

   c. Women cannot be trusted to get the overall idea.

   d. Perceptions can cause misunderstandings.

Time (after reading selection and completing all specific skill comprehension questions):

Post-Reading Questions

1. The text was (underline your selection):

    • reader-friendly   • not reader-friendly

2. Did the topic/title provide me with enough information to predict a main idea? Did I have enough background knowledge on the subject that facilitated my reading?

3. a. This excerpt came from a college textbook. The college course I think this excerpt corresponds with is:

    Underline your selection for both b and c below.

    b. I was familiar with **most/some/none** of the subject-specific vocabulary.

    c. I was familiar with **most/some/none** of the nonsubject-specific vocabulary.

4. I think that the readability of this excerpt was on my (underline one): **Independent (comfort) level, learning level, frustration level**. (For information about readability levels, refer to "Sink or Swim! English Language Learner and Reading Strategies," Part One.)

    Score based on percentage of the number correct:

    Rating of reading material (circle your selection): good   fair   poor

    Rating of reading material (circle your selection): reader-friendly   not reader-friendly

    Number of incorrect answers: Literal ___   Inferential ___   Critical ___

    (**Literal:** phonics, vocabulary; **Inferential:** main idea, implied main idea, supporting details, relationship between and within sentences, patterns of organization, inferences; **Critical:** author's purpose, tone, fact and opinion, bias, argument, figurative language)

Follow-Up Exercises

1. Write an outline of this selection.

2. Draw a diagram using the information from the outline. As an example of what is expected, you may consider the "roof with pillars" figures that I used in the chapter "Get to the Point! Main Ideas, Implied Main Ideas, and Supporting Details" (Part Two).

Accounting for Individuals in the Stress Process

Jason Colquitt, Jeffrey A. Lepine, and Michael J. Wesson

Pre-Reading Questions

1. What background knowledge do I have on this topic/title?

2. What subject-specific words do I know on this topic/title?

3. Based on the topic/title, I think that I will not find opportunities to apply the following skills. (Hint: for example, in a Biology text excerpt, you are not likely to find an opinion):

4. What implied main idea can I predict from the topic/title?

5. Based on the predicted implied main idea, what pattern of organization do I expect to find in this excerpt?

6. Based on the predicted implied main idea, what author's purpose and tone do I expect?

time started:

Accounting for Individuals in the Stress Process

1   So far in this chapter, we've discussed how the typical or average person reacts to different sorts of stressors. Of course, people differ in terms of how they typically react to stressful demands. One way that people differ in their reaction to stress depends on whether they exhibit the **Type A Behavior Pattern**. "Type A" people have a strong sense of time urgency and tend to be impatient, hard-driving, competitive, controlling, aggressive, and even hostile. If you walk, talk, and eat at a quick pace, and if you find yourself constantly annoyed with people who do things too slowly, chances are that you're a Type A person.

2   The Type A Behavior Pattern is important because it can influence each variable in our general model of stress. First, the Type A Behavior Pattern may have a direct influence on the level of stressors that a person confronts. To understand why this connection might be true, consider that Type A persons tend to be hard-driving and have a strong desire to achieve. Because the behaviors that reflect these tendencies are valued by the organization, Type A individuals receive "rewards" in the form of increases in the amount and level of work required. Second the Type A Behavior Pattern influences the appraisal process. In essence, Type A individuals are simply more likely to appraise demands as being stressful rather than being benign. Third, and perhaps most important, the Type A Behavior Pattern has been directly linked to coronary heart disease and other physiological, psychological, and behavioral strains. The size of the relationship between the Type A Behavior Pattern and these strains is not so strong as to suggest that if you're a Type A person, you should immediately dial 911. However, the linkage is strong enough to suggest that the risk of these problems is significantly higher for Type A people.

3   Another individual factor that affects the way people manage stress is the degree of social support that they receive from supervisors, peers, friends and family members. Social support refers to the help that people receive when they are confronted with stressful demands, and there are at least two major types. One type of social support is called instrumental support, which refers to the assistance people receive that can to address the stressful demand directly. For example, if a person is overloaded with work, a coworker could provide instrumental support by taking over some of the work or offering suggestions about how to do the work more efficiently. A second type of social support is called emotional support. This type of support refers to the help people receive in addressing the emotional distress that accompanies stressful demands. As an example, the supervisor of the individual who is overloaded with work might provide emotional support by showing interest in the employee's situation and appearing to be understanding and empathetic.

4   Most research on social support focuses on the ways that social support buffers the relationship between stressors and strains. According to this research, higher levels of social support provide a person with instrumental or emotional resources that are useful for coping with the stressor, which tends to reduce the harmful consequences of the stressor to that individual. With lower levels of social support, the person does not have extra coping resources available, so the stressor tends to have effects that are more harmful. Although not every research study has found support for the buffering effect of social support, the majority of research evidence has been supportive.

Specific Skill Comprehension Questions

1. The main idea of paragraph two that begins with *The Type A Behavior Pattern …* is:

    a. Type A individuals risk coronary heart disease.

    b. Type A individuals are more stressed than others.

    c. Type A individuals have physiological, psychological, and behavioral problems.

    d. The Type A Behavior Pattern is important because it can influence each variable in our general model of stress.

2. All the following are major supporting details from paragraph two that begins with *The Type A Behavior Pattern ...* **except**:

    a. First, the Type A Behavior Pattern may have a direct influence on the level of stressors that a person confronts.

    b. Second, the Type A Behavior Pattern influences the appraisal process.

    c. Type A individuals receive "rewards" in the form of increases in the amount and level of work required.

    d. Third, and perhaps most important, the Type A Behavior Pattern has been directly linked to coronary heart disease.

3. What is the relationship within the sentence below:

With lower levels of social support, the person does not have extra coping resources available, so the stressor tends to have effects that are more harmful.

    a. cause and effect

    b. compare and contrast

    c. illustration

    d. addition

4. What is the relationship between the sentences below:

One type of social support is called instrumental support, which refers to the assistance people receive that can be used to address the stressful demand directly. For example, if a person is overloaded with work, a coworker could provide instrumental support by taking over some of the work or offering suggestions about how to do the work more efficiently.

    a. addition

    b. time

    c. cause and effect

    d. definition and example

5. The word **empathetic** as used in the last sentence of the third paragraph that begins with *Another individual factor ...* means:

    a. helpful.

    b. optimistic.

    c. sensitive.

    d. pessimistic.

6. The word **confronted** as used in the third paragraph that begins with *Another individual factor ...* means:

    a. shirk.

    b. faced.

    c. plagued.

    d. surprised.

7. *However, the linkage is strong enough to suggest that the risk of these problems is significantly higher for Type A people.*

The above statement is:

a. fact.

b. opinion.

c. fact and opinion.

8. The pattern of organization in paragraph three that begins with *Another individual factor … can best be described as:

a. compare and contrast.

b. definition and example.

c. cause and effect.

d. problem and solution.

9. It can be concluded that:

a. Type A people are not good to be around.

b. Having Type A Behavior Pattern can be detrimental to your health.

c. Instrumental support refers to the assistance people receive.

d. Social support helps alleviate stress.

10. What is the relationship within the following sentence:

Social support refers to the help that people receive when they are confronted with stressful demands, and there are at least two major types.

a. spatial

b. contrast

c. compare

d. addition

Time (after reading selection and completing all specific skill comprehension questions): _____

Post-Reading Questions

1. The text was (underline your selection):

   • reader-friendly   • not reader-friendly

2. Did the topic/title provide me with enough information to predict a main idea? Did I have enough background knowledge on the subject that facilitated my reading?

3. a. This excerpt came from a college textbook. The college course I think this excerpt corresponds with is:

   Underline your selection for both b and c below.

   b. I was familiar with **most/some/none** of the subject-specific vocabulary.

   c. I was familiar with **most/some/none** of the nonsubject-specific vocabulary.

4. I think that the readability of this excerpt was on my (underline one): **Independent (comfort) level**, **learning level**, **frustration level**. (For information about readability levels, refer to "Sink or Swim! English Language Learner and Reading Strategies," Part One.)

Score based on percentage of the number correct:

Rating of reading material (circle your selection):   good   fair   poor

Rating of reading material (circle your selection):   reader-friendly   not reader-friendly

Number of incorrect answers: Literal ___   Inferential ___   Critical ___

(**Literal:** phonics, vocabulary; **Inferential:** main idea, implied main idea, supporting details, relationship between and within sentences, patterns of organization, inferences; **Critical:** author's purpose, tone, fact and opinion, bias, argument, figurative language)

Follow-Up Exercises

1. Write a summary of this selection in no more than five sentences.

2. Paraphrase paragraph two that begins with *The Type A Behavior Pattern* … in no more than five sentences

Reduce Your Procrastination

Dianna L. Van Blerkom

Pre-Reading Questions

1. What background knowledge do I have on this topic/title?

2. What subject-specific words do I know on this topic/title?

3. Based on the topic/title, I think that I will not find opportunities to apply the following skills. (Hint: for example, in a Biology text excerpt, you are not likely to find an opinion):

4. What implied main idea can I predict from the topic/title?

5. Based on the predicted implied main idea, what pattern of organization do I expect to find in this excerpt?

6. Based on the predicted implied main idea, what author's purpose and tone do I expect?

time started:

Reduce Your Procrastination

1   *Procrastination*, putting things off, is a common behavior pattern for many students. It's often the result of not wanting to start a task that seems difficult or time consuming. Unfortunately, procrastination can become a habit. The more you avoid the task, the more daunting it becomes; the more you tend to dwell on the negative aspects of the task, the more it's blown all out of proportion. After a while you may feel that you can't ever complete the task because you don't have the time to finish it.

Main Causes of Procrastination

2   According to Albert Ellis and William Knaus, the three main causes of procrastination are self-downing, low frustration tolerance, and hostility. Learning more about each of these causes may help you learn to control your own procrastination problems.

Self-Downing

3   *Self-downing* refers to putting yourself down—telling yourself you can't do it or you're not smart enough. When you don't complete tasks successfully or on time, you may begin to doubt your ability to succeed. If you set unrealistic goals such as planning to study the entire weekend or getting an A in every class, you may begin to worry about whether you can really achieve them, This can result in procrastination or avoidance caused by self-downing.

Low Frustration Tolerance

4   A second cause of procrastination is low frustration tolerance. Students who experience low frustration tolerance are easily frustrated; they tend to give up or have trouble starting on a task when it appears to be difficult or too time consuming. Having to read two long chapters in your Economics text may feel like it will take forever to complete. Instead of getting to work, some students think, "It's too hard." Some students experience a great deal of frustration when they attempt to complete certain assignments or projects. Writing a twenty-page term paper for your Political Science class, for example, may be extremely difficult for you. The task may appear to be too difficult or require too much of your time, and just thinking about it may become a very unpleasant experience. Your low tolerance for frustration may lead you to put off this difficult task and do something else instead. Before you know it, you've fallen into the procrastination trap. The next time you decide that you had better start that paper, you may experience even more feelings of anxiety and panic because by that time you have even less time available to complete the paper.

Hostility

5   Ellis and Knaus's third cause of procrastination is *hostility* toward others. You may put off doing that term paper because of your anger toward your professor. Comments like "He just expects too much of our class" or "She didn't even assign us that paper until two weeks before the end of the term" or "That assignment is so unfair" are indicative of angry feelings toward your instructors. If you're angry at one of your instructors for giving you a difficult assignment, because you received a poor test grade, or for embarrassing you in class, you may find it unpleasant to work on the assignment for that class. Your angry feelings can in fact increase your feelings of frustration about the task. Together, these feelings lead to procrastination.

Other Reasons Students Procrastinate

6   Some students put off studying for exams until it's almost too late. Have you? You may be procrastinating for another reason—to protect yourself from feelings of inadequacy. By not studying well enough, you can protect your ego because you can blame your failure on your lack of preparation rather than on your lack of ability. For example, you

might say, "Well, if I had studied, I would have gotten a B, but I just didn't have time." In this way you tell yourself that you *could* have done a good job if you had chosen to. Students procrastinate for many other reasons. Some are listed below.

- **Overscheduling.** When you plan more tasks than you can actually complete, you won't get them all done. This leads to putting some of them off to the next day. Then you have those tasks to complete along with new tasks, and that leads to even more overscheduling.

- **Lack of clear, specific goals.** When you haven't set clear, specific goals—when you haven't decided exactly what you want to accomplish—it's easy to decide to do it later.

- **Not planning ahead.** If you don't work on long-range assignments in advance, you may find that you're in a time crunch when the deadline is approaching.

- **Getting behind in your work.** Once you begin to put work off, things pile up. As your workload increases, it becomes even harder to get it all done.

- **The task isn't relevant.** Many students have difficulty getting started on tasks that they think are not relevant to their own lives.

- **The task lacks value.** Some students have difficulty seeing the value in some of the assignments they are given. When students see tasks as busy work or decide that they have no or little value, it's easy to put them off.

- **Lack of motivation.** Some students just can't get motivated to start a particular assignment. They may think it's irrelevant, unimportant, boring, too difficult, too big, or they just may not want to do it because they got a low grade on the last assignment in that class.

- **Unclear about what to do.** Many students procrastinate on an assignment when they're confused about what they need to do to correctly complete the assignment.

- **They're tired or don't feel well.** When students are tired or aren't feeling well, it's easy to put off completing or even starting some of their work. A common thought is, "I'll work on it when I'm feeling better."

- **There are better things to do.** Many students procrastinate because they seem to find better things to do with their time. Have you ever decided to clean your room, catch up on your e-mail, pay bills, or go out with friends instead of doing your work?

- **They're waiting for the perfect time, place, or mood.** Some students have difficulty starting an assignment because they are waiting for the perfect time or place to do it or aren't in the right mood. Have you ever felt that way about an assignment?

Strategies for Overcoming Procrastination

7   Because so many people have problems with procrastination, many books, articles, and Web sites are devoted to the topic. They include hundreds of suggestions for dealing with procrastination. Below, you'll find a number of strategies and techniques that will help you overcome procrastination related to your academic work

- **Just get started.** The best way to overcome procrastination is simply to get started—to take action. Do anything. Take out paper and write anything. Work for five to ten minutes. At the end of that time, you can decide whether you want to work for another ten minutes.

- **Set realistic goals.** If you set reasonable expectations for yourself, you're more likely to accomplish your goals and less likely to have negative feelings about your capabilities.

- **Clarify the directions.** Make sure that you know how to do the assignment before you begin. If you're unsure, check with the professor, a tutor, or another classmate. It's hard to get started when you really aren't sure what it is you're expected to do.

- **Start with the easiest part of the task.** Do the easiest part of the assignment or only a small part of it. Once you start the assignment, you're likely to continue. Remember, getting started is half the battle.

- **Avoid overscheduling.** Estimate how much time it will take to complete your daily tasks. If you plan only what you can accomplish in the time you have available for study, you won't have a long list of tasks to carry over to the next day.

- **Create "To Do" lists.** Putting your tasks in writing helps you see exactly what you must accomplish and strengthens your commitment to complete your work.

- **Set priorities.** If you complete your most important tasks first, you won't feel as though you have failed or let yourself down.

- **Break down large tasks.** Breaking down large tasks makes them appear less difficult and time consuming. It's always easier to get yourself motivated to do a small task.

- **Recognize that not all assignments are easy.** If you can accept the fact that not all your tasks will be pleasant experiences, that in itself will help you approach them more willingly.

- **Recognize that all courses are relevant.** Learning to see the relevance of your courses and assignments also can motivate you to do your work. A college education will help prepare you for a career, but it is also your opportunity to become an educated person (something that will serve you well in *any* career).

- **Use positive self-talk.** Tell yourself that you can complete the task, that you want to do it, and that you can be successful. Think about how completing the task will benefit you or help you achieve your goals. Telling yourself that it's too hard, too big, or that you won't do it right leads to procrastination.

- **Identify escapist techniques.** You also can help yourself avoid procrastination by identifying your *escapist techniques*—things you do to keep from doing your work. Do you suddenly decide to clean the house, take a nap, check your e-mail, watch television, or visit a friend when you should be doing assignments?

- **Plan rewards.** Planning to do something you really enjoy after completing a task you don't like may help you overcome your tendency to procrastinate.

Specific Skill Comprehension Questions

1. The implied main idea of this selection is:

   a. There are many reasons for procrastination and many ways to overcome it.

   b. There are several causes for procrastination and students must learn about them.

   c. There are many strategies for overcoming procrastination if you use them.

   d. Students can reduce their problems with procrastination easily.

2. A major supporting detail is:

   a. Instead of getting to work, some students think, "It's too hard."

   b. A common thought is, "I'll work on it when I'm feeling better."

   c. A second cause of procrastination is low frustration tolerance.

   d. There are many reasons for procrastination and many ways to overcome it.

3. *Unfortunately, procrastination can become a habit.*

   The above statement is:

   a. fact.

   b. opinion.

   c. fact and opinion.

4. *Your angry feelings can in fact increase your feelings of frustration about the task.*

    The above statement is:

    a. fact.

    b. opinion.

    c. fact and opinion.

5. *Planning to do something you really enjoy after completing a task you don't like may help you overcome your* **tendency** *to procrastinate.*

    The word **tendency** as used in the above sentence means:

    a. habit.

    b. propensity.

    c. appreciation.

    d. desire.

6. *Ellis and Knaus's third cause of procrastination is* **hostility** *toward others. You may put off doing that term paper because of your anger toward your professor.*

    The word **hostility** as used in the above sentence means:

    a. friendship.

    b. appreciation.

    c. ill will.

    d. hospitality.

7. The author's purpose can best be described as:

    a. to entertain.

    b. to incite.

    c. to discourage.

    d. to encourage.

8. The author's tone can best be described as:

    a. worried.

    b. pessimistic.

    c. superior.

    d. instructive.

9. The author is:

    a. in favor of procrastination.

    b. against procrastination.

    c. not biased at all.

10. An inference that can be drawn from this selection is:

   a. Procrastination, putting things off, is a common behavior pattern for many students.

   b. Some students put off studying for exams until it's almost too late.

   c. No one other than the procrastinator can help himself/herself overcome his/her procrastination problems.

   d. All college students are procrastinators.

Time (after reading selection and completing all specific skill comprehension questions):

Post-Reading Questions

1. The text was (underline your selection):

   • reader-friendly   • not reader-friendly

2. Did the topic/title provide me with enough information to predict a main idea? Did I have enough background knowledge on the subject that facilitated my reading?

3. a. This excerpt came from a college textbook. The college course I think this excerpt corresponds with is:

   Underline your selection for both b and c below.

   b. I was familiar with **most/some/none** of the subject-specific vocabulary.

   c. I was familiar with **most/some/none** of the nonsubject-specific vocabulary.

4. I think that the readability of this excerpt was on my (underline one): **Independent (comfort) level, learning level, frustration level**. (For information about readability levels, refer to "Sink or Swim! English Language Learner and Reading Strategies," Part One.)

   Score based on percentage of the number correct:

   Rating of reading material (circle your selection):   good   fair   poor

   Rating of reading material (circle your selection):   reader-friendly   not reader-friendly

   Number of incorrect answers: Literal ___   Inferential ___   Critical ___

   (**Literal:** phonics, vocabulary; **Inferential:** main idea, implied main idea, supporting details, relationship between and within sentences, patterns of organization, inferences; **Critical:** author's purpose, tone, fact and opinion, bias, argument, figurative language)

Follow-Up Exercises

1. The information in this selection is organized as a list of items. Illustrate this list in graphic form.

2. What is the implied main idea for the section under *Strategies for Overcoming Procrastination?*

The Moral Issues

Judith A. Boss

Pre-Reading Questions

1. What background knowledge do I have on this topic/title?

2. What subject-specific words do I know on this topic/title?

3. Based on the topic/title, I think that I will not find opportunities to apply the following skills. (Hint: for example, in a Biology text excerpt, you are not likely to find an opinion):

4. What implied main idea can I predict from the topic/title?

5. Based on the predicted implied main idea, what pattern of organization do I expect to find in this excerpt?

6. Based on the predicted implied main idea, what author's purpose and tone do I expect?

time started:

The Moral Issues

Human Dignity and Individual Moral Worth

1   Jorge Garcia defines racism in terms of ill will and a disregard for the dignity and welfare of certain people based on their assigned race. The victims of Hurricane Katrina (2005), mostly poor and black, were left for days without adequate food and water and in unsanitary conditions before FEMA finally took action to assist them. Failure to take their plight as seriously as that of richer, white victims of natural disasters reflects a history of both institutional and individual racism on the part of the government employees and those in power.

2   One of the problems in overcoming institutional racism is how to restore the dignity of groups that have suffered discrimination without violating the equal moral worth of members of groups who have historically benefited from that discrimination. This is particularly an issue in the debate on affirmative action.

Justice and Equality

3   According to the principle of equality, "it is unjust to treat people differently in ways that deny them significant social benefits unless we can show that there is a difference between them that is relevant to the differential treatment." This principle requires that differential treatment be based only on real and relevant differences.

4   Michael Levin in "Race, Biology, and Justice" argues that discrimination against blacks is justified based on what he claims are real differences between whites and blacks in terms of intelligence and aggressiveness. Others argue that even if it can be shown that members of one race are, on the average, more intelligent or more aggressive than members of another, this tells us nothing about a particular individual. The principle of equality requires that people be judged on their individual merits, not on their membership in a particular group. Bernard R. Boxill questions whether color-conscious programs, such as affirmative action, are necessarily unjust. He maintains that there are times when race, like talent, is relevant in creating public policy.

5   On a global level, Pogge maintains that wealthy nations have a duty based on justice to work toward alleviating severe poverty in the world. As it stands now, corporations from wealthy nations can take advantage of workers in poorer nations without regard for the labor and environmental laws that protect workers in richer nations.

6   Currently, the international market exists, for the most part, in a "state of nature"—to use Hobbes's term—in which the powerful are free to exploit the weak.

Utilitarian Considerations

7   Racism hurts. In the 1954 *Brown v. Board of Education* ruling, the U.S. Supreme Court spoke of the irrevocable damage to the "hearts and minds" of black children who were compelled to attend segregated schools. Delays in responses to disasters that affect mainly people of color, or failure to provide a decent standard of living, can also result in long-term harms and even death, as in the case of Hurricane Katrina.

8   Affirmative action programs are both defended and opposed on utilitarian grounds. Some people argue that preferential treatment of minorities works against their best interests by fostering social tension and resentment against minorities. It also creates the impression that minorities can't make it on their own merits. In their enthusiasm to diversify, some universities have admitted minority students who are poorly qualified academically, thus setting them up for failure. Furthermore, it is argued, strong affirmative action programs waste the talents of those who are most qualified. Defenders of preferential hiring, in response, maintain that it helps minorities who are less qualified because of racism to develop their talents, thus creating a greater pool of qualified workers.

Reparation and Restitution

9   **Restitution** is payment made to a group of people for past harms. Restitution is a type of reparation. Blacks, Native Americans, and Japanese Americans have all sought restitution from the U.S. government. In 1988 Congress passed the Civil Liberties Act authorizing the payment of $20,000 to every living Japanese American who was interned in federal camps during World War II. No similar restitution, however, has been offered to blacks or Native Americans.

10   What do we owe to blacks and Native Americans, if anything, for a legacy of slavery, genocide, and degradation? Is an apology enough? Should the U.S. government return Indian lands or monetarily compensate Native Americans for the loss of their lands? Should descendants of slaves be compensated monetarily, as were the Japanese Americans for their loss of freedom during World War II? Or do we owe only an indirect debt to contemporary blacks, since it was their ancestors, not they, who were brought to this country against their will? Or is it now time to make peace with the past and just put it behind us?

11   In his controversial anti-reparations ad, David Horowitz argues that the United States does not owe restitution to blacks. Among his reasons are that blacks who are alive today were not enslaved and that American slavery actually benefited today's African Americans, because they have a much higher standard of living than they would have had if they were living in the African countries from which their ancestors were kidnapped and sold into slavery. His ad has been censored by several college newspapers and student groups. Boxill agrees with Horowitz that the argument for compensation to blacks for harm to their slave ancestors is weak. However, he maintains that blacks living now have a claim for compensation for harms from current injustices.

Care Ethics

12   The analytical utilitarian approach is often contrasted with a care ethics that emphasizes sentiment and human relationships. Racism prevents the development of caring relationships between people of different races. Care ethics, however, can also be used to justify paternalistic caring and colonialism.

13   One of the weaknesses of care ethics is that it does not provide a strategy for overcoming racism in a segregated society. When a commitment to caring is absent it is our commitment to an ideal or principle that must motivate us to do what is right.

Conclusion

14   Because racism is woven into the very fabric of society and reinforced by personal prejudices, it is difficult to eliminate. We need to carefully examine ways in which society today normalizes racism. The racism of the Jim Crow era seemed normal and rational to the majority of white Americans, just as slavery was once regarded as part of the natural order, at least by those who benefited from it.

15   Some people argue that those affected by racist policies should take responsibility for changing the system. The problem of racism, however, is not a "black problem" or a "Hispanic problem"; the problem is white racism. The people who created and maintain racism bear the main responsibility for eradicating it. Those who have the most power to change institutional racism are the very people who have the power to perpetuate it.

16   Racism needs to be addressed at all levels. Being "tolerant" or "color-blind" is not enough. The majority of whites state that they strongly believe in the ideal of racial equality; but, even though we may not personally feel racial hatred, our actions can be infected by the hatred of others. It is not enough to simply change our own personal attitudes or substitute a politically correct ideology for action. Unless we actively work toward eliminating racism, we are still part of the problem. Martin Luther King Jr. once said that "the choice is ours, and though we might prefer it otherwise, we must choose."

Specific Skill Comprehension Questions

1. The implied main idea under the section *Reparation and Restitution* is:

   a. Blacks are not owed any restitution for slavery.

   b. Blacks, Native Americans, and Japanese Americans have all sought restitution from the U.S. government.

   c. Reparation and restitution to Blacks and Native Americans is a controversial moral issue.

   d. Blacks living now have a claim for compensation for harms from current injustices.

2. The word **alleviating** as used in the fifth paragraph that begins *On a global level ...* means:

   a. exacerbating.

   b. relieving.

   c. aggravating.

   d. compounding.

3. The word **preferential** as used in paragraph 8 that begins with *Affirmative action programs ...* means:

   a. giving advantage.

   b. disadvantageous.

   c. courteous.

   d. obnoxious.

4. What is the relationship within the following sentence:

   The victims of Hurricane Katrina (2005), mostly poor and black, were left for days without adequate food and water and in unsanitary conditions before FEMA finally took action to assist them.

   a. cause and effect

   b. time

   c. addition

   d. illustration

5. What is the relationship within the following sentence:

   Delays in responses to disasters that affect mainly people of color, or failure to provide a decent standard of living, can also result in long-term harms and even death, as in the case of Hurricane Katrina.

   a. compare and contrast

   b. addition

   c. time

   d. cause and effect

6. The pattern of organization for the section under *Reparation and Restitution* can best be described as that of:

   a. definition and explanation.

   b. cause and effect.

   c. classification.

   d. compare and contrast.

7. *We need to carefully examine ways in which society today normalizes racism.*

   The above statement is:

   a. fact.

   b. opinion.

   c. fact and opinion.

8. In the *Conclusion* section, the author provides:

   a. relevant support for eliminating racism.

   b. irrelevant support for eliminating racism.

9. The author is:

   a. for racism.

   b. against racism.

   c. not biased.

10. An inference that can be drawn from this selection is:

    a. eliminating racism is a complicated matter.

    b. racism needs to be addressed at all levels.

    c. racism hurts.

    d. racism prevents the development of caring relationships between people of different races.

Time (after reading selection and completing all specific skill comprehension questions):

Post-Reading Questions

1. The text was (underline your selection):

   • reader-friendly   • not reader-friendly

2. Did the topic/title provide me with enough information to predict a main idea? Did I have enough background knowledge on the subject that facilitated my reading?

3. a. This excerpt came from a college textbook. The college course I think this excerpt corresponds with is:

   Underline your selection for both b and c below.

   b. I was familiar with **most/some/none** of the subject-specific vocabulary.

   c. I was familiar with **most/some/none** of the nonsubject-specific vocabulary.

4. I think that the readability of this excerpt was on my (underline one): **Independent (comfort) level**, **learning level**, **frustration level**. (For information about readability levels, refer to "Sink or Swim! English Language Learner and Reading Strategies," Part One.)

Score based on percentage of the number correct:

Rating of reading material (circle your selection):   good   fair   poor

Rating of reading material (circle your selection):   reader-friendly   not reader-friendly

Number of incorrect answers: Literal ___   Inferential ___   Critical ___

(**Literal:** phonics, vocabulary; **Inferential:** main idea, implied main idea, supporting details, relationship between and within sentences, patterns of organization, inferences; **Critical:** author's purpose, tone, fact and opinion, bias, argument, figurative language)

Follow-Up Exercises

1. Write a summary of this reading material of no more than seven sentences.

2. Paraphrase the section under *Justice and Equality*.

Job Characteristics Theory

Jason Colquitt, Jeffrey A. Lepine, and Michael J. Wesson

Pre-Reading Questions

1. What background knowledge do I have on this topic/title?

2. What subject-specific words do I know on this topic/title?

3. Based on the topic/title, I think that I will not find opportunities to apply the following skills. (Hint: for example, in a Biology text excerpt, you are not likely to find an opinion):

4. What implied main idea can I predict from the topic/title?

5. Based on the predicted implied main idea, what pattern of organization do I expect to find in this excerpt?

6. Based on the predicted implied main idea, what author's purpose and tone do I expect?

time started:

Job Characteristics Theory

1   Given how important enjoyable work tasks are to overall job satisfaction, it's worth spending more time describing the kinds of tasks that most people find enjoyable. Researchers began focusing on this question in the 1950s and 1960s, partly in reaction to practices based in the "scientific management" perspective. Scientific management focuses on increasing the efficiency of job tasks by making them more simplified and specialized and using time and motion studies to plan task movements and sequences carefully. The hope was that such steps would increase worker productivity and reduce the breadth of skills required to complete a job, ultimately improving organizational profitability. Instead, the simplified and routine jobs tended to lower job satisfaction while increasing absenteeism and turnover. Put simply: Boring jobs may be easier, but they're not necessarily better.

2   So what kinds of work tasks are especially satisfying? Research suggests that three "critical psychological states" make work satisfying. The first psychological state is believing in the *meaningfulness of work,* which reflects the degree to which work tasks are viewed as something that "counts" in the employee's system of philosophies and beliefs. Trivial tasks tend to be less satisfying than tasks that make employees feel like they're aiding the organization or society in some meaningful way. The second psychological state is perceiving *responsibility for outcomes,* which captures the degree to which employees feel that they are key drivers of the quality of the unit's work. Sometimes employees feel like their efforts don't really matter because work outcomes are dictated by effective procedures, efficient technologies, or more influential colleagues. Finally, the third psychological state is *knowledge of results,* which reflects the extent to which employees know how well (or how poorly) they are doing. Many employees work in jobs in which they never find out about their mistakes or never fully realize that they've performed well.

Specific Skill Comprehension Questions

1. The main idea of paragraph two is:

    a. Employees feel that their efforts don't really matter.

    b. Trivial tasks seem less satisfying.

    c. Certain jobs are more satisfying than others.

    d. Research suggests that three "critical psychological states" make work satisfying.

2. All the following are major supporting details from paragraph two except:

    a. The second psychological state is perceiving responsibility for outcomes.

    b. Sometimes employees feel like their efforts don't really matter.

    c. Finally, the third psychological state is knowledge of results.

    d. The first psychological state is believing in the meaningfulness of work.

3. What is the relationship between the sentences below:

    The hope was that such steps would increase worker productivity and reduce the breadth of skills required to complete a job, ultimately improving organizational profitability. Instead, the simplified and routine jobs tended to lower job satisfaction while increasing absenteeism and turn-over.

    a. addition

    b. contrast

    c. compare

    d. cause and effect

4. What is the relationship within the sentence below:

   Put simply: Boring jobs may be easier, but they're not necessarily better.

   a. contrast

   b. compare

   c. addition

   d. illustration

5. The author's tone can best be described as:

   a. scheming.

   b. tolerant.

   c. uncertain.

   d. objective.

6. The author's purpose can best be described as:

   a. to inspire.

   b. to inform.

   c. to persuade.

   d. to convince.

7. The author is:

   a. biased.

   b. not biased.

8. *Put simply: Boring jobs may be easier, but they're not necessarily better.*

   The above statement is:

   a. fact.

   b. opinion.

   c. fact and opinion.

9. *Research suggests that three "critical psychological states" make work satisfying.*

   The above statement is:

   a. fact.

   b. opinion.

   c. fact and opinion.

10. *Sometimes employees feel like their efforts don't really matter because work outcomes are dictated by effective procedure, efficient technologies, or more influential **colleagues**.*

    The word **colleagues** as used in the above sentence means:

    a. college worker.

    b. assembly line worker.

    c. supervisor.

    d. fellow worker.

Time (after reading selection and completing all specific skill comprehension questions): _____

Post-Reading Questions

1. The text was (underline your selection):

   • reader-friendly   • not reader-friendly

2. Did the topic/title provide me with enough information to predict a main idea? Did I have enough background knowledge on the subject that facilitated my reading?

3. a. This excerpt came from a college textbook. The college course I think this excerpt corresponds with is:

   Underline your selection for both b and c below.

   b. I was familiar with **most/some/none** of the subject-specific vocabulary.

   c. I was familiar with **most/some/none** of the nonsubject-specific vocabulary.

4. I think that the readability of this excerpt was on my (underline one): **Independent (comfort) level**, **learning level**, **frustration level**. (For information about readability levels, refer to "Sink or Swim! English Language Learner and Reading Strategies," Part One.)

   Score based on percentage of the number correct:

   Rating of reading material (circle your selection):   good   fair   poor

   Rating of reading material (circle your selection):   reader-friendly   not reader-friendly

   Number of incorrect answers: Literal ___   Inferential ___   Critical ___

   (**Literal:** phonics, vocabulary; **Inferential:** main idea, implied main idea, supporting details, relationship between and within sentences, patterns of organization, inferences; **Critical:** author's purpose, tone, fact and opinion, bias, argument, figurative language)

Follow-Up Exercises

1. Write a summary of the selection in no more than three sentences.

2. In your own words tell what is the Job Characteristics Theory?

Skin Color

Elaine
Nicpon
Marieb

Pre-Reading Questions

1. What background knowledge do I have on this topic/title?

2. What subject-specific words do I know on this topic/title?

3. Based on the topic/title, I think that I will not find opportunities to apply the following skills. (Hint: for example, in a Biology text excerpt, you are not likely to find an opinion):

4. What implied main idea can I predict from the topic/title?

5. Based on the predicted implied main idea, what pattern of organization do I expect to find in this excerpt?

6. Based on the predicted implied main idea, what author's purpose and tone do I expect?

time started:

Skin Color

Skin Color

1   Three pigments contribute to skin color: melanin, carotene, and hemoglobin. Of these, only melanin is made in the skin. **Melanin** is a polymer made of tyrosine amino acids. Its two forms range in color from yellow to tan to reddish-brown to black. Its synthesis depends on an enzyme in melanocytes called tyrosinase (ti-rosă-nās) and, as noted earlier, it passes from melanocytes to the basal keratinocytes. Eventually, the melanosomes are broken down by lysosomes, so melanin pigment is found only in the deeper layers of the epidermis.

2   Human skin comes in different colors. However, distribution of those colors is not random—populations of darker-skinned people tend to be found nearer the equator (where greater protection from the sun is needed), and those with the lightest skin are found closer to the poles. Since all humans have the same relative number of melanocytes, individual and racial differences in skin coloring reflect the relative kind and amount of melanin made and retained. Melanocytes of black- and brown-skinned people produce many more and darker melanosomes than those of fair-skinned individuals, and their keratinocytes retain it longer. *Freckles* and *pigmented nevi* (*moles*) are local accumulations of melanin.

3   Melanocytes are stimulated to greater activity by chemicals secreted by the surrounding keratinocytes when we expose our skin to sunlight. Prolonged sun exposure causes a substantial melanin buildup, which helps protect the DNA of viable skin cells from UV radiation by absorbing the rays and dissipating the energy as heat. Indeed, the initial signal for speeding up melanin synthesis seems to be a faster rate of repair of photo-damaged DNA. In all but the darkest people, this response causes visible darkening of the skin (a tan).

Homeostatic Imbalance

4   Despite melanin's protective effects, excessive sun exposure eventually damages the skin. It causes clumping of elastic fibers which results in leathery skin; temporarily depresses the immune system; and can alter the DNA of skin cells and in this way lead to skin cancer. The fact that dark-skinned people get skin cancer less often than fair-skinned people and get it in areas with less pigment—the soles of the feet and nail beds— attests to melanin's effectiveness as a natural sunscreen.

5   Ultraviolet radiation has other consequences as well. It destroys the body's folic acid stores necessary for DNA synthesis, which can have serious consequences, particularly in pregnant women because the deficit may impair the development of the embryo's nervous system. Many chemicals induce photosensitivity; that is, they heighten the skin's sensitivity to UV radiation, setting sun worshippers up for an unsightly skin rash. Such substances include some antibiotic and antihistamine drugs, and many chemicals in perfumes and detergents. Small, itchy, blisterlike lesions erupt all over the body; then the peeling begins, in sheets!

6   **Carotene** (kar'o-tēn) is a yellow to orange pigment found in certain plant products such as carrots. It tends to accumulate in the stratum corneum and in fatty tissue of the hypodermis. Its color is most obvious in the palms and soles, where the stratum corneum is thickest (for example the skin of the heels), and most intense when large amounts of carotene-rich foods are eaten. However, the yellowish tinge of the skin of some Asian peoples is due to variations in melanin, as well as to carotene. In the body, carotene can be converted to vitamin A, a vitamin that is essential for normal vision, as well as for epidermal health.

7   The pinkish hue of fair skin reflects the crimson color of the oxygenated pigment **hemoglobin** (he'mo-glo"bin) in the red blood cells circulating through the dermal capillaries. Because Caucasian skin contains only small amounts of melanin, the epidermis is nearly transparent and allows hemoglobin's color to show through.

8   When hemoglobin is poorly oxygenated, both the blood and the skin of Caucasians appear blue, a condition called *cyanosis* (si"ah-no'sis; cyan = dark blue). Skin often becomes cyanotic during heart failure and severe respiratory disorders. In dark-skinned individuals, the skin does not appear cyanotic because of the masking effects of melanin, but cyanosis is apparent in their mucous membranes and nail beds (the same sites where the red cast of normally oxygenated blood is visible).

Many alterations in skin color signal certain disease states, and in many people emotional states:

- *Redness,* or *erythema* (er"ĭ-the'mah): Reddened skin may indicate embarrassment (blushing), fever, hypertension, inflammation, or allergy.

- *Pallor,* or *blanching:* During fear, anger, and certain other types of emotional stress, some people become pale. Pale skin may also signify anemia or low blood pressure.

- *Jaundice* (jawn'dis), or *yellow cast:* An abnormal yellow skin tone usually signifies a liver disorder, in which yellow bile pigments accumulate in the blood and are deposited in body tissues. [Normally, the liver cells secrete the bile pigments (bilirubin) as a component of bile.]

- *Bronzing:* A bronze, almost metallic appearance of the skin is a sign of Addison's disease, in which the adrenal cortex is producing inadequate amounts of its steroid hormones; or a sign of the presence of pituitary gland tumors that inappropriately secrete melanocyte-stimulating hormone (MSH).

- *Black-and-blue marks,* or *bruises:* Black-and-blue marks reveal where blood escaped from the circulation and clotted beneath the skin. Such clotted blood masses are called *hematomas* (he"mah-to'mah; "blood swelling").

Specific Skill Comprehension Questions

1. The main idea for this selection is:

   a. Ultraviolet radiation has negative consequences.

   b. Carotene is a yellow to orange pigment found in certain plant products.

   c. Despite melanin's protective effects, excessive sun exposure eventually damages the skin.

   d. Three pigments contribute to skin color: melanin, carotene, and hemoglobin.

2. The pattern of organization of this selection can best be described as:

   a. list of items.

   b. cause and effect.

   c. compare and contrast.

   d. time order.

3. *Prolonged sun exposure causes a substantial melanin buildup, which helps protect the DNA of viable skin cells from UV radiation by absorbing the rays and **dissipating** the energy as heat.*

   The word **dissipating** as used in the above sentence (in paragraph three) means:

   a. breaking up.

   b. assembling.

   c. congregating.

   d. keeping.

4. *Small, itchy, blisterlike lesions* **erupt** *all over the body; then the peeling begins, in sheets!*

The word **erupt** as used in the above sentence (in paragraph five) means:

a. show up.

b. break out.

c. stay.

d. smell.

5. *The fact that dark-skinned people get skin cancer less often than fair-skinned people and get it in areas with less pigment–the soles of the feet and nail beds–attests to melanin's effectiveness as a natural sunscreen.*

The above statement is:

a. opinion.

b. fact.

c. fact and opinion.

6. What is the relationship within the sentence below:

Despite melanin's protective effects, excessive sun exposure eventually damages the skin.

a. contrast

b. compare

c. addition

d. cause and effect

7. What is the relationship within the sentence below:

Because Caucasian skin contains only small amounts of melanin, the epidermis is nearly transparent and allows hemoglobin's color to show through.

a. compare and contrast

b. cause and effect

c. illustration

d. addition

8. The author is:

a. in favor of ultraviolet radiation.

b. against ultraviolet radiation.

c. is neutral about the topic.

9. One conclusion that can be drawn is:

a. People with lighter skin should live closer to the poles.

b. People with darker skin should live closer to the equator.

c. The yellowish tinge of the skin of some Asians is due to tans.

d. None of the above

10. What is the relationship between the two sentences below:

Black-and-blue marks reveal where blood escaped from the circulation and clotted beneath the skin. Such clotted blood masses are called hematomas.

a. contrast

b. cause and effect

c. spatial

d. definition and illustration

<u>Time</u> (after reading selection and completing all specific skill comprehension questions):

Post-Reading Questions

1. The text was (underline your selection):

   • reader-friendly   • not reader-friendly

2. Did the topic/title provide me with enough information to predict a main idea? Did I have enough background knowledge on the subject that facilitated my reading?

3. a. This excerpt came from a college textbook. The college course I think this excerpt corresponds with is:

   Underline your selection for both b and c below.

   b. I was familiar with **most/some/none** of the subject-specific vocabulary.

   c. I was familiar with **most/some/none** of the nonsubject-specific vocabulary.

4. I think that the readability of this excerpt was on my (underline one): **Independent (comfort) level, learning level, frustration level.** (For information about readability levels, refer to "Sink or Swim! English Language Learner and Reading Strategies," Part One.)

   Score based on percentage of the number correct:

   Rating of reading material (circle your selection):   good   fair   poor

   Rating of reading material (circle your selection):   reader-friendly   not reader-friendly

   Number of incorrect answers: Literal ___   Inferential ___   Critical ___

   (**Literal:** phonics, vocabulary; **Inferential:** main idea, implied main idea, supporting details, relationship between and within sentences, patterns of organization, inferences; **Critical:** author's purpose, tone, fact and opinion, bias, argument, figurative language)

Follow-Up Exercises

1. Write a summary of the selection in no more than five sentences.

2. In your own words explain the consequences of ultraviolet radiation. Limit your answer to no more than three sentences.

The Contemporary Debate over Euthanasia

Judith A. Boss

Pre-Reading Questions

1. What background knowledge do I have on this topic/title?

2. What subject-specific words do I know on this topic/title?

3. Based on the topic/title, I think that I will not find opportunities to apply the following skills. (Hint: for example, in a Biology text excerpt, you are not likely to find an opinion):

4. What implied main idea can I predict from the topic/title?

5. Based on the predicted implied main idea, what pattern of organization do I expect to find in this excerpt?

6. Based on the predicted implied main idea, what author's purpose and tone do I expect?

time started:

The Contemporary Debate over Euthanasia

1   It was not until the end of the nineteenth century that the public began questioning the prohibition of euthanasia. Public debate over euthanasia turned to horror when was learned that in Nazi Germany up to a hundred thousand mentally ill and disabled children and adults "considered incurable according to the best available human judgment" were, to use official language, "granted a mercy death." The memory of this terrible event still haunts Germany, which now prohibits euthanasia.

2   The public debate over euthanasia resumed with the development of new life sustaining technologies such as the mechanical respirator. In 1957, troubled by the ethical problems involved in resuscitating unconscious individuals, the International Congress of Anesthesiology sought moral guidance from Pope Pius XII. The pope responded that physicians should not act without the consent of the family. Physicians also have a moral duty to use ordinary, but not "extraordinary," measures to prolong life. The pope's position was supported by the Catholic Church's "principle of double effect."

3   The **principle of double effect** states that if an act has two effects, one intended (in this case to end pain and suffering) and the other unintended (the death of the patient), terminating treatment may be morally permissible if it is the only way to bring about the intended effect. This distinction between passive euthanasia, where death is an unintended effect, and active euthanasia, where the intention is to directly bring about the death of the patient, has remained unchallenged for years.

4   Public opinion began shifting in favor of legalized euthanasia in the early 1970s. In 1973, 53 percent of Americans supported legalized euthanasia. By 2005 this figure had risen to 75 percent. The debate gained momentum with the 2005 Terri Schiavo case. Terri Schiavo had suffered irreversible brain damage and had been in a persistent vegetative state since 1990. Her husband requested that the feeding tube be removed. Her parents disagreed with the decision. The courts repeatedly rejected parents' request to make the hospital reinsert the feeding tube that kept their daughter alive.

5   Support for physician-assisted suicide, on the other hand, is somewhat lower, having declined since reaching a high of 65 percent in 2001 to 49 percent in 2007. Men significantly more likely than women to support legalized euthanasia and physician assisted suicide. Support for legalizing euthanasia and physician-assisted suicide tends to be higher in other Western countries. Support for euthanasia is especially high in France and in the Netherlands, where active voluntary euthanasia has been legal for several years.

6   Support for euthanasia of incurably ill people is also high in China, where there is a tradition in some parts of euthanizing unwanted infant girls. There is currently a movement afoot to legalize and regulate euthanasia. Although Japanese views on euthanasia have been influenced by the Buddhist repugnance of killing, the influence of the Shinto religion's glorification of self-willed death for the benefit of the country has led to a more permissive attitude toward euthanasia than in other Buddhist countries.

7   Muslims are opposed to euthanasia on the grounds that human life is sacred and belongs to Allah. The Qur'an states, "Do not take life, which Allah made sacred, other than in the course of justice" (*Qur'an* 17:33) and "And no person can ever die except by Allah's leave and at an appointed term" (*Qur'an* 3:145).

8   Judaism likewise forbids active euthanasia as murder. Israel recently passed a law that will allow euthanasia by a timer machine, which shuts down a patient's respiratory system, and hence does not violate Jewish law. The Roman Catholic Church, as well as some other Christian denominations, also prohibits euthanasia. However, some Catholics support euthanasia in cases of unremitting and severe pain or irreversible brain damage.

Specific Skill Comprehension Questions

1. The word **prolong** as used in paragraph two which begins with *The public debate over ...* means:

   a. abbreviate.

   b. lengthen.

   c. abridge.

   d. shorten.

2. The word **unremitting** as used in the last sentence of this selection means:

   a. discontinuing.

   b. tolerable.

   c. constant.

   d. painful.

3. The main idea for this selection is:

   a. Public opinion began shifting in favor of legalized euthanasia in the early 1970s.

   b. Support for euthanasia of incurably ill people is also high in China.

   c. Many people are opposed to euthanasia based on their religious beliefs.

   d. It was not until the end of the 19th century that the public began questioning the prohibition of euthanasia.

4. The pattern of organization of this selection can best be described as:

   a. time order and illustration.

   b. list of items.

   c. compare and contrast.

   d. cause and effect.

5. What is the relationship between the following sentences:

   Public opinion began shifting in favor of legalized euthanasia in the early 1970s. In 1973, 53 percent of Americans supported legalized euthanasia.

   a. addition

   b. contrast

   c. compare

   d. time

6. What is the relationship between the following sentences:

   Her husband requested that the feeding tube be removed. Her parents disagreed with the decision.

   a. compare

   b. spatial

   c. addition

   d. cause and effect

7. Based on the last three paragraphs of this selection, it can be concluded that:

    a. Muslims are opposed to euthanasia.

    b. Support for euthanasia of incurably ill people is high in China.

    c. The Shinto religion's glorification of self-willed death has led to a more permissive attitude toward euthanasia in Japan than in other Buddhist countries.

    d. Some Roman Catholics do not follow the church's teachings.

8. *There is currently a movement afoot to legalize and regulate euthanasia.*

    The above statement is:

    a. fact.

    b. opinion.

    c. fact and opinion.

9. The tone of this selection can best be described as:

    a. critical.

    b. tragic.

    c. matter-of-fact.

    d. tolerant.

10. The pattern or organization of paragraph four which begins with Public opinion began shifting … can best be described as that of:

    a. cause and effect.

    b. spatial.

    c. problem and solution.

    d. time order.

Time (after reading selection and completing all specific skill comprehension questions): _____

Post-Reading Questions

1. The text was (underline your selection):

    • reader-friendly   • not reader-friendly

2. Did the topic/title provide me with enough information to predict a main idea? Did I have enough background knowledge on the subject that facilitated my reading?

3. a. This excerpt came from a college textbook. The college course I think this excerpt corresponds with is:

    Underline your selection for both b and c below.

    b. I was familiar with **most/some/none** of the subject-specific vocabulary.

    c. I was familiar with **most/some/none** of the nonsubject-specific vocabulary.

4. I think that the readability of this excerpt was on my (underline one): **Independent (comfort) level, learning level, frustration level**. (For information about readability levels, refer to "Sink or Swim! English Language Learner and Reading Strategies," Part One.)

Score based on percentage of the number correct:

Rating of reading material (circle your selection):   good   fair   poor

Rating of reading material (circle your selection):   reader-friendly   not reader-friendly

Number of incorrect answers: Literal ___   Inferential ___   Critical ___

(**Literal:** phonics, vocabulary; **Inferential:** main idea, implied main idea, supporting details, relationship between and within sentences, patterns of organization, inferences; **Critical:** author's purpose, tone, fact and opinion, bias, argument, figurative language)

Follow-Up Exercises

1. Based on the information in this selection, write a paragraph making an argument for or against the use of euthanasia. Support your choice by the information provided in this selection.

2. Summarize this selection in no more than six sentences.

Final Note

Did you notice that the author's purpose for most of these selections is to inform? It makes sense, does it not, that this is content (reading material particular to a subject area) and, therefore, in all probability, the author is providing information on subject-related topics that the reader should learn or know. This is because most textbooks that you are likely to encounter in college are for sharing information on a subject. However, depending on the subject, reading material in some instances may be presented for other purposes, such as to persuade or to inspire. If the primary purpose of a text is to provide information, it would make sense that the author's tone would probably be best described in terms such as *straightforward, objective,* and *neutral* (sometimes you may find informational text that is biased—not neutral). Although in some cases information in texts may be presented in a humorous tone, the author's purpose will likely be to inform and not to entertain. Remember that there are no absolutes when we discuss language!

Reason to Reason

Part Three (B)

Foreword

Dear Student:

1   Section B is devoted to poems such as the ones you may find in literary texts. I have also added an excerpt from a musical play. Again, just as in section A, you'll find that in addition to some specific skill comprehension questions involving application of skills, I have asked you pre- and post-reading questions not related to the type of reading comprehension questions you'll find in reading comprehension tests. The purpose for these types of questions is to engage you in the reading material by focusing you on what you know, and what you do not know, and therefore, need to know. Refer to the *Foreword* to Part Three A for a more thorough explanation.

2   In Part Four, you will find three analyses of song lyrics (courtesy of Jeffrey Fraser). I trust that you will read them and reflect on what you would add or subtract from those analyses and why. In doing so, I hope that you will discover the importance of having prior knowledge about the songwriter, his/her agenda, the era in which the song was released, as well as the importance of vocabulary and knowledge of literary tools. In the excerpt of the musical play *May the Circle Be Unbroken*, for example, Althea Beneby-Duren has provided brief information on both the playwright and the play. When you read these, you must ask yourself whether that background knowledge was helpful in analyzing the excerpt of the play. Likewise, I hope that you will make the connections between song lyrics and poems and find that writing an analysis of lyrics is similar to writing an analysis for a poem.

3   You may want to refresh your memory by rereading the chapters "Imaginary vs. Real: Fiction vs. Non-fiction" (Part One) and "Say What? The Nuances of English" (Part Two). You will want to be particularly familiar with denotation and connotation of words, figures of speech, and the difference between literal and figurative language.

4   You'll notice that for literary work such as poems and plays, you will seldom be asked for application of specific skills such as main idea, major and minor supporting details, fact and opinion, relationships, argument, and author's purpose. Instead, you will be asked for inferences, tone, and analyses, as these types of writings are typically conducive to application of such higher-order thinking skills and processes. However, I have added questions on main ideas, relationships, and so on to the exercises I have provided here so that you can apply what you've learned to literary texts such as poems and plays. You'll notice that not all poems were conducive to my providing you with comprehension questions on every skill addressed in Part Two. If you decide to score your answers, the score will have to be calculated based on the number of questions correct versus the number of questions asked. If you have 10 questions, then you can follow the directions given in the *Foreword* of Part Three A.

5   As I mentioned in "Let Me Introduce Myself ...," we are fortunate to have easy access to much reading material. I trust that what you'll realize by now is that what you have learned in your course can be applied to make sense of any reading material and that reading is not such a daunting task after all!

6   I hope you continue to enjoy the benefits of being a member of a literate society!

Much Regards,

2011

The Voice You Hear When You Read Silently

Thomas Lux

Pre-Reading Questions

1. What background knowledge do I have on this title?

2. What background knowledge do I have on this poet and his/her style of poetry?

3. What subject-specific words do I know on this type of reading (poem/play) (Hint: For example, what literary tools would I be able to identify?)

4. What implied main idea can I predict from the topic/title?

5. Based on the predicted implied main idea, what pattern of organization do I expect to find in this poem?

6. Based on the predicted implied main idea, what poet's purpose and tone do I expect?

time started:

The Voice You Hear When You Read Silently

is not silent, it is a speaking-
out-loud voice in your head; it is *spoken,*
a voice is *saying* it
as you read. It's the writer's words,
of course, in a literary sense   5
his or her *voice,* but the sound
of that voice is the sound of your voice.
Not the sound your friends know
or the sound of a tape played back
but your voice   10
caught in the dark cathedral
of your skull, your voice heard
by an internal ear informed by internal abstracts
and what you know by feeling,
having felt. It is your voice   15
saying, for example, the word barn
that the writer wrote
but the barn you say
is a barn you know or knew. The voice
in your head, speaking as you read,   20
never says anything neutrally—some people
hated the barn they knew,
some people love the barn they know
so you hear the word loaded
and a sensory constellation   25
is lit: horse-gnawed stalls,
hayloft, black heat tape wrapping
a water pipe, a slippery
spilled chirr of oats from a split sack,
the bony, filthy haunches of cows. ...   30
And barn is only a noun—no verb
or subject has entered into the sentence yet!
The voice you hear when you read to yourself
is the clearest voice: you speak it
speaking to you.

Specific Skill Comprehension Questions

1. In line 11 *dark cathedral* is an example of a/an:

   a. oxymoron.

   b. euphemism.

   c. idiom.

   d. metaphor.

2. In lines 25 and 26, *sensory constellation is lit* is an example of a/an:

   a. oxymoron.

   b. euphemism.

   c. idiom.

   d. metaphor.

3. The main idea of this poem is:

   a. The barn is what we make of it.

   b. The voice we hear in our head when we read silently is the clearest voice.

   c. Our voice is the voice we hear in our head.

   d. Our experiences are important in interpreting the poet's message.

4. The poet's tone can best be described as:

   a. scheming.

   b. mocking.

   c. superior.

   d. impassioned.

5. The poet's purpose can best be described as:

   a. to inform.

   b. to entertain.

   c. to convince.

   d. to inspire.

6. One inference that can be drawn is that:

   a. The voice we hear in our head when reading silently is the clearest one.

   b. Our experiences play a part in making sense of things.

   c. Our internal ear is informed by the internal abstracts we know.

   d. *Home* would mean different things to different people.

7. The word *constellation* in the context of this poem means:

   a. collection of stars.

   b. collection of thoughts and ideas.

   c. brilliant.

   d. having to do with astronomy.

8. The denotative meaning of the word *cathedral* is:

   a. big mansion.

   b. big dungeon.

   c. big church.

   d. huge building.

9. When the poet refers to *voice*, he means:

    a. reading.

    b. thinking.

    c. singing.

    d. saying.

10. When the poet refers to *you speak it speaking to you,* he means:

    a. You are thinking.

    b. You are reading.

    c. You are stating.

    d. You are mimicking the voice of the poet.

Time (after reading selection and completing all specific skill comprehension questions): _____

Post-Reading Questions

1. The text was (underline your selection):

    • reader-friendly   • not reader-friendly

2. Did the title of the poem provide me with enough information to predict a main idea? Did I have enough background knowledge on the topic and/or the poet that facilitated my reading?

3. a. This poem could be found in a college textbook. The college course I think this excerpt would correspond with is:

    Underline your selection for both b and c below.

    b. I was familiar with **most/some/none** of the subject-specific vocabulary.

    c. I was familiar with **most/some/none** of the nonsubject-specific vocabulary.

4. I think that the readability of this poem was on my (underline one): **Independent (comfort) level**, **learning level**, **frustration level**. (For information about readability levels, refer to "Sink or Swim! English Language Learner and Reading Strategies," Part One.)

    Score based on percentage of the number correct (You will have to calculate this for each selection based on the

    number of questions right versus the number of questions asked): _____

    Rating of reading material (circle your selection):   good   fair   poor

    Rating of reading material (circle your selection):   reader-friendly   not reader-friendly

    Number of incorrect answers: Literal ___   Inferential ___   Critical ___

    (**Literal:** phonics, vocabulary; **Inferential:** main idea, implied main idea, supporting details, relationship between and within sentences, patterns of organization, inferences; **Critical:** author's purpose, tone, fact and opinion, bias, argument, figurative language)

Follow-Up Exercises

1. How would you describe the *voice* in your head when you read silently?

2. Do you think that the poet explained this *voice* sufficiently well? Do you agree with the poet's description? Give reasons for your answers.

Richard Cory

Edwin
Arlington
Robinson

Pre-Reading Questions

1. What background knowledge do I have on this title?

2. What background knowledge do I have on this poet and his/her style of poetry?

3. What subject-specific words do I know on this type of reading (poem/play) (Hint: For example, what literary tools would I be able to identify?)

4. What implied main idea can I predict from the topic/title?

5. Based on the predicted implied main idea, what pattern of organization do I expect to find in this poem?

6. Based on the predicted implied main idea, what poet's purpose and tone do I expect?

time started:

Richard Cory

Whenever Richard Cory went down town,
We people on the pavement looked at him:
He was a gentleman from sole to crown,
Clean favored, and imperially slim.

And he was always quietly arrayed,   5
And he was always human when he talked;
But still he fluttered pulses when he said,
"Good-morning," and he glittered when he walked.

And he was rich—yes, richer than a king—
And admirably schooled in every grace: 10
In fine, we thought that he was everything
To make us wish that we were in his place.

So on we worked, and waited for the light,
And went without the meat, and cursed the bread;
And Richard Cory, one calm summer night,   15
Went home and put a bullet through his head.

Specific Skill Comprehension Questions

1. The implied main idea of this poem is:

   a. Richard Cory was admired by people.

   b. Richard Cory was a happy man.

   c. Richard Cory was well-mannered.

   d. Richard Cory killed himself despite having things others envied.

2. What word/s in what line in the poem gives some initial indication that Richard Cory did not have everything:

   a. fluttered pulses (line 7)

   b. imperially slim (line 4)

   c. cursed the bread (line 14)

   d. we thought that (line 11)

3. What is the relationship within the sentences below:

   And he was always quietly arrayed,
   And he was always human when he talked;

   a. compare

   b. illustration

   c. addition

   d. contrast

4. What is the relationship between the sentences below:

> *And he was always quietly arrayed,*
> *And he was always human when he talked;*
> *But still he fluttered pulses when he said,*
> *"Good-morning," and he glittered when he walked.*

    a. compare

    b. contrast

    c. cause and effect

    d. illustration

5. The pattern of organization of this poem can best be described as:

    a. spatial.

    b. classification.

    c. generalization and example.

    d. time order.

6. In the context of this poem, what does the word *imperially* in line 4 mean?

    a. stately.

    b. unimpressively.

    c. extremely.

    d. slightly.

7. In the context of this poem, what does the word *arrayed* in line 5 mean?

    a. portrayed

    b. mannered

    c. dressed splendidly

    d. answering questions

8. This poem is an example of:

    a. sarcasm.

    b. situational irony.

    c. propaganda.

    d. glittering generalities.

9. One inference we can draw from this poem is:

    a. Richard Cory was admired by people who knew him.

    b. Richard Cory was a violent man.

    c. Richard Cory was wealthy.

    d. Richard Cory was unhappy despite his wealth.

10. The poet may have intended one moral of this poem to be:

   a. It's important to be liked.

   b. It's important to have good manners.

   c. Do not assume that someone who appears to have everything is happy.

   d. It's best not to compare ourselves to others.

Time (after reading selection and completing all specific skill comprehension questions):

Post-Reading Questions

1. The text was (underline your selection):

   • reader-friendly   • not reader-friendly

2. Did the title of the poem provide me with enough information to predict a main idea? Did I have enough background knowledge on the topic and/or the poet that facilitated my reading?

3. a. This poem could be found in a college textbook. The college course I think this excerpt would correspond with is:

   Underline your selection for both b and c below.

   b. I was familiar with **most/some/none** of the subject-specific vocabulary.

   c. I was familiar with **most/some/none** of the nonsubject-specific vocabulary.

4. I think that the readability of this poem was on my (underline one): **Independent (comfort) level**, **learning level**, **frustration level**. (For information about readability levels, refer to "Sink or Swim! English Language Learner and Reading Strategies," Part One.)

   Score based on percentage of the number correct (You will have to calculate this for each selection based on the

   number of questions right versus the number of questions asked):

   Rating of reading material (circle your selection):   good   fair   poor

   Rating of reading material (circle your selection):   reader-friendly   not reader-friendly

   Number of incorrect answers: Literal ___   Inferential ___   Critical ___

   (**Literal:** phonics, vocabulary; **Inferential:** main idea, implied main idea, supporting details, relationship between and within sentences, patterns of organization, inferences; **Critical:** author's purpose, tone, fact and opinion, bias, argument, figurative language)

Follow-Up Exercises

1. Write a five-sentence analysis of this poem.

2. Is there someone whose lifestyle you admire/envy? Give reasons for your answer.

A Man Said to the Universe

Stephen Crane

Pre-Reading Questions

1. What background knowledge do I have on this title?

2. What background knowledge do I have on this poet and his/her style of poetry?

3. What subject-specific words do I know on this type of reading (poem/play) (Hint: For example, what literary tools would I be able to identify?)

4. What implied main idea can I predict from the topic/title?

5. Based on the predicted implied main idea, what pattern of organization do I expect to find in this poem?

6. Based on the predicted implied main idea, what poet's purpose and tone do I expect?

<u>time started:</u>

A Man Said to the Universe

A man said to the universe:
"Sir, I exist!"
"However," replied the universe,
"The fact has not created in me
A sense of obligation."

Specific Skill Comprehension Questions

1. The poet's tone can best be described as:

   a. indignant.

   b. scornful.

   c. bewildered.

   d. humorous.

2. The conversation between the man and the universe suggests that:

   a. The man needs recognition of his existence.

   b. The universe is obligated to recognize the man's existence.

   c. The man does not realize that he exists in a universe.

   d. The universe recognizes the man's existence.

3. Based on the universe's response to the man, we can infer that:

   a. The man does not realize that he exists in a universe.

   b. The universe recognizes the man's existence.

   c. The universe does not assume responsibility for the man's well-being.

   d. The universe is obligated to recognize the man's existence.

Time (after reading selection and completing all specific skill comprehension questions): _____

Post-Reading Questions

1. The text was (underline your selection):

   • reader-friendly   • not reader-friendly

2. Did the title of the poem provide me with enough information to predict a main idea? Did I have enough background knowledge on the topic and/or the poet that facilitated my reading?

3. a. This poem could be found in a college textbook. The college course I think this excerpt would correspond with is:

Underline your selection for both b and c below.

b. I was familiar with **most/some/none** of the subject-specific vocabulary.

c. I was familiar with **most/some/none** of the nonsubject-specific vocabulary.

4. I think that the readability of this poem was on my (underline one): **Independent (comfort) level, learning level, frustration level**. (For information about readability levels, refer to "Sink or Swim! English Language Learner and Reading Strategies," Part One.)

Score based on percentage of the number correct (You will have to calculate this for each selection based on the

number of questions right versus the number of questions asked):

Rating of reading material (circle your selection):   good   fair   poor

Rating of reading material (circle your selection):   reader-friendly   not reader-friendly

Number of incorrect answers: Literal ___   Inferential ___   Critical ___

(**Literal:** phonics, vocabulary; **Inferential:** main idea, implied main idea, supporting details, relationship between and within sentences, patterns of organization, inferences; **Critical:** author's purpose, tone, fact and opinion, bias, argument, figurative language)

Follow-Up Exercises

1. This poem is an example of cosmic irony in literature. It's referred to as cosmic irony because there is a discrepancy between what the man expects (recognition) from the universe and what the universe actually provides (anonymity). Tell in your own words what message the poet was trying to portray.

2. Look for another example of cosmic irony in literature. Tell about it in no more than 10 sentences. **OR** Tell about another poem by Stephen Crane in no more than five sentences.

A Bird Came Down the Walk

Emily Dickinson

Pre-Reading Questions

1. What background knowledge do I have on this title?

2. What background knowledge do I have on this poet and his/her style of poetry?

3. What subject-specific words do I know on this type of reading (poem/play) (Hint: For example, what literary tools would I be able to identify?)

4. What implied main idea can I predict from the topic/title?

5. Based on the predicted implied main idea, what pattern of organization do I expect to find in this poem?

6. Based on the predicted implied main idea, what poet's purpose and tone do I expect?

<u>time started:</u>

A Bird Came Down the Walk

A bird came down the walk:
He did not know I saw;
He bit an angle-worm in halves
And ate the fellow, raw,

And then he drank a dew   5
From a convenient grass,
And then hopped sidewise to the wall
To let a beetle pass.

He glanced with rapid eyes
That hurried all abroad,—   10
They looked like frightened beads, I thought—
He stirred his velvet head

Like one in danger; cautious,
I offered him a crumb,
And he unrolled his feathers   15
And rowed him softer home

Than oars divide the ocean,
Too silver for a seam,
Or butterflies, off banks of noon,
Leap, plashless, as they swim.   20

Specific Skill Comprehension Questions

1. *They looked like frightened beads* is an example of a/an:

   a. cliché.

   b. oxymoron.

   c. alliteration.

   d. simile.

2. The poet's comparison of the bird's flight to that of oars movements in the ocean is an example of a/an:

   a. euphemism.

   b. personification.

   c. analogy.

   d. hyperbole.

3. In *And ate the fellow, raw*, the poet refers to the angle-worm as a "fellow." This is an example of a/an:

   a. personification.

   b. euphemism.

   c. metaphor.

   d. irony.

4. The pattern of organization can best be described as:

   a. list of items.

   b. compare and contrast.

   c. time order.

   d. cause and effect.

5. What does the word *cautious* in line 13 mean?

   a. heedless.

   b. careful.

   c. unwary.

   d. terrified.

6. We can conclude that the bird flew away because:

   a. He was afraid of the beetle.

   b. He was afraid of the poet.

7. When the author writes *Like one in danger, cautious,* she is referring to:

   a. the bird.

   b. the beetle.

   c. herself.

8. The tone of this poem can best be described as both:

   a. amusing and awe-inspiring.

   b. optimistic and solemn.

   c. sentimental and tolerant.

   d. lighthearted and ambivalent.

9. The implied main idea of this poem is:

   a. A bird flew away.

   b. A bird moved on the ground.

   c. A bird flew away gracefully and effortlessly.

   d. A bird moves on the ground and then, frightened, flies gracefully away.

10. The poet's purpose can best be described as:

   a. to inform.

   b. to convince.

   c. to entertain.

   d. to incite.

Time (after reading selection and completing all specific skill comprehension questions):

Post-Reading Questions

1. The text was (underline your selection):

   • reader-friendly   • not reader-friendly

2. Did the title of the poem provide me with enough information to predict a main idea? Did I have enough background knowledge on the topic and/or the poet that facilitated my reading?

3. a. This poem could be found in a college textbook. The college course I think this excerpt would correspond with is:

   Underline your selection for both b and c below.

   b. I was familiar with **most/some/none** of the subject-specific vocabulary.

   c. I was familiar with **most/some/none** of the nonsubject-specific vocabulary.

4. I think that the readability of this poem was on my (underline one): **Independent (comfort) level**, **learning level**, **frustration level**. (For information about readability levels, refer to "Sink or Swim! English Language Learner and Reading Strategies," Part One.)

   Score based on percentage of the number correct (You will have to calculate this for each selection based on the

   number of questions right versus the number of questions asked):

   Rating of reading material (circle your selection):   good   fair   poor

   Rating of reading material (circle your selection):   reader-friendly   not reader-friendly

   Number of incorrect answers: Literal ___   Inferential ___   Critical ___

   (**Literal:** phonics, vocabulary; **Inferential:** main idea, implied main idea, supporting details, relationship between and within sentences, patterns of organization, inferences; **Critical:** author's purpose, tone, fact and opinion, bias, argument, figurative language)

Follow-Up Exercises

1. Did you like the poem? Tell why.

2. Research Emily Dickinson. Write one paragraph about her literary works.

Scarborough Fair

Anonymous

Pre-Reading Questions

1. What background knowledge do I have on this title?

2. What background knowledge do I have on this poet and his/her style of poetry?

3. What subject-specific words do I know on this type of reading (poem/play) (Hint: For example, what literary tools would I be able to identify?)

4. What implied main idea can I predict from the topic/title?

5. Based on the predicted implied main idea, what pattern of organization do I expect to find in this poem?

6. Based on the predicted implied main idea, what poet's purpose and tone do I expect?

time started:

Scarborough Fair

Where are you going? To Scarborough Fair?
Parsley, sage, rosemary, and thyme,
Remember me to a bonny lass there,
For once she was a true lover of mine.

Tell her to make me a cambric shirt,   5
Parsley, sage, rosemary, and thyme,
Without any needle or thread work'd in it,
And she shall be a true lover of mine.

Tell her to wash it in yonder well,
Parsley, sage, rosemary, and thyme,   10
Where water ne'er sprung nor a drop of rain fell,
And she shall be a true lover of mine.

Tell her to plough me an acre of land,
Parsley, sage, rosemary, and thyme,
Between the sea and the salt sea strand,   15
And she shall be a true lover of mine.

Tell her to plough it with one ram's horn,
Parsley, sage, rosemary, and thyme,
And sow it all over with one peppercorn,
And she shall be a true lover of mine.   20

Tell her to reap it with a sickle of leather,
Parsley, sage, rosemary, and thyme,
And tie it all up with a tom tit's feather,
And she shall be a true lover of mine.

Tell her to gather it all in a sack,   25
Parsley, sage, rosemary, and thyme,
And carry it home on a butterfly's back.
And then she shall be a true lover of mine.

Specific Skill Comprehension Questions

1. What does *lass* in line 3 mean?

   a. young lady

   b. young wife

   c. young mistress

   d. young lover

2. What does *yonder* in line 9 mean?

   a. here

   b. over there

   c. place in another village

   d. place in another town

3. What does *plough* in line 13 mean?

   a. sow seeds

   b. plant trees

   c. fix land for construction

   d. prepare land for planting

4. An inference that we can draw from this poem is that:

   a. Herbs are good for you.

   b. A former lover does not expect the lass to fulfill his demands.

   c. His demands are reasonable.

   d. She will want to fulfill his demands.

5. The tone of this poem can best be described as:

   a. remorseful.

   b. solemn.

   c. bewildered.

   d. amusing.

6. The implied main idea of this poem can best be stated as:

   a. Several impossible demands are made of a former lover.

   b. Several achievable demands are made of a former lover.

   c. Parsley, sage, rosemary, and thyme are good for lovers.

   d. Shirt, land, and peppercorn are demands made by the ex-lover.

7. The pattern of organization of this poem can best be described as:

   a. list of items.

   b. cause and effect.

   c. definition and example.

   d. compare and contrast.

Time (after reading selection and completing all specific skill comprehension questions):

Post-Reading Questions

1. The text was (underline your selection):

   • reader-friendly   • not reader-friendly

2. Did the title of the poem provide me with enough information to predict a main idea? Did I have enough background knowledge on the topic and/or the poet that facilitated my reading?

3. a. This poem could be found in a college textbook. The college course I think this excerpt would correspond with is:

Underline your selection for both b and c below.

b. I was familiar with **most/some/none** of the subject-specific vocabulary.

c. I was familiar with **most/some/none** of the nonsubject-specific vocabulary.

4. I think that the readability of this poem was on my (underline one): **Independent (comfort) level**, **learning level**, **frustration level**. (For information about readability levels, refer to "Sink or Swim! English Language Learner and Reading Strategies," Part One.)

Score based on percentage of the number correct (You will have to calculate this for each selection based on the

number of questions right versus the number of questions asked):

Rating of reading material (circle your selection):   good   fair   poor

Rating of reading material (circle your selection):   reader-friendly   not reader-friendly

Number of incorrect answers: Literal ___   Inferential ___   Critical ___

(**Literal:** phonics, vocabulary; **Inferential:** main idea, implied main idea, supporting details, relationship between and within sentences, patterns of organization, inferences; **Critical:** author's purpose, tone, fact and opinion, bias, argument, figurative language)

Follow-Up Exercises

1. Why would the man make these unreasonable demands of his ex-lover?

2. This poem is a traditional ballad from England. Although the poet is unknown, this poem was made into a song in 1966 by singer-songwriter Paul Simon and singer Art Garfunkel. They were popular in the 1960s. If you recall, much earlier in this book I had mentioned how song lyrics are similar to poems set to music. *Scarborough Fair* is an example of what I meant.

Simon and Garfunkel became popular for hits such as *The Sound of Silence* that was released in 1964. The lyrics of this song can be found on the Internet. Write an analysis of *The Sound of Silence* lyrics while taking into account the changes the U.S. was undergoing at the time. In the 1960s many of your parents or your grandparents were probably the same age as you are now. Ask these relatives about the social and political climate of the country back then, and the impact these songs may have had in their lives. BTW: You can listen to Simon and Garfunkel's songs, *Scarborough Fair* and *The Sound of Silence* on YouTube.

When I Was One-and-Twenty

A. E. Housman

Pre-Reading Questions

1. What background knowledge do I have on this title?

2. What background knowledge do I have on this poet and his/her style of poetry?

3. What subject-specific words do I know on this type of reading (poem/play) (Hint: For example, what literary tools would I be able to identify?)

4. What implied main idea can I predict from the topic/title?

5. Based on the predicted implied main idea, what pattern of organization do I expect to find in this poem?

6. Based on the predicted implied main idea, what poet's purpose and tone do I expect?

time started:

When I Was One-and-Twenty

When I was one-and-twenty
    I heard a wise man say,
"Give crowns and pounds and guineas
    But not your heart away;
Give pearls away and rubies   5
    But keep your fancy free."
But I was one-and-twenty,
    No use to talk to me.

When I was one-and-twenty
    I heard him say again,   10
"The heart out of the bosom
    Was never given in vain;
'Tis paid with sighs a plenty
    And sold for endless rue."
And I am two-and-twenty,   15
    And oh, 'tis true, 'tis true.

Specific Skill Comprehension Questions

1. In line 4 *heart* is used as a:

   a. metaphor for feelings.

   b. simile for feelings.

   c. personification for feelings.

   d. euphemism for feelings.

2. What is the relationship between the following two thoughts:

   Give pearls away and rubies
   But keep your fancy free.

   a. addition

   b. cause and effect

   c. contrast

   d. compare

3. What is the relationship between the following two thoughts:

   But I was one-and-twenty,
   No use to talk to me.

   a. addition

   b. cause and effect

   c. contrast

   d. compare

4. As used in line 11, the word *bosom* means:

    a. ribs.

    b. body.

    c. chest.

    d. place where emotions reside.

5. In the context of this poem the word *bosom's* definition is:

    a. connotative.

    b. denotative.

6. As used in line 6, the word *fancy* means:

    a. inclination to like.

    b. aversion.

    c. thoughts.

    d. admiration.

7. As used in line 14, the word *rue* means:

    a. monetary reward.

    b. precious jewelry.

    c. sorrow.

    d. joy.

8. The pattern of organization of the poem from line 9 through 16 is:

    a. spatial.

    b. definition and example.

    c. illustration.

    d. time order.

9. The poem's tone can best be described as:

    a. pessimistic.

    b. regretful.

    c. prideful.

    d. indignant.

10. The poet's purpose is to:

    a. convince.

    b. inspire.

    c. entertain.

    d. incite.

Time (after reading selection and completing all specific skill comprehension questions):

Post-Reading Questions

1. The text was (underline your selection):

   - reader-friendly   • not reader-friendly

2. Did the title of the poem provide me with enough information to predict a main idea? Did I have enough background knowledge on the topic and/or the poet that facilitated my reading?

3. a. This poem could be found in a college textbook. The college course I think this excerpt would correspond with is:

   Underline your selection for both b and c below.

   b. I was familiar with **most/some/none** of the subject-specific vocabulary.

   c. I was familiar with **most/some/none** of the nonsubject-specific vocabulary.

4. I think that the readability of this poem was on my (underline one): **Independent (comfort) level**, **learning level**, **frustration level**. (For information about readability levels, refer to "Sink or Swim! English Language Learner and Reading Strategies," Part One.)

   Score based on percentage of the number correct (You will have to calculate this for each selection based on the

   number of questions right versus the number of questions asked):

   Rating of reading material (circle your selection):   good   fair   poor

   Rating of reading material (circle your selection):   reader-friendly   not reader-friendly

   Number of incorrect answers: Literal ___   Inferential ___   Critical ___

   (**Literal:** phonics, vocabulary; **Inferential:** main idea, implied main idea, supporting details, relationship between and within sentences, patterns of organization, inferences; **Critical:** author's purpose, tone, fact and opinion, bias, argument, figurative language)

Follow-Up Exercises

1. In the last sentence the poet states *'tis true, 'tis true*. What is true? Why is it repeated?

2. Do you agree with the poet? Give reasons why.

Jabberwocky

Lewis Carroll
(Charles
Lutwidge
Dodgson)

Pre-Reading Questions

1. What background knowledge do I have on this title?

2. What background knowledge do I have on this poet and his/her style of poetry?

3. What subject-specific words do I know on this type of reading (poem/play)? (Hint: For example, what literary tools would I be able to identify?)

4. What implied main idea can I predict from the topic/title?

5. Based on the predicted implied main idea, what pattern of organization do I expect to find in this poem?

6. Based on the predicted implied main idea, what poet's purpose and tone do I expect?

time started:

Jabberwocky

'Twas brillig, and the slithy toves
    Did gyre and gimble in the wabe:
All mimsy were the borogoves,
    And the mome raths outgrabe.

"Beware the Jabberwock, my son!   5
    The jaws that bite, the claws that catch !
Beware the Jubjub bird, and shun
    The frumious Bandersnatch!"

He took his vorpal sword in hand;
    Long time the manxome foe he sought—   10
So rested he by the Tumtum tree,
    And stood awhile in thought.

And, as in uffish thought he stood,
    The Jabberwock, with eyes of flame,
Came whiffling through the tulgey wood,   15
    And burbled as it came!

One, two! One, two! And through and through
    The vorpal blade went snicker-snack!
He left it dead, and with its head
    He went galumphing back.   20

"And hast thou slain the Jabberwock?
    Come to my arms, my beamish boy!
O frabjous day! Callooh, Callay!"
    He chortled in his joy.

'Twas brillig, and the slithy toves   25
    Did gyre and gimble in the wabe:
All mimsy were the borogoves,
    And the mome raths outgrabe.

Specific Skill Comprehension Questions

1. As used in line 16, the word *burbled* means:

   a. making bubbling sounds.

   b. making loud noises.

   c. slithering.

   d. swaying about.

2. As used in line 21, the word *slain* means:

   a. beat.

   b. sent away.

   c. whipped.

   d. killed.

3. As used in line 24, the word *chortled* means:

   a. danced.

   b. laughed.

   c. screamed.

   d. cried.

4. This poem can be *best* described as a work of:

   a. nonfiction.

   b. fantasy.

5. As used in line 18, the words *snicker-snack* can be described as a/an:

   a. alliteration.

   b. hyperbole.

   c. onomatopoeia.

   d. euphemism.

6. We can infer that:

   a. The Jabberwock was killed.

   b. The father was pleased that the son killed the Jabberwock.

   c. The Jabberwock was killed with a sword.

   d. The father warned the son about the Jabberwock.

<u>Time</u> (after reading selection and completing all specific skill comprehension questions):

Post-Reading Questions

1. The text was (underline your selection):

   • reader-friendly   • not reader-friendly

2. Did the title of the poem provide me with enough information to predict a main idea? Did I have enough background knowledge on the topic and/or the poet that facilitated my reading?

3. a. This poem could be found in a college textbook. The college course I think this excerpt would correspond with is:

   Underline your selection for both b and c below.

   b. I was familiar with **most/some/none** of the subject-specific vocabulary.

   c. I was familiar with **most/some/none** of the nonsubject-specific vocabulary.

4. I think that the readability of this poem was on my (underline one): **Independent (comfort) level**, **learning level**, **frustration level**. (For information about readability levels, refer to "Sink or Swim! English Language Learner and Reading Strategies," Part One.)

   Score based on percentage of the number correct (You will have to calculate this for each selection based on the

   number of questions right versus the number of questions asked):

   Rating of reading material (circle your selection):   good   fair   poor

   Rating of reading material (circle your selection):   reader-friendly   not reader-friendly

   Number of incorrect answers: Literal ___   Inferential ___   Critical ___

   (**Literal:** phonics, vocabulary; **Inferential:** main idea, implied main idea, supporting details, relationship between and within sentences, patterns of organization, inferences; **Critical:** author's purpose, tone, fact and opinion, bias, argument, figurative language)

Follow-Up Exercises

1. Look up Lewis Carroll and *Jabberwocky* and write at least a five-sentence paragraph on this author and this poem.

2. Did you like this poem? Give reasons why.

3. I saved this poem for last because I thought that this poem would present you with a challenge, especially because of its made-up words. Perhaps you had to read it a few times to make sense of it. But you did make some sense of it. How?

May the Circle Be Unbroken

Lehman Beneby

April 30, 1950–
February 17, 2001

Pre-Reading Questions

1. What background knowledge do I have on this title?

2. What background knowledge do I have on this playwright?

3. What subject-specific words do I know on this type of reading (play)
   (Hint: For example, what literary tools would I be able to identify?)

4. What implied main idea can I predict from the topic/title?

5. Based on the predicted implied main idea, what pattern of organization
   do I expect to find in this play?

6. Based on the predicted implied main idea, what playwright's purpose and
   tone do I expect?

time started:

May The Circle Be Unbroken

Excerpt from Gospel Musical, copyright 1994
Contributed by Althea Beneby-Duren

Foreword

by Althea Beneby-Duren

The Playwright

Lehman Beneby was a native of Miami, Florida. He attended the public schools of Miami-Dade County and graduated from Miami Northwestern Senior High School in June of 1969. He earned his Bachelor's degree from Bethune-Cookman College in Daytona Beach, Florida, with postgraduate work at the University of Miami and Philadelphia School of the Performing Arts. For over six years, he served as assistant director and director of the Dade County (African Heritage) Cultural Arts Center.

At an early age his musical and theatrical "gifts" were discovered and nurtured through his Christian upbringing, high school, and college career, and were to be his signature in later pursuits. He formed several musical groups, including the LeBene Ensemble, Voices of Spring, and The Sounds of Exaltation.

He began his professional career in the Broadway National Tour of *Your Arms Too Short to Box with God*. He also performed in *Bubbling Brown Sugar*, and toured South America with *The Big Apple Review*. Mr. Beneby was Minister of Music for *Mama, I Want to Sing* and was an AUDELCO Award Nominee for Outstanding Male Performer in *Abyssinia*. He wrote *May the Circle Be Unbroken*, which was performed at the Billie Holiday Theater in Brooklyn, NY, the National Black Theater in Harlem, NY, and The Miami Shores Theater of the Performing Arts. *May the Circle Be Unbroken* was nominated for an AUDELCO Award as Best New Gospel Musical in 1994.

Synopsis

The gospel musical *May the Circle Be Unbroken* presents a selection of vignettes that pay tribute in song to gospel greats such as The Clara Ward Singers, Albertina Walker, Shirley Caesar, and James Cleveland. The first act of the play tells the story of Clara Ward who started singing publicly at the age of eight in the Baptist churches. She later became a national star with her group known as "The Famous Ward Singers" who performed at clubs, jazz festivals, on national television, radio, and in foreign countries. As a songwriter composing many gospel hits, she established her own publishing firm. Clara was known for her unusual wigs and ravishing robes.

Other characters include Ruth Davis and The Davis Sisters, one of the most intriguing and exciting groups in gospel music; Dorothy Love Coates, who organized the group, The Gospel Harmonettes, recording on the RCA label from out of Birmingham, Alabama; and The Caravans, composed of James Cleveland, Albertina Walker, Inez Andrews, and Shirley Caesar, one of the top groups that became rising stars in the 60s. Gospel music contests were one of the most exciting festivities in the 60s through the 70s. The contests included singing groups such as The Barrett Singers and The Roberta Martin Singers; these groups competed for the celebrity status associated with winning the first prize.

The last act, which features songs of several contemporary artists and today's gospel rap music, illustrates how gospel music presently has made a great transition from the past.

1   MAY THE CIRCLE BE UNBROKEN
     BY AND BY, LORD, BY AND BY
     THERE'S A BETTER HOME AWAITING
     IN THE SKY, LORD, IN THE SKY

ACT 1

2   The staging of the introduction takes place on a large record. On the label of the record stands an upright honky-tonk piano. The record is designed to be mobile and rotates periodically.

3   The curtain opens with a reflection of light beaming on a large center stage record (slightly raked). Through the theater we hear the sound of a honky-tonk piano playing the theme song, *May the Circle Be Unbroken,* in a ragtime style. The record on stage begins to rotate (clockwise). On the label stands a honky-tonk piano with five women standing around it. They begin singing the theme song with the piano playing in the background. The song begins to speed up as if it moves from the meter 17–33–45 speed. Before the ending, the music is now high speed and with a "churchified" rhythm. Lights fade on record. The song ends and a dark shadow appears across stage with space sounds in the background. Out of the darkness comes a bright shining light that rolls across stage and ends at center stage. A man dressed in black formal attire suddenly appears in the light. (He speaks)

MR. TIME

4   My name is Mr. Time. Time of the past, the present, and future. Yesterday, today, and your tomorrow. Within my recall, there is good, in spite of the bad. There is love, although there is hate. There is the just and the unjust. Night and day, peace, war, happy times and sad times. I am rhythm that syncopates from your head down to your feet, from half-note to whole. With me, you hear the music everywhere; there's nothing besides me that can compare. With me you dance to the rhythm of the marching band, to choirs on Sunday that make you clap your hands. (Mr. Time demonstrates. The drummer plays a military beat as Mr. Time falls into the rhythm. After four measures, the piano begins to play *"We're Marching Up to Zion."* Mr. Time continues his demonstration.) From the old-time gospel music, that soothes men, women, boys and girls, to today's contemporary style (Mr. Time dances to contemporary gospel music), I'll rock your world. Let's take a look back in time, beginning in the 1940's when gospel music played a most intricate part of our walk through history. (Change of lights to full-stage lights.)

5   Years ago, churches used to be filled with Dr. Watts-style singing, which Isaac Watts originated. The music was taken from the 18th-century English hymns accompanied by the emotions of wailing, mourning, lamentations, the yearning for God's deliverance.

6   Traditionally, the Head Deacon or Deaconess of the church, prestigious, distinguished, would recite the lines after which the congregation would sing in a slow, languid manner called long or common meter.

7   Let's move into the circle where Deacon John is about to approach the mourner's bench. (Mr. Time gives a wave of hand and the church scene appears. During the song, members of the church begin entering the stage and starts singing *"I Love the Lord."* The Deacon and Deaconess take their respective places across stage.)

8   I LOVE THE LORD. HE HEARD MY CRY
AND PITIED MY EVERY GROAN.
LONG AS I LIVE AND TROUBLES RISE,
I'LL HASTEN TO HIS THRONE.
(Deacon John approaches the mourner's bench.)

DEACON JOHN

9   We are gathered here today in your name. We're asking you to hear the prayers of your children. Remove all doubts and fears. Keep us in the Circle of Thy love. This we ask in your Son's name. MAY THE CIRCLE BE UNBROKEN. (Deacon John returns back to seat. Song continues.)

10   LONG AS I LIVE AND TROUBLES RISE,
I'LL HASTEN TO HIS THRONE.
(Mr. Time waves his hands and the church scene goes to a freeze. He continues.)

MR. TIME

11   Blues created an outpouring of feelings in music, but nothing could beat that old down-home gospel. Baptist and other denominations were widespread, but holiness churches, you know what we use to call "Sanctified," "Holy Rollers," "Pentecostal Fire," or the "Latter Rain Churches" were springing up all over the place. Man, there was no way you could get out of there without feeling the heat. The memory of those old saints never leaves my mind. They had these unusual instruments in song service, just to keep the rhythm going and on occasion, they would place their instruments to the side and get happy!" (Mr. Time waves his hands again and the church service continues. Each member has an instrument: tambourine, wash board, triangular, shekere, and bell. They began singing *"Jesus on the Main Line."*)

12   JESUS ON THE MAIN LINE,
TELL HIM WHAT YOU WANT.
JESUS ON THE MAIN LINE,
TELL HIM WHAT YOU WANT.
JESUS ON THE MAIN LINE,
TELL HIM WHAT YOU WANT.
CALL HIM UP AND TELL HIM WHAT YOU WANT.

13   (1) IF YOU WANT YOUR BODY HEALED…
(2) IF YOU WANT THE HOLY GHOST…
(Under the music, Mr. Time begins to speak.)

Specific Skill Comprehension Questions

contributed by Althea Beneby-Duren

1. In Mr. Time's introduction, he states that rhythm *syncopates from your head down to your feet* … The meaning of *syncopates* is "shifts from place to place with a beat." All of the following words are synonyms of *syncopate* **except**:

   a. move.

   b. swing.

   c. travel.

   d. immobile.

2. It appears from Mr. Time's introductory statements that this gospel play will focus on:

   a. Dr. Watts–style singing.

   b. the head deacon/ess.

   c. the history of gospel music from the past to present.

   d. the feelings created by the blues.

3. Mr. Time's character speaks, marches, and:

   a. sings.

   b. claps.

   c. dances.

   d. prays.

4. Mr. Time points out that one could not get out of the holiness churches *without feeling the heat*. The *heat* he is most likely referring to is:

   a. high body temperatures.

   b. heated discussions on different topics.

   c. fire within the "soul."

   d. the lack of fans in the building.

5. What is the relationship between the following statements recited by Mr. Time?

Within my recall, there is good, in spite of the bad. There is love, although there is hate.

   a. cause-and-effect

   b. compare and/or contrast

   c. addition

   d. list of items

6. The overall organizational pattern of this portion of the play is:

   a. cause-and-effect.

   b. compare and/or contrast.

   c. time order.

   d. list of items.

7. In this portion of the play, it can be inferred that time is:

   a. a period when something happened.

   b. the rate of speed while marching.

   c. the rhythm as determined by beats in music.

   d. all of the above.

8. The author uses education and entertainment ("edutainment") in the storyline of the play and the overall tone is:

   a. cynical.

   b. indignant.

   c. sardonic.

   d. jovial.

9. Having Mr. Time dressed in black formal attire adds to his credibility and our acceptance of his authority on the subject of time. This is an example of how our thinking can be influenced by the technique of:

   a. transfer.

   b. false comparison.

   c. glittering generalities.

   d. hasty generalization.

10. In this play thus far, Mr. Time is both the protagonist and the:

   a. antagonist.

   b. persona.

   c. oxymoron.

   d. unreliable narrator.

Time (after reading selection and completing all specific skill comprehension questions):

Post-Reading Questions

1. The text was (underline your selection):

    • reader-friendly   • not reader-friendly

2. Did the title of the play provide me with enough information to predict a main idea? Did the background knowledge on the play and the playwright facilitate my reading?

3. a. This play could be found in a college textbook. The college course I think this excerpt would correspond with is

    Underline your selection for both b and c below.

    b. I was familiar with **most/some/none** of the subject-specific vocabulary.

    c. I was familiar with **most/some/none** of the nonsubject-specific vocabulary.

4. I think that the readability of this poem was on my (underline one): **Independent (comfort) level**, **learning level**, **frustration level**. (For information about readability levels, refer to "Sink or Swim! English Language Learner and Reading Strategies," Part One.)

    Score based on percentage of the number correct (You will have to calculate this for each selection based on the

    number of questions right versus the number of questions asked):

    Rating of reading material (circle your selection):   good   fair   poor

    Rating of reading material (circle your selection):   reader-friendly   not reader-friendly

    Number of incorrect answers: Literal ___   Inferential ___   Critical ___

    (**Literal:** phonics, vocabulary; **Inferential:** main idea, implied main idea, supporting details, relationship between and within sentences, patterns of organization, inferences; **Critical:** author's purpose, tone, fact and opinion, bias, argument, figurative language)

Follow-Up Exercise

1. Read another play and write a two-paragraph summary of it.

Read to Read

Part Four

Pronunciation Guide

Sherrie L. Nist

Long Vowel Sounds		Consonant Sounds	
ā	age	b	big
ē	easy	d	do
ī	ice	f	fall
ō	open	g	get
o͞o	ooze	h	he
yo͞o	use	j	jump
Short Vowel Sounds		k	kiss
ă	apple	l	let
ĕ	end	m	meet
ĭ	ill	n	no
ŏ	odd	p	put
o͝o	book	r	red
ŭ	up	s	sell
yo͝o	cure	t	top
Other Vowel Sounds		v	vote
â	area	w	way
ä	art	y	yes
îr	ear	z	zero
ô	all	ch	church
oi	oil	sh	shell
ou	out	th	then
ûr	urge	th	thick
ə	ago, item, easily, gallop, circus	zh	usual

1   Note that each pronunciation symbol above is paired with a common word that shows the sound of the symbol. For example, the symbol ā has the sound of the *a* in the common word *age*. The symbol ă has the sound of the *a* in the common word *apple*. The symbol ə, which looks like an upside-down *e* and is known as the schwa, has the unaccented sound in the common word *ago*. It sounds like the "uh" a speaker often says when hesitating.

2   Accent marks are small black marks that tell you which syllable to emphasize as you say a word. A bold accent mark (´) shows which syllable should be stressed. A lighter accent mark (´) in some words indicates a secondary stress. Syllables without an accent mark are unstressed.

Reading MATTERS: A Parent-Child Booksharing Guide

Althea Beneby-Duren

Foreword

by Alda Noronha-Nimmo, Ed.D.

I know you are interested in your child's or children's literacy development. By reading this material, you are taking the first step to ensure that your child receives literacy experiences to which all children are entitled. When I refer to literacy, I mean the intimate knowledge of reading, writing, speaking, and listening. These create the environment in which a child learns to become a critical thinker and a contributing member of our society.

In this section, we focus on reading to your young child and nurturing in him/her the love of reading and the potential of learning through reading.

Dr. Beneby-Duren guides you through the steps that have been proven to be effective in developing these skills and attitudes in young children. Research has found that children who are read to from infancy are more inclined to read well and develop an appetite for reading. Similarly, these children are likely to do well in school. Therefore, it is hoped that this section will serve as a handy household "recipe" to provide hours of family literacy enjoyment.

I taught Special Education and English as a second language (ESOL) to students for seven years in the Miami-Dade County Public School System. I presently teach developmental reading courses at a large college in Miami. These classes are mandatory for students who do not test into college-level courses. This means these students' reading levels are lower than what is expected to process college-reading material. Students placed in developmental reading classes often feel resentful that it is going to take them longer to graduate because of these required courses.

I often ask students, by a show of hands, if they were read to as young children. After 10 years of teaching in the college system, I still feel a sense of despair when I see only two or three hands go up (and sadly sometimes no hands are raised) in a classroom full of young adults. Although some students feel that the school system failed them, others blame the significant adults in their lives who did not instill in them the importance of reading and writing from an early age.

I encourage you to make a commitment today to read to your child. After all, you are your child's first teacher. You and your child will be more enriched for having had these reading experiences. Most importantly, the parent-child bonding that is an intrinsic part of reading to your child will forever be a part of your child's favorite memories—and yours too! May you and your child discover the joys of reading together.

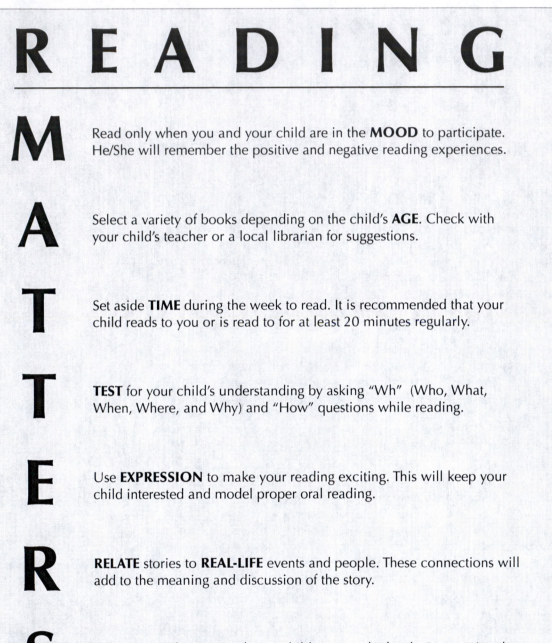

R E A D I N G

M — Read only when you and your child are in the **MOOD** to participate. He/She will remember the positive and negative reading experiences.

A — Select a variety of books depending on the child's **AGE**. Check with your child's teacher or a local librarian for suggestions.

T — Set aside **TIME** during the week to read. It is recommended that your child reads to you or is read to for at least 20 minutes regularly.

T — **TEST** for your child's understanding by asking "Wh" (Who, What, When, Where, and Why) and "How" questions while reading.

E — Use **EXPRESSION** to make your reading exciting. This will keep your child interested and model proper oral reading.

R — **RELATE** stories to **REAL-LIFE** events and people. These connections will add to the meaning and discussion of the story.

S — **SIT** in a way that you and your child can see the book. An emotional bond is established as you and your child sit together to read.

Figure 15

Parent-to-Child Reading Checklist	Always	Sometimes	Never
1. I choose books my child can understand.			
2. I sit in a position to allow my child to see the book.			
3. I point to the pictures.			
4. I point to the words.			
5. I use expression in my voice.			
6. I make motions and/or sounds when appropriate.			
7. I ask "Wh" and "How" questions about the book I'm reading.			
8. I relate the stories in the books to real-life events and people.			
9. I praise my child when he/she answers questions.			
10. I stop reading when my child loses interest.			
11. I read to my child on a regular basis.			
12. I get different types of books for my child from the library.			
13. I get different types of books for my child from a bookstore.			
14. I enjoy reading to my child.			

Shared Reading

1   At a relaxed time and in a comfortable place, the parent introduces the book to the child by

- showing the cover of the book,
- reading the title, the author's and the illustrrator's names,
- showing the pictures before reading ("picture walk")
- pointing to the words,
- asking the child to join in and read certain words or repetitive phrases as he or she is able.

2   Select a variety of books depending on the child's *age*.

Choosing Books

3   **"Five Finger Rule"** If your child misses more than 5 words per page, the book is too hard. Set aside *time* during the week to read to your child as often as possible.

Babies & Toddlers (Ages 0–2)

Board books with few words
Bold, familiar pictures

Preschoolers (Ages 3–4)

Picture books with simple sentences or rhyming words

Grades K-2 (Ages 5–7)

Picture books with a plot and some multisyllable words

Grades 3-5 (Ages 8–10)

Chapter books with few or no pictures and challenging text

Benefits of 20 Minutes

4   The American Heart Association recommends 20 minutes of vigorous aerobic activity at least three days per week to help maintain a healthy heart. Equally important is the American Academy of Pediatrics' statement that 20 minutes of routinely reading aloud to children helps to stimulate infant and child brain development.

5   *Test* your child for understanding by asking "Wh" and "How" questions.

Comprehension Check

6   (Examples Only—Feel free to add to the list)

- *Who* are the characters?
- *When* does the story take place?
- *Where* does the story take place?
- *What* do you think will happen next?
- *What* was the problem in the story?
- *Why* was there a problem in the story?
- *How* was the problem solved?

7   At the end of the story ask: *What* was your favorite part of the story?
How would you change the ending of the story (or solve the problem)?
Use *expression* to make your reading exciting.

Echo Reading

1. The parent reads a sentence in the book at the appropriate rate and with expression, changing his or her tone of voice based on punctuation (periods, question marks, and exclamation points).

2. The child repeats (echoes) the sentence the parent has read, imitating the parent's reading, with the appropriate rate and expression.

3. Repeat often while reading.

8   *Relate* stories to real-life events and people.

Compare Story to Self or Child, Another Story, and the World

Text-to-Self or Child

How does this story remind you of your life? Your child's life?

Text-to-Text

How does this story remind you or your child of another story?

Text-to-World

What does this story remind you or your child of the world around you?
Sit in a way that you and your child can see the book.

Creating an Emotional Bond

9   As the parent and child read through the book together, the parent enables the child to learn to read well, instills a love of reading in the child, and satisfies the child's need to spend quality time with the parent.

10   Positive attitudes for books and reading promote classroom and lifelong achievement.

11   Read the statements below to determine if you are using these techniques while reading to your child. The more "Always" answers you check, the more you are providing a positive booksharing, read-aloud session with your child and contributing to classroom and lifelong achievement.

References

Anderson, R. C., Hiebert, E. H., Scott, J. A., & Wilkinson, I. A. G. (1985). *Becoming a nation of readers: The report of the Commission on Reading.* Champaign-Urbana, IL: A Center for the Study of Reading.

Edwards, P. A. (2004). *Children's literacy development: Making it happen through school, family, and community involvement.* Boston: Allyn & Bacon.

Goodman, Y. (1984). The development of initial literacy. In H. Goelman, A. Oberg, & F. Smith (Eds.), *Awakening to literacy* (pp. 102–109). Exeter, NH: Heinemann.

Hart, B., & Risley, T. R. (1995). *Meaningful differences in the everyday experience of young American children.* Baltimore: Paul H. Brookes Publishing Co.

Noria, C. W., Weed, K., & Keogh, D. (2007). The fate of adolescent mothers. In J. G. Borkowski, J. R. Farris, T. L. Whitman, S. S. Carothers, K. Weed, & D. A. Keogh (Eds.), *Risk and resilience: Adolescent mothers and their children grow up.* Mahwah, NJ: Erlbaum.

Shore, R. (2003). *Rethinking the brain: New insights into early development.* New York: Families and Work Institute.

Tompkins, G. E. (2009). *Literacy for the 21st century: A balanced approach* (5th ed.). Upper Saddle River, NJ: Merrill Prentice Hall.

American Proverbs

Robert A. Mathews

1. "Necessity is the mother of invention." We are more likely to make new things when we have a need for them.

2. "A penny saved is a penny earned." What you save by being thrifty is like earning that money.

3. "Ignorance is bliss." Being unaware of some things can produce happiness.

4. "Look before you leap." Consider consequences before you make big decisions.

5. "Search others for their virtues, and yourself for your vices." You should look for the good in other people and for the bad in yourself.

6. "Actions speak louder than words." What we do matters a lot more than what we say we are going to do.

7. "Discretion is the better part of valor." It makes sense to use discretion to avoid a dangerous situation.

8. "Practice what you preach." A person needs to do the things that they are telling other people to do.

9. "A man is judged by the company he keeps." The friends a person has reveals a lot about what kind of person he/she is.

10. "You reap what you sow." You get out of life what you put into it.

11. "A guilty conscience needs no accuser." A person with a guilty conscience feels bad about what he/she did.

12. "Where there's a will there's a way." If a person really wants something, he/she will find a way to get it.

13. "Too many cooks spoil the broth." Too many people involved in a project can ruin it.

14. "Lost time is never found." If you waste your time, you can never get it back.

15. "Loose lips sink ships." Too much talking can cause a great disaster.

16. "Empty vessels make the most noise." People who know the least about something talk the most about it.

17. "A clean conscience makes a soft pillow." It's easier for a person to live with himself/herself when he/she has a clear conscience.

18. "One man's meat is another man's poison." What is healthy for one person could be unhealthy for someone else.

19. "Make hay while the sun shines." You should do your work while you are able to do it.

20. "Pleasant hours fly fast." Time goes quickly when you are having a good time.

Rock Your World with Idioms!

Jennifer Nimmo

1. "Down to the wire." Being at the final stages to complete something, and time is running out.

2. "A blessing in disguise." Something beneficial that was not recognized initially.

3. "Back to square one." Having to start over again from the beginning.

4. "Keep an eye on him." Watch him carefully.

5. "Under the weather." Not feeling well.

6. "Tie the knot." Get married.

7. "Hit the books." Study.

8. "Stop cold turkey." Stop a behavior suddenly.

9. "All bark and no bite." A person who says things that he or she will not follow through with.

10. "Go out on a limb" Take a risk.

11. "Beating around the bush" Being vague; not speaking directly about a topic.

12. "A piece of cake" Simple and easy.

13. "When pigs fly" Wishful thinking.

14. "Wear your heart on your sleeve" Expressing emotions frequently and freely.

15. "Saved by the bell" Saved at the very last moment.

16. "To steal someone's thunder" Trying to take someone else's credit as your own success.

17. "The third time is a charm" Hopeful that you are successful on the third attempt.

18. "Caught with your pants down" Caught in the act of doing something.

19. "It's all Greek to me" Something spoken that is not understood.

20. "Pull the plug" To bring everything to a halt.

21. "Keep your chin up" Still be hopeful in a tough situation.

22. "Get up on the wrong side of the bed" Someone who is having a bad day.

23. "Excuse my French" Apologizing for cursing.

24. "The best of both worlds" Having the best of two situations.

25. "When it rains, it pours" Many things going wrong at the same time.

26. "Hit the sack" Go to bed.

27. "All in the same boat" Everyone is encountering the same challenges.

28. "At the drop of a hat" Being able to act immediately.

Motivate Your Spirit with Quotes

1   I was privileged to work with Professor Jerry Fackrell, who started every day with a quote or proverb. It made him think about the world and his life a little differently. He shared them with his students to spark conversation and motivate them to write. Often I walked into a room and found that day's selection written on the board. In this way, he shared them with his colleagues. In honor of his memory, I now share some with you by invitation of Dr. Noronha-Nimmo. Thank you for inviting me to share some of these.

2   Motivation comes from two sources: inside ourselves (intrinsic) and from outside ourselves (extrinsic). If you need a boost to your intrinsic motivation, try a dose of quotations or proverbs. Some can be attributed to specific authors while some are unknown. Cultures around the world have their own proverbs but they can apply to anyone, anywhere.

3   According to Wikipedia, a quotation is the repetition of an expression, especially when the quoted expression is well known or attributed specifically to its original source. Wikiquote defines a proverb as "a simple and concrete saying popularly known … which expresses a truth based on common sense or the practical experience of humanity. They are often metaphorical. A proverb that describes a basic rule of conduct may also be known as a maxim. A *maxim* is a ground rule or subjective principle of action; in that sense, a maxim is a thought that can motivate individuals. It is generally any simple and memorable rule or guide for living."

4   I have found quotes in many places: books, movies, speeches, news and interviews, television, greeting cards, and websites. I have named a few websites here just to get you started. You can browse quotes by topic, author type, or author name or even play games at the proverbs site.

http://www.manythings.org/proverbs
http://www.brainyquote.com
http://thinkexist.com/quotation
http://www.memorablequotes.net

5   Try Prof. Fackrell's strategy, or you might want to adopt one as your motto. Stoke your fire! Recharge your battery! Have fun!

6   "Deal with the faults of others as gently as your own."—Chinese proverb

7   "Not to know is bad. Not to wish to know is worse."—Nigerian proverb

8   "God gives every bird its proper food, but all must fly for it."—Dutch proverb

9   "Necessity can make us surprisingly brave."—Latin proverb

10   "Sleep faster. We need the pillows."—Yiddish proverb

11   "Concealing a disease is no way to cure it."—Ethiopian proverb

12   "Good medicine always tastes bitter."—Japanese proverb

13   "A lucky man thrown into the sea emerges with a fish in his mouth."—Arab proverb

14   "An elephant never forgets an injury."—American proverb

15   "The burden of proof lies on the plaintiff."—Legal maxim

16   "One arrow does not bring down two birds."—Turkish proverb

17   "In the eyes of its mother, every beetle is a gazelle."—Moorish proverb

18   "Do not scald your tongue in other people's broth."—English proverb

19   "Love your neighbor, but don't pull down the hedge."—Swiss proverb

20   "Do not use a hatchet to remove a fly from your friend's forehead."—Chinese proverb

21   "Your best teacher is your last mistake."—Ralph Nader (1934–present), American attorney, author, lecturer, political activist (of consumer rights, humanitarianism, environmentalism, and democracy), candidate for President of the U.S. in five elections

22   "Thou shalt not be a victim. Thou shalt not be a perpetrator. Above all, thou shalt not be a bystander."—Holocaust Museum

23   "My father used to say, 'Don't raise your voice. Improve your argument.'"—Desmond Tutu (1931–present), South African cleric (Anglican Archbishop) and activist, Nobel Peace Prize 1984

24   This is the essence of Olympianism expressed in the *Olympic Creed:* "The most important thing in the Olympic Games is not to win but to take part, just as the most important thing in life is not the triumph but the struggle. The essential thing is not to have conquered but to have fought well."

25   "A man who views the world the same at 50 as he did at 20 has wasted 30 years of his life."—Muhammad Ali (born Cassius Marcellus Clay Jr., 1942–present), American boxer, Olympic gold medalist

26   "Fair play is not blaming others for anything that is wrong with us. We tend to rub our guilty conscience against others the way we wipe dirty fingers on a rag."—Eric Hoffer (1902–1983), social writer, awarded Presidential Medal of Freedom 1983

27   "I have always strenuously supported the right of every man to his own opinion, however different that opinion might be to mine. He who denies another this right makes a slave of himself to his present opinion because he precludes himself the right of changing it."—Thomas Paine (1737–1809), English pamphleteer *(Common Sense),* revolutionary, radical, classical liberal, intellectual

28   "Excellence is an art won by training and habituation. We do not act rightly because we have virtue or excellence, but we rather have those because we have acted rightly. We are what we repeatedly do. Excellence, then, is not an act but a habit."—Aristotle (384–322 BCE), Greek philosopher and writer, student of Plato, teacher of Alexander the Great

29   "Education is an ornament in prosperity and a refuge in adversity."—Aristotle

30   "Education is a progressive discovery of our own ignorance."—Will Durant (1885–1981), American philosopher, historian, writer, Pulitzer Prize in 1967 for literature, Presidential Medal of Freedom 1977

31   "You can say the nastiest things about yourself without offending anyone."—Phyllis Diller (born Phyllis Ada Driver, 1917–present) actor, comedian

Humor for the Soul

Karen Taghi Zoghi

1   My friend Dr. Noronha-Nimmo has a wonderful sense of humor. She always tickles my funny bone! I suspect that she inherited it from her dad, whom I was privileged to meet and who made me laugh, as well. My father also loved a good joke and often poked fun at himself. In honor of the memories of our fathers and by Dr. N's request, I contribute these jokes.

2   Humor is a uniquely human experience. It balances our lives and refreshes our soul. Laughter is healthy! Understanding jokes and puns requires knowledge of vocabulary and culture. Here are a few to practice your inference skills and that I hope will also lighten your day.

Jokes

3   I'm a high school geometry teacher, and I started one lesson on triangles by reading a theorem. "If an angle is an exterior angle of a triangle, then its measure is greater than the measure of either of its corresponding remote interior angles." When I saw that one student wasn't taking notes and looked confused, I asked him why. He answered honestly, "Well, I'm waiting until you start speaking English."

4   Teacher: "Give me a sentence starting with 'I.'"
5   Student: "I is ..."
6   Teacher: "No, Ellen. Always say, 'I am.'"
7   Student: "All right. I am the ninth letter of the alphabet."

8   Teacher: "How do you spell 'crocodile'?"
9   Student: " k-r-o-k-o-d-a-i-l"
10   Teacher: "No, that's wrong."
11   Student: "It may be wrong, but you asked me how I spell it!"

12   Two flies are in the porch. Which one is the actor? The one on the screen.

Funny Signs

13   Toilet out of order. Please use floor below.
14   Automatic washing machines: Please remove all your clothes when the light goes out.
15   After a tea break, staff should empty the teapot and stand upside down on the draining board.
16   For anyone who has children and doesn't know it, there is a daycare on the first floor.
17   The farmer allows walkers to cross the field for free, but the bull charges.

18   If you cannot read, this leaflet will tell you how to get lessons.
19   We can repair anything. (Please knock hard on the door—the bell doesn't work).
20   Bargain basement upstairs.
21   We exchange anything—bicycles, washing machines, etc. Why not bring your wife along and get a wonderful bargain?
22   Would the person who took the step ladder yesterday please bring it back, or further steps will be taken.

Puns

23   A backward poet writes inverse.
24   A man's home is his castle, in a manor of speaking.
25   Dijon vu is the same mustard as before.
26   The definition of a shotgun wedding is a case of wife or death.
27   A man needs a mistress just to break the monogamy.
28   A hangover is the wrath of grapes.
29   In democracy, your vote counts. In feudalism, your count votes.
30   She was engaged to a boyfriend with a wooden leg but broke it off.
31   A chicken crossing the road is poultry in motion.
32   A lot of money is tainted. It taint yours and it taint mine.
33   Those who get too big for their britches will be exposed in the end.
34   Once you've seen one shopping center, you've seen a mall.
35   Bakers trade bread recipes on a knead-to-know basis.
36   Santa's helpers are subordinate clauses.

Bob Marley— "Concrete Jungle" Analysis

Jeffrey Fraser

1   The following is an analysis of Bob Marley's *Concrete Jungle*. Due to copyright law, I am unfortunately unable to directly quote lyrics from the song or provide the entire lyrics to the song as a reference for this analysis. Instead, I have listed two websites where the lyrics may be read. In the event such websites are no longer active, the lyrics are easily obtainable with a simple Internet search in most search engines.

2   Bob Marley and the Wailers' *Concrete Jungle* is arguably one of the most impactful songs ever written in any genre of music. To analyze the "Jungle," it is important to define what Marley was referring to. The answer is actually a multifaceted one, up for multiple interpretations.

3   It is very likely that the *jungle* referred to are the slums in Jamaica, in particular, Trenchtown, where Bob Marley spent a large portion of his adolescence. Ultimately, when referring to the slums, *Concrete Jungle* portrays the ubiquitous plight of the everyday resident in such areas. Beyond a dense collection of tropical vegetation, the term *jungle* can also be described as a huge mass of confusion, or a maze. The *jungle* has also been said to refer to the Wailers' challenging stint in Europe and the helplessness of being trapped in a foreign land where "the living is hard." Regardless of the physical location Marley was referring to, I believe his primary intent was to portray the notion of a confused maze, nearly impossible to escape from.

4   Analyzing the *jungle* through Marley's lyrics exemplifies the sentiment of the day. Marley begins by describing a life absent of both sunlight and moonlight. He uses symbolism in the form of light to exemplify the lack of opportunity for individuals living in the slums. Light is a representative of hope and opportunity. No form of light, whether the sun or the moon, shines on slums. The sun, the light, the hope, and the opportunity are designated for the rich and the tourists who visit Jamaica. The darkness and overall desolation encompass the slums, forming a metaphoric jungle, a "concrete jungle." The slums are a collection of stone buildings, full of confusion, and largely devoid of upward mobility.

5   Marley later provides the listener with a captivity image, where he conveys the notion of being trapped without physical restraint. Slum society, alone, has bound the residents of the *Concrete Jungle*. In essence, life is an endless cycle of plight and redundancy. Ultimately, he proclaims that a sweeter life must be found somewhere. While Bob Marley and the Wailers eventually found that "sweet life," escaping the jungle through fame and reggae music, *Concrete Jungle* represents the sentiment of the period, and its message can certainly be applied to the slums of today. The message of *Concrete Jungle* can appropriately be described by one phrase—brilliant melancholy.

Website references for lyrics:

http://www.lyricsty.com/bob-marley-concrete-jungle-lyrics/
http://www.songlyrics.com/bob-marley/concrete-jungle-lyrics/

Jill Scott— "My Petition" Analysis

Jeffrey Fraser

1   What follows is an analysis of Jill Scott's *My Petition*. Due to copyright law, I am unfortunately unable to directly quote lyrics from the song or provide the entire lyrics to the song as a reference for this analysis. Instead, I have listed two websites where the lyrics may be read. If the websites are no longer active, the lyrics are easily obtainable with a simple Internet search in most search engines.

2   Jill Scott is a queen within the largely unheralded musical genre of Neo Soul. With most of her music, Scott displays a jazzy and sometimes funky style, always highlighting her unique and powerful voice. Displaying the importance of social awareness in a brilliant allegorical song, Scott demonstrates her range as an artist when she composed *My Petition* during the 2004 presidential election.

3   A simile is an indirect comparison of two different things linked either by "like" or "as." For example, "your love is like a river" or "she is smooth as silk." Similes are unique devices and easily incorporated into poetry and songs. Allegories, on the other hand, are more sophisticated. Operating as an extended metaphor, an allegory, in addition to making comparisons, allows artists to communicate their message through symbolism. In *My Petition*, Scott employs this literary device by seemingly singing about a constrained love relationship with a man (a common theme in Rhythm & Blues ["R&B"] and Neo Soul), but in reality using this common theme as a symbolic representation of a constrained love relationship with the government. An examination of the lyrics displays such a connection.

4   At the onset, the title of the song exhibits duality. A petition is a formal request or an appeal for change. Certainly, a woman can petition her significant other to change his ways; however, the following will display how Scott, instead, directs her formal request to the government. In the first verse, she describes how her significant other constantly says that he means good for her and has a plan for "us," yet he never follows through with his plan. She goes on to say that all the empty promises have left her hollow. With a familiarity of Scott (and most female R&B artists) the preceding description instantly triggers the listener to believe this song is about a man, who has made mistakes a number of times by continually failing to keep his word. The next few lines of the song also convey the same theme. She pleads with the significant other, begging him to explain why she should trust and have faith in him when he lies to her repeatedly, and continually fails to live up to his many promises.

5   The next line (Scott cleverly uses the first line of America's national anthem) serves as a preview to the listener. At this point, the lyrical content starts to shift. Instead of common relationship issues, she switches gears to a more political undertone by saying that she has a right to state her opinion and that there will be no laws abridging such right. Scott brilliantly displays political expression, while maintaining the constrained intimate love relationship theme by using the term "babe"—a common pet name for couples in relationships.

6   If there existed any doubt regarding the political direction of the song, Scott alleviates such doubt in her final verse. She expresses her desire for fresh fruit, clean water, and the need to feel safe in her neighborhood—all government responsibilities. Finally, she pleads for a life where she simply can live free with the assurance that her children will be adequately educated. The imagery is relatable to anyone, and the message transcends race, gender, or sexual orientation. Fresh fruit, clean water, feeling safe—all legitimate citizen concerns. Further, freedom is fundamental to the fabric of the American culture. While the importance of these concerns is always relevant, election years amplify such concerns. Thus, Jill Scott's allegorical *My Petition* is not only well composed, but timely.

7   Website references for lyrics:

http://www.elyrics.net/read/j/jill-scott-lyrics/my-petition-lyrics.html

http://www.azlyrics.com/lyrics/jillscott/mypetition.html

Sam Cook— "A Change Gonna Come" Analysis

1   The following is an analysis of Sam Cooke's song *A Change Gonna Come*. Due to copyright law, I am unfortunately unable to directly quote lyrics from the song or provide the entire lyrics to the song as a reference for this analysis. Instead, I have listed two websites where you may read the lyrics. If the websites are no longer active, the lyrics are easily obtainable with a simple Internet search in most search engines.

2   To understand and appreciate Sam Cooke's *A Change Gonna Come* requires an understanding of the man, Sam Cooke, himself, and the era in which he wrote such a timeless classic. While *A Change Gonna Come* fully embraces the plight, the struggle, and foreshadowes the imminent social breakthroughs of the Black individual during the Civil Rights Era; an essential uniqueness of the song stems from the fact that its author was already widely accepted by the "White America" of the day.

3   *A Change Gonna Come,* written in December 1963 and released in 1964; was presented to the ears of America during the height of the Civil Rights Movement. While individuals like Malcolm X (and his followers) preached resistance, segregation, and an overall black vs. white mentality, Sam Cooke actually "enjoyed" a role as a "safe" black entertainer. Prior to Cooke's revolutionary song, his primary hits were race neutral, if not white friendly. He composed cheerful songs such as *Twisting the Night Away* and, during the Civil Rights Era, whites accepted Black entertainers who composed nonthreatening material (although Cooke did not completely escape racism).

4   Cooke's frustration with the second-class status of his race coupled with his influence as a popular musician provided him with the ideal platform to create his own personal impact regarding the struggles of the time. Thus, *A Change Gonna Come* became the unofficial anthem of the Civil Rights Movement. The lyrics are simple, yet timeless. Cooke begins by drawing a similarity between a running river and the constant "running" of a black man during and before this era. He is not literally running, but rather taking strides, which were often elusive, in the direction of equal rights in America.

5   Cooke then represents the overall sentiment and emotion of this song by describing how difficult it is to live, yet the fear of death outweighs life's daily struggles. Cooke simply, but brilliantly, conveys the struggle of the black individual, but the importance of continuing the struggle for equality. Although Cooke seems to indicate that he fears death because life after death is unknown, I believe his true fear is perishing without having made an impact or, at the very least, an effort, toward equality for Blacks.

6   Later in the lyrics, Cooke portrays the overall feeling of existing, but not belonging. Although Cooke was highly regarded as an entertainer, a certain level of success and/or status was still unavailable to him because of his race. Finally, he proclaims that he must carry on, despite the hardships that plagued him during his life. This verse, in particular, conveys his struggles with the death of his child along

with his personal experiences with racism. Such life circumstances left Cooke devoid of hope; however, the Civil Rights Movement (and Cooke's personal drive to make an impact) provided the catalyst for Cooke to "carry on" and pen such a groundbreaking song.

7   Although tragically/controversially killed before he had the opportunity to appreciate the role that his music played in the Civil Rights Movements, Sam Cooke's *A Change Gonna Come* left an indelible mark on the era. The song continues to be a reference to monumental achievements of the past, the present, and hopefully, the future.

8   Website references for lyrics:
    http://www.metrolyrics.com/a-change-is-gonna-come-lyrics-sam-cooke.html
    http://www.lyricsmode.com/lyrics/s/sam_cooke/a_change_is_gonna_come.html

Invisible Disabilities

Karen Taghi Zoghi

1   When Dr. Noronha-Nimmo saw a PowerPoint presentation I had created to introduce my students to the concept of learning disabilities and the resources available to them at the institution where I teach, she encouraged me to include a brief overview in her new book. This is a topic dear to my heart, so I obliged her "wholeheartedly"! Thank you, Dr. N.

2   All people learn in highly individual ways. Sometimes, though, learning, reading, writing, and solving math problems may be especially difficult—with good reason.

What is a learning disability?

3   A learning disability (LD) is more than a difference in learning or communication style or a difficulty with learning. In the 1990s, scientists discovered a link between these difficulties and neurological disorders in the brain. These disorders affect people's ability either to interpret what they see and hear or to associate information from various parts of the brain. These disorders can upset the brain's ability to receive, process, store, and recall, respond to, and communicate information, and can interfere with learning to read, write, or do math. One may observe the effects in many areas of learning, including specific difficulties with spoken and written language, coordination, self-control, and/or attention. It's important to make the distinction that a learning disability is not mental retardation (please note that the "R" word is no longer used), mental illness, autism, deafness, blindness, a behavioral disorder, hyperactivity, lack of educational opportunities (for example, from changing schools often or poor attendance), an attention disorder, or lack of knowledge of English.

Who is affected?

- 15–20% of the U.S. population
- Males and females (nearly equally)
- People from all ethnic and socioeconomic backgrounds
- Famous people with a learning disability include Whoopi Goldberg, Orlando Bloom, Cher, Walt Disney, and Einstein!

What is the cause?

4   No one knows the cause of learning disabilities. Many possibilities and theories have been explored. A leading theory among scientists is that learning disabilities stem from subtle disturbances in the brain structures and functions. Other possibilities include neurological deficits, genetics, medications, and illicit drug use.

What are the types of learning disabilities?

5   LD is a broad term that covers a wide range of possible causes, symptoms, treatments, and outcomes. LD can be divided into three broad categories, each of which includes a number of more specific disorders, each with its own set of unique characteristics. Practically everyone has shown some of these characteristics at one time or another.

1. Developmental speech and language disorders, such as dyslexia (which is the most common cause of reading, writing, and spelling difficulties)

2. Academic skills disorders

3. "Other," a catch-all that includes certain coordination disorders and learning handicaps not covered by the other terms

What are some general characteristics?

- Average or above-average intelligence
- Unexpected underachievement
- Math difficulties
- Difficulty with language processing: reading, writing, spelling, listening, oral expression, processing information, recall, thinking and reasoning, organizing information
- Social difficulties or social withdrawal
- Emotional difficulties
- Frustration
- Low self-esteem

What to do?

6   Because a learning disability isn't a disease, there is no "cure." However, many programs exist to assist people. Seek assessment. Find out what is wrong. Find support services. Often your local college or university offers support services and even has professionals available to work with you. Learn about your local educational system. You can begin to appreciate more about learning disorders, find out how to overcome obstacles, gain strategies for dealing with specific difficulties, and uncover your hidden aptitudes and gifts!

Resources

- International Dyslexia Association
- National Center for Learning Disabilities
- American Speech-Language-Hearing Association
- LD Online at http://www.ldonline.org/index.php

- Help Read online software tool at http://www.ldpride.net/helpread.htm
- American Association of Intellectual and Developmental Disabilities
- National Institutes of Health

Tips to Improve Your Comprehension

Ildiko Barsony

Suggestions	Explanations
Annotate (during reading)	Take notes (such as topic/main idea of the paragraph) on the margins. Reread your notes before going to class or answering questions.
Ask questions (during reading)	During reading, ask questions such as "Why does the author say that?", "Why am I so confused about this?", or "Why did this happen?" Once you form a question, try answering it.
Highlight (during reading)	Underline or highlight the most important points in the passage, but remember to highlight in moderation.
Monitor your comprehension (during reading)	Check your understanding. If you don't do this automatically, make yourself stop at the end of each paragraph and ask yourself if you understood what you just read. If you didn't understand the paragraph, what are you going to do about it?
Motivate yourself (before reading)	You have to read a lot in college. Find at least one reason to read the assignment. Reading is much easier when you are motivated!
Scan (after reading)	Scanning is looking for specific information in the text. Scanning is different from reading because when you are scanning, you are looking for specific information and not paying attention to other details. For example, when you are looking for the answer to a question, you are not reading everything carefully and therefore your eyes are moving quickly across the page. However, when you get to the section you are looking for, you slow down and read carefully. When you are taking a test, you should read the passage first. Then, read the first question and scan the passage for the answer.
Skim (before reading)	Skimming helps you get an idea of what the passage is about. When skimming, read the title, subtitles, and the first sentence of each paragraph. It's easier to ask questions and set a purpose for reading if you skim first.

Use graphic organizers (before, during, and after reading)	Use a graphic organizer to take notes before, during, and after reading. A graphic organizer is a chart that helps you see the information from the text in a different way. Some graphic organizers can also help you to see the relationship of that information to your previous ideas about the topic. There are many types of graphic organizers. What organizers you use depends on the type of text. For narrative texts (stories), draw a timeline and mark events from the story on it. For expository texts, the KWL chart (developed by Donna Ogle and explained in this book) works well. For comparison and contrast, you can use a Venn-diagram. On this website, you can find some great printable organizers for different types of texts: http://www.educationoasis.com/curriculum/graphic_organizers.htm
Use sticky notes (during reading)	Have a sticky note pad handy while you are reading. Take notes and stick them to the pages you want to revisit.
Use your first language (during reading)	If you find that a foreign word reminds you of a word in your native language, try the meaning of the word you know in the context. Words that have the same origin and similar form and meaning in different languages are called *cognates*. For example, the English word *adjacent*, the Spanish word *adyacentes*, and the French word *adjacents* are cognates. This strategy will not always work, however. For example, the English word *embarrassed* and the French word *embarrassé* are cognates, but the Spanish word *embarazada* (pregnant woman) is not a cognate. Therefore, exercise caution when you use your native language to aid your comprehension in your second language.
Visualize (during reading)	Imagine the elements of the story in your head as you read, such as the setting and characters.

Online Reading Exercises

Ildiko Barsony

ESL Resources

1   Accent Reduction Exercises: http://www.trainyouraccent.com/
2   American English Pronunciation Exercises: http://www.manythings.org/pp/
3   Listening Practice: http://www.esl-lab.com/

Vocabulary in Context and Vocabulary Building

4   Words in Context: http://english-zone.com/vocab/vic01.html
5   http://www.pc.maricopa.edu/rdg/tutorials/vocless/vocab1.htm
6   Free Rice Vocabulary from the UN World Food Program:
     http://www.freerice.com/
7   Academic Word List Exercises: http://www.academicvocabularyexercises.com/
     index.htm

Main Ideas and Supporting Details

8   http://english.glendale.cc.ca.us/topic.html
9   http://www.pc.maricopa.edu/rdg/tutorials/paraless/paragraph1.htm

Patterns and Transitions

10   http://www2.actden.com/writ_den/tips/paragrap/index.htm
11   http://www.pasadena.edu/divisions/english/writing/documents/
     dbdistin_525.pdf
12   http://academicenglishcafe.com/HotChocolateCoolQuotesBetaT.aspx

Inferences

13   http://www.philtulga.com/Riddles.html
14   http://www.quia.com/pop/43335.html?AP_rand=1569636179

The Author's Tone

15   http://www.studystack.com/menu-11420

The Author's Purpose

16   http://www.woodland.k12.mo.us/faculty/rgarner/Reading/Authors%20puropse.htm

Outline 101: The Basics

Cherie Canon

1   Good writing depends on the following factors: clarity, conciseness, completeness, and accuracy. The key to achieving these factors, and thereby making your writing good, is organization. The best way to organize for writing is the development of an outline.

2   Outlines are similar to structural blueprints (an architect's rendering of how a building will be erected and look when complete). Blueprints are used by contractors while constructing a building to guide them with exacting dimensions, materials, and placement of structural components for the newly rising structure. Similarly, an outline becomes your final, organized plan of your paper. The outline, therefore, allows for a structured order to be followed, so that you will know what to write, how to write, and where to place your ideas in a clearly ordered and inclusive way.

3   There are many styles of outlining: Some people use key words to organize their outline, while others prefer to use phrases. Most writers, however, prefer to write outlines in full sentences because people think in sentences rather than in discrete words. Additionally, by writing sentences in an outline, many students find that their paper "almost writes itself." It is important to remember that, regardless of which style you chose to write your outline in, you *must* maintain that style throughout the outline. For example, an outline written in full-sentence style would *not* make use of any paragraphs within it.

4   Outlines can be simple or complex. A simple outline is basic, meaning it does not contain a lot of information. A simple outline may contain only major ideas or concepts. A complex outline, on the other hand, will contain much more information, including details, supports, and/or examples, when compared to the simple outline. The longer and more complex an outline is, the longer the paper will be that you will write from the outline.

5   Outlines use Roman numerals, capital letters, numbers, lowercase letters, parenthetic numbers, and parenthetic lowercase letters. Each of these is a denotative marking, and it represents a specific structural item used as the outline is developed. A key rule to remember that applies when using denotative markings in an outline is that ***everything in an outline must minimally come in pairs***.

Outlining and Writing the Five-Paragraph Essay

Cherie Canon

1   By this point in time, while working in this textbook, you have learned basic outline structure and how to outline a paragraph. You have gained knowledge about expanding an outline and have been enlightened about reinforcing main ideas with additional information and added details and/or supports. All the information presented in your outline helps you to write organized paragraphs that are at least five sentences. It is now time to expand your outline once again and to learn how this expanded outline will help you write essays and eventually even longer papers.

2   According to today's English class definition, essays are at least five paragraphs in length. However, many famous essays are longer and some are actually shorter. An essay revolves around a central theme, known as the central idea, which can be written in various ways. These include narratives, comparisons, descriptives, and process essays. All essays must be written clearly, completely, accurately, and concisely. To achieve these writing goals, one must invoke the use of an outline to help with organization.

3   Before you begin to write this outline, however, there are a few things you should know about an essay. An essay is composed of three easily recognizable sections. These sections are commonly referred to as the introduction, the body, and the conclusion. To envision how these sections are formatted, imagine a sandwich. Think of the introduction and the conclusion as representing the pieces of bread that make up the sandwich. Although necessary, the bread is not the main focus of the sandwich; in fact, it is only thick enough to hold the sandwich together. Similarly, while absolutely necessary, the introduction, and the conclusion in a paper are usually relatively short when compared to the rest of the text.

4   What becomes the focus of the sandwich is what actually goes into it—the body of your text. The more ingredients you put into your sandwich, the better it becomes. The same concept applies to your writing. The more "meat and other fixings" you add to your writing, the more appealing, filling, and interesting your work is to your reader. Therefore, the body is really the substantive portion of your essay.

5   These three sections—the introduction, body, and conclusion—are outlined prior to writing the actual paper. Each section's outline contains specific components to ensure the section is identifiable and complete.

Chart of Common Prefixes, Roots, and Suffixes

Cherie Canon

Vocabulary Prefixes	
Prefix	Meaning
a-, ac-, ad-, af-, ag-, al-, an-, ap-, as-, at-	to, toward, near, in addition to
a-, an-	not, without
ab-, abs-	away from, off
ante-	before
anti-	against
auto-	self
be-	all over, all around, completely, covered with, affect with
bi-	two
cat-, cata-, cath-	down, with
circum-	around, on all sides
co-, cog-, col-, com-, con-, car-	together, with
contra-	against, opposite
counter-	opposition, opposite direction
de-	to do the opposite, to take away from
dia-	through, across
di-, dif-, dis-	apart, separate, two, opposite, not
dis-	not, opposite of, exclude, away from
e-, ex-	out, out of, from
en-, em-	put into, cause to

epi-	upon, beside, over
extra-	beyond
fore-	before
hemi-	half
hyper-	beyond, more than, more than normal
hypo-	under
il-, im-, in-, ir-	not, in
in-, im-, il-	in, into
infra-	below
inter-	between, among
intra-	inside, within
intro-	into
mal-	bad, wrongly, ill
mid-	middle
mis-	wrong, wrongly
mono-	one
multi-	many
non-	not, no
ob-, oc-, of-, op-	toward, against, in the way
omni-	all
out-	surpassing, exceeding, external, away from
over-	excessive, above, over
para-	beside
per-	through
peri-	round, about
post-	after
pre-	before
pro-	for, forward
re-	back, again
retro-	backward
se-	apart, move away from
semi-	half
sub-, suc-, suf-, sup-, sur-, sus-	under, beneath, near, from below, below, secretly, above, up
super-	over, above

syn-, sym-	together, at the same time
trans-	across, beyond, change
tri-	three
ultra-	beyond, extreme
un-	not, against, opposite
under-	under, below
uni-	one

Vocabulary Roots

Root	Meaning
-act-, -ag-	do, act, drive
-am-, -ami-	love, like
-anim-	mind, life, spirit, anger
-annu-, -enni-	yearly
-auc-, -aug-, -aut-	originate, increase
-aud-, -audit-,-aur-	hear
-bene-, -ben-	good, well, gentle
-bibli-, -biblio-	book
-bio-, -bi-	life
-brev-	short
-cad-, -cap-, -cas-, -ceiv-, -cept-, -cid-	to take, to seize, to hold
-ceas-, -cede-, -ceed-, -cess-	go, yield
-chron-	time
-cis-	cut
-clam-, -claim-	call or cry out, shout
-clar-	clear
-cogn-, -gnos-	know, to know
-corp-	body
-cre-, -cresc, -cret-	grow
-cred-	trust, believe
-cour-, -cur-, -curr-, -curs-	run, course
-dic-, -dict-, -dit-	say, speak
-doc-, -doct-	teach, prove
-dog-, -dox-	thought, idea

-dec-, -dign-	suitable
-duc-, -duct-	draw or lead
-dur-	hard
-ev-, -et-	time, age
-fac-, -fact-, fec-, -fic-, -fas-, -fea-	make do, do
-fer-	bear, carry
-fict-, -feign-, -fain-	shape, make, fashion
-fid-	faith
-fig-	shape, form
-fin-	end
-flu-, -fluct-, -flux-	flow
-form-	shape
-fract-, -frag-, -frai-	break
-gen-, -gin-	to give birth, kind
-geo-	earth
-gor-	gather, bring together
-grad-, -gress-, -gree-	step, go, move
-graph-, -graf-	write, draw
-her-, -hes-	stick
-jac-, -ject-, -jet-	throw
-jug-, -junct-, -just-	join
-lab-	work
-lect-, -leg-, -lig-	choose, gather, select, read
-lex-, -leag-, -leg-	law
-loc-	place, area
-log-	say, speech, word, reason, study
-luc-, -lum-, -lust-	light
-man-	hand, make, do
-mem-	recall, remember
-ment-	mind
-min-	little, small
-mit-, -miss-	send
-mob-, -mov-, -mot-	move
-nasc-, -nat-, -gnant-, -nai-	be born
-nom-, -nym-	name

-nov-	new
-oper-	work
-pat-, -pass-	feel, suffer
-path-	feel
-ped-	foot
-pod-	foot
-pel-, -puls-	drive, push
-pend-, -pens-, -pond-	hang, weigh
-phan-, -phas-, -phen-, -fan-, -phant-, -fant-	show, make visible
-phil-	love
-phon-	sound
-pict-	paint, show, draw
-pli-, -ply-	fold
-pon-, -pos-	put, place
-port-	carry
-psych-	mind
-quir-, -quis-, -quest-, -quer-	seek, ask
-rupt-	break
-sci-, -scio-	know
-scrib-, -scrip-, -script-	write
-sent-, -sens-	feel, think
-sequ-, -secut-, -sue-	follow
-sist-	withstand, make up
-soci-	join, companions
-sol-	alone
-solv, -solu-, -solut-	loosen, explain
-spec-, -spi-, -spic-, -spect-	look
-spir-	breath, soul
-stab-, -stat-	stand
-strain-, -strict-, -string-, -stige-	bind, pull
-stru-, -struct-, -stroy-	build
-tact-, -tang-, -tig-, -ting-	touch
-tain-, -ten-, -tent-, -tin-	keep, have
-tele-	far away
-tend-, -lens-	stretch

-term-	end, boundary, limit
-terr-	earth
-test-	see, witness
-therm-	heat
-tor-, -tors-, -tort-	twist
-tract-, -trai-, -treat-	pull, draw
-uni-	one
-vac-	empty
-ven-, -vent-	come
-ver-	true
-verb-, -verv-	word
-vers-, -vert-	turn, change
-vid-, -vie-, -vis-	see
-vit-, -viv-	live
-voc-, -voke-	call
-volv-, -volt-, -vol-	roll, turn

Vocabulary Suffixes

Suffix	Meaning
Nouns	
-acy, -cy	state or quality
-age	activity, result of action
-al	action, result of action
-an	person
-ance, -ence	action, state of being, quality, process
-ancy, -ency	state of being, quality, capacity
-ant, -ent	an agent, something that performs an action
-ate	state of being, office, function
-ation	action, resulting state
-dom	place, state of being
-er, -or	person or thing that does something
-ful	amount or quantity that fills
-ia	names, diseases
-ian, -an	related to, one that is

-iatry	art of healing
-ic, -ics	related to the arts and sciences
-ice	act
-ing	material made for, activity, result of an activity
-ion, -tion, -ation, -ition	condition or action
-ism	doctrine, theory, belief, action, conduct
-ist	person or member
-ite	product or part
-ity, -ty	state of being, quality
-ive	condition
-ment	condition, result, action, slate
-ness	state, condition, quality
-ology	study of
-or	condition, activity
-ory	place for, serves for
-s, -es	plural
-ship	status, condition
-ure	act, condition, process, function
-y	state, condition, result of an activity, characterized by
Verbs	
-ate	cause to be
-ed	past tense
-en	cause to become
-er, -or	action
-ify, -fy	cause, make
-ing	present participle
-ize	cause
-ure	act
Adjectives	
-able, -ible	worth, ability, capable of
-al, -ial, -ical	quality, relation, having a characteristic of
-ant, -ent, -ient	kind of agent, indication
-ar, -ary	resembling, related to, pertain, connected with
-ate	kind of state
-ed	having the quality of

-en	material, made
-er	comparative
-est	superlative, comparison
-ful	having, giving, marked by
-ic	quality, relation
-ile	having the qualities of
-ing	activity
-ish	having the character of
-ive, -ative, -itive	having the quality of, performing an action
-less	without, missing
-ly	characteristic
-ous, -eous, -ose, -ious	having the quality of, relating to
-y	marked by, having
Adverbs	
-fold	in a manner of, marked by
-ly	in the manner of
-ward	in a direction or manner
-wise	in the manner of, with regard to

Adapted from the TOEFL Vocabulary Preparation Guide (South Hampton–Long Island University).

Confused or Misused Words

Cherie Canon

1   The following list represents some of the words that are often misused or confused in English. Always consult a dictionary if you are unsure you are using the right word in your writing. The common definition of each word is provided for your convenience.

accept	take willingly
except	exclude
advice	suggestion, recommendation
advise	show the way, to give advice
affect	have an influence on
effect	a result, to bring about, cause
aggravate	make worse
irritate	provoke impatience or anger
allusion	indirect reference
illusion	deceiving image or perception
all ready	prepared
already	by this time
alternatively	giving a choice between two or more things
alternately	occurring by turns
altogether	entirely
all together	gathered with everything in one place
amiable	agreeable
amicable	peaceful, not hostile
among	surrounded by
between	in the middle
assure	make sure or certain
insure	arrange for monetary compensation
ensure	make sure

awhile	for a short period of time
a while	space of time
apart	be separated
a part	be joined with
ascent	climb
assent	agreement
breath	air inhaled
breathe	the act of inhaling or exhaling
by	show location
buy	purchase
beside	next to
besides	also
bimonthly	every two months
semimonthly	happening twice a month
classic	of extremely high standard
classical	of or relating to ancient Greece and Rome
compliment	said to praise a person
complement	completes, fills in, makes something perfect
compose	form parts of
comprise	consist of
corroborate	confirm
collaborate	aid or cooperate
credible	believable
credulous	too ready to believe
capital	accumulation of wealth, capital letter
capitol	building where the legislative assembly meets
cite	quote authority or give example
site	location
sight	vision
concurrent	simultaneous
consecutive	successive, following one after the other
connote	imply, suggest
denote	indicate or refer specifically
council	assembly called together for discussion
counsel	give advice or guidance

conscience	sense of right and wrong
conscious	awake
deduce	infer from a general rule
deduct	take away from a total
discrete	separate, individual, distinct
discreet	prudent and tactful
desert	a large area of sand, arid and dry
dessert	a sweet, after-meal treat
disinterested	impartial, fair
uninterested	not interested
either	one of the other two
neither	not one or the other of two
enormity	outrageous, evil, unexpected
enormousness	having a huge size
elicit	draw out
illicit	unlawful
emigrant	one who leaves one's native country
immigrant	one who enters and settles into a new country
eminent	famous, respected
immanent	inherent or intrinsic
imminent	ready to take place
figuratively	metaphorically or symbolically
literally	actually
flaunt	show off shamelessly
flout	show scorn or contempt
foreword	introductory note or preface
forward	toward the front
founder	fail utterly; person who starts something
flounder	move about clumsily; a fish
farther	more physical distance
further	bring to a new level, moreover, to a greater extent
hanged	execute by suspending by the neck
hung	suspend from above with no support from below

historic	what is important in history
historical	whatever existed in the past, whether it was important or not
hear	listen
here	location
its	of or belonging to it
it's	contraction for *it is*
ingenious	clever, skillful
ingenuous	sincere and genuine, simple, natural, innocent
lead	type of metal
led	past tense of *lead*
lie	lie down; falsehood
lay	lay an object down, to place
lose	misplace or not win
loose	not be tight; release
lightening	illuminate
lightning	electrical charges, the cause of flashes of light during storms
libel	written statement intended to damage a person's reputation
slander	oral statement intended to damage a person's reputation
like	having the chacteristics of, similar to
as	to the same degree or extent, in the same manner
masterful	fond of power or authority
masterly	expert, skillful
partake	eat or drink some
participate	take part in
prescribe	lay down as a rule
proscribe	prohibit or condemn
passed	past tense of *pass*
past	time gone by
precede	come before
proceed	move forward
principal	person who holds high position or plays and important role
principle	rule or standard

quote	cite
quotation	the act of citing
right	correct or proper
write	action of communication of thought on paper
reticent	reserved in speech
reluctant	reserved, unwilling, hesitant
stationary	standing still
stationery	writing paper
supposed to	be obligated to or presumed to
supposed	accepted as such, ought, should
suppose	guess or make a conjecture
thankful	be or give thanks for something
grateful	be or give thanks for someone's action or service
their	belonging to them
there	reference to a location
they're	contraction for *they are*
than	shows comparison
then	shows a time sequence or order, at that time, next
to	shows movement or direction, toward
too	also or to a greater degree
two	the number 2
through	by means of, finished, into or out of
threw	past tense of throw
thru	abbreviated slang of *through*
thorough	careful or complete
though	however, nevertheless
use	utilize
used	past tense of *use*; also, used to ___
venal	corruptible
venial	slight flaw
who	referring to a person
which	replaces singular or plural things but never people
that	used to refer to things in a group or class of people

whom	used as object
whose	asks question about belonging, person to whom it belongs
who's	contraction for *who is*
your	belonging to you
you're	contraction for *you are*

Collegiate-Level Vocabulary

Cherie Canon

1   The following list of words is only a beginning directory of the types of vocabulary words you will come across, and be required to know during your collegiate experience. These words have come from numerous lists to help students learn vocabulary for the TOEFL, SAT, and ACT tests, and from English professors' vocabulary lists. While not complete, as far as a list goes, notice that the words provided include their common definitions. To further assist you in learning these words, or any other words you may be unfamiliar with, think about additionally learning a synonym and an antonym of the word.

2   Maintain a *vocabulary notebook* in which you can write any new words you come across. Include in this notebook a definition of the word, as well as a synonym and an antonym for it. Then begin to use all of the new words you have learned, whenever and wherever you can. By using your new terms when speaking and writing, you will be surprised to see how quickly your vocabulary increases. Remember, effective use of vocabulary is an important indicator of intelligence in adults.

abet	encourage or assist in committing an offense
abstemious	moderate in eating
acerbity	sharpness in speech or manner
acquiesce	assent, to agree without protest
adamant	obstinate, stubborn
admonition	warning
affliction	suffering
agape	wonder
anemic	weak, insipid
anomalous	irregular, abnormal
apathetic	lack of interest or concern
arboreal	of trees, living in trees
argot	slang for class or group of criminals
audacious	bold, daring
baleful	menacing, destructive
ballast	weight for stability in character

bicameral	two legislative chambers
biliousness	sickness caused by too much bile
bivouac	temporary unsheltered encampment
bowdlerized	censored words or scenes considered improper
bucolic	rural, pastoral
cacophonous	jarring, incongruous, harsh, unpleasant sound, noise
cahoots	questionable collaboration or partnering
cajole	coax, persuade
capitulation	surrender, submission
caprice	whim, impulse
capricious	unpredictable
capriciousness	indecisiveness, unpredictability
cavil	carping, insignificant hurtful criticism
chicanery	trickery, deceit
complacent	satisfied, unworried
compunction	misgiving, feeling guilty, qualm
conclave	secret meeting or convention
convalesce	recover
credulous	ready to believe things
dearth	lack
debacle	disaster
debauched	morally wrong
debauchery	wickedness, depravity, extreme indulgence in sensual pleasure
diffident	timid
dilatory	procrastinating
discrete	discontinuous, individually distinct
disparate	different in kind
dour	stern, severe, gloomy
droll	amusing in an odd way
efface	wipe out
effervescence	fizz, bubbles
efficacious	effective
efficacy	effectiveness, produce desired effect
egregious	outrageously bad, notice negatively

enervate	cause to lose vitality
errant	out of place
esoteric	arcane
ethereal	light and delicate
façade	an artificial or deceptive front
facile	achieved easily without attention to quality, superficial
farcical	ridiculous, ludicrous
fastidious	fussy, picky, choosey
faux	fake, artificial, imitation
felicitous	well chosen, apt (of words)
foment	stir up trouble
fulminate	protest loudly and bitterly
fulsome	nauseatingly overabundant
flaunt	display proudly or ostentatiously
flippant	frivolous, lacking depth, seriousness
flout	disobey openly and scornfully
gauze	haze
geniality	friendliness
gelid	icy
glib	persuasive
gregarious	outgoing, sociable
haughty	proud of oneself and looking down on others
heeding	paying attention to
hegemony	domination, control
hermetic	with an airtight closure
highbrow	intellectual
hirsute	extremely hairy or bristly
histrionic	overly theatrical
homogenization	to blend into a uniform mixture
iconoclastic	one who attacks settled beliefs
ignominious	bring contempt or disgrace, humiliating
immaculate	perfect, clean, tidy
impartial	neutral
impeccable	perfect
impecunious	having little or no money

imperceptible	hardly noticed
impervious	not able to be penetrated, not influenced
incredulous	skeptical, disbelieving
ineffable	difficult to describe
ineluctable	cannot be avoided or overcome
iniquitous	great injustice, wicked act
insipid	stupidly dull or silly
inure	accustomed to something unpleasant
inveterate	habitual, firmly established
laconic	brief, terse, not talkative
latent	hidden, dormant
lauded	praised
lax	not tense, slack
levied	tax, charge
ligneous	wooden
loquacious	wordy
lugubrious	dismal, mournful
maelstrom	powerful whirlpool
magnanimity	nobility, fairness
malfeasance	wrongdoing, especially by public officials
malignant	evil, hateful
mercurial	unpredictable
meretricious	gaudy, glitzy, showy but cheap or insincere
motley	diversified in color, of varied character
munificent	rich, lavish, splendidly generous
naysayer	one who denies, refuses, opposes, or is skeptical or cynical about something
nefarious	evil, wicked
neurotic	anxious, fearful
nonchalant	casual, indifference, unconcern
noxious	harmful, toxic
obdurate	stubborn
obstreperous	noisy, unruly
ominous	warning, threatening
omnipresent	present in all places at all times

ornery	bad-tempered
ostensibly	apparently
osculate	kiss
oubliette	secret dungeon with entrance only by a trap door at the top
paltriness	lacking in importance or worth, wretched
panache	style, flamboyant
panegyric	warm, glowing praise
pantomime	communication by means of gesture and facial expression
parsimonious	stingy, cheap
patent	obvious, unconcealed
patrician	high class, aristocratic
pertinent	relevant
perfunctory	done as duty or routine without care
peremptory	masterful in a haughty, dictatorial way
pertinacious	holding firm to opinion or action
pernicious	having a very harmful effect
petulant	rude, cranky, ill-tempered
perfidious	treacherous
pulchritudinous	beautiful
pusillanimous	cowardly
philistine	doesn't understand or appreciate aesthetics
pretentious	pompous, ambitious
prevarication	telling lies or speaking evasively
prosaic	unpoetic, plain
probity	integrity
psychedelic	state produced by drugs
putsch	revolt against the government
putative	reputed, supposed
quaffable	drinkable
quaint	old-fashioned, charming
querulous	complaining in an irritable way
recalcitrant	strongly against authority, tough handle
recondite	obscure
redolent	smelling strongly, full of memories

relegate	send away
reneged	go back on
reprieve	to bring relief to, pardon
reproach	disapproval, admonish
repudiation	denial
rue	feel remorse or sorrow
saccade	twitch
salubrious	health-giving
sanguine	hopeful, optimistic
sardonic	sarcastic, mocking
saturnine	sluggish, gloomy
sedulous	particular, diligently careful
serendipitous	making a pleasant discovery by accident
sentient	capable of perceiving and feeling things
sobriquet	nickname
solipsism	philosophical theory that the self is the only knowable
suborn	to incite, cause to happen
supercilious	an air of superiority, haughty, scornful
surreptitious	sneaky
scant	slight, barely sufficient
scrutinized	inspected with great care, examined, studied
scrupulous	careful, reliable
specious	false, but attractively so
splenetic	ill-tempered, grouchy
spurious	not genuine or authentic
telegenic	well suited to television
tenacious	stubborn
tenebrous	obscure, dark, gloomy
tenuous	having little substance or strength, weak
tepid	lukewarm, lacking in passion
torrid	hot
truculent	brutal, aggressive
turpitude	wickedness
unequivocally	clearly, plainly

unction	act of anointing as part of a religious, ceremonial, or healing ritual
unctuous	insincere, oily
uncouth	awkward, clumsy in manner
unilateral	one-sided
unfathomably	difficult or impossible to understand
vagary, vagaries	unpredictable, unexpected, or capricious acts or occurrences
verisimilitude	an appearance of being true
vindictive	spiteful, unforgiving
virile	characteristics of adult male
virulent	marked by rapid, severe, malignant course
visceral	natural, instinctive
vitiate	to make imperfect, spoil, weaken force
whimsy	sudden turn of mind
windfall	bonus, extra
wrest	extort, extract
zealous	enthusiastic, obsessive
zeitgeist	spirit of the times

Commonly Misspelled Words

Cherie Canon

1 Spelling matters! This is especially true if you are trying to make a good impression with your writing. *Always consult a dictionary if you do not know how to spell a word.*

2 The list presented here represents many of the most commonly misspelled words in English. However, do not try to memorize all the words on this list. Simply find a few words that you know cause you trouble; then, learn their proper spelling.

A			
absence	abundance	accessible	accidentally
accessory	aggression	alcohol	amend
acclaim	accommodate	accomplish	accordion
accumulate	achievement	acquaintance	across
address	advertisement	aggravate	alleged
annual	apparent	appearance	argument
apologize	average	acceptable	acquire
atheist	athletics	attendance	auxiliary
a lot	amateur		

B			
balloon	barbecue	barbiturate	bargain
basically	beggar	beginning	believe
biscuit	bouillon	boundary	Britain
Buddha	business	beautiful	belief
burglar			

C			
calendar	camouflage	cantaloupe	category
cemetery	chagrined	challenge	characteristic
changeable	consensus	controversy	committed
changing	chief	cigarette	climbed
collectible	colonel	colossal	column

From *Speaking of Writing: A Guide to Effective Written Communication* by Cherie Cannon.
Copyright © 2008 by Kendall Hunt Publishing Company. Reprinted by permission.

coming	committee	commitment	comparative
competent	completely	concede	conceive
condemn	condescend	conscientious	consciousness
consistent	continuous	controlled	convenient
coolly	corollary	correlate	correspondence
counselor	courteous	courtesy	criticize
conscience			

D			
deceive	defendant	deferred	dependent
descend	description	desirable	despair
desperate	develop	dispensable	dissatisfied
difference	dilemma	dining	dispensable
disastrous	discipline	disease	development
dissatisfied	drunkenness	definite	daiquiri
doesn't	dominant	disappearance	disappoint
dumbbell			

E			
easily	ecstasy	efficiency	eighth
either	eligible	emperor	enemy
entirely	equipped	equivalent	especially
exaggerate	exceed	excellence	excellent
exhaust	exhilarate	existence	expense
experience	experiment	explanation	extremely
exuberance	embarrass	extraordinary	equipment

F			
fallacious	fallacy	familiar	fascinate
feasible	fictitious	fiery	finally
financially	fluorescent	forcibly	foreign
foresee	forfeit	formerly	forty
fourth	fulfill	fundamentally	

G			
gauge	generally	genius	government
governor	grievous	guarantee	guerrilla
guidance			

H			
handkerchief	happily	harass	height
heinous	hemorrhage	heroes	hesitancy
hierarchy	hindrance	hoarse	hoping
humorous	hypocrisy	hypocrite	

I			
ideally	idiosyncrasy	ignorance	imaginary
immediately	implement	incidentally	incredible
independence	independent	indicted	indispensable
inevitable	influential	information	inoculate
installment	insurance	intelligence	intercede
interference	interrupt	introduce	irrelevant
irresistible	island	itinerary	

J			
jealousy	jewelry	judgment	judicial

K			
kernel	knowledge		

L			
laboratory	legitimate	leisure	length
lenient	liaison	license	lieutenant
lightning	likelihood	likely	longitude
loneliness	losing	lovely	luxury
library			

M			
magazine	maintain	maintenance	manageable
maneuver	marriage	mathematics	medicine
millennium	millionaire	miniature	minuscule
minutes	mischievous	missile	misspelled
mortgage	mosquito	mosquitoes	murmur
muscle	mysterious	medieval	memento

N			
naïve	narrative	naturally	necessary
necessity	negligible	neighbor	neutron

niece	ninety	ninth	noticeable
nowadays			
nuisance			

O			
obedience	obstacle	occasion	occasionally
occurred	occurrence	official	omission
omit	omitted	opinion	opponent
opportunity	oppression	optimism	ordinary
origin	original	outrageous	overrun

P			
panicky	parallel	parliament	particularly
pavilion	peaceable	peculiar	penetrate
perceive	performance	permanent	permissible
permitted	perseverance	persistence	physical
physician	picnicking	piece	pilgrimage
pitiful	planning	pleasant	portray
possess	possessive	potato	potatoes
practically	prairie	performance	preference
preferred	prejudice	preparation	prescription
prevalent	primitive	privilege	probably
procedure	proceed	professor	prominent
pronounce	pronunciation	propaganda	psychology
publicly	pursue	practice	presence
pastime	personnel	playwright	precede

Q			
quandary	quarantine	questionnaire	quizzes

R			
realistically	realize	really	recede
receipt	receive	recognize	recommend
reference	referred	relevant	relieving
religious	remembrance	reminiscence	renege
repetition	representative	resemblance	reservoir
resistance	restaurant	rheumatism	rhythm
rhythmical	roommate	restaurateur	rhyme

S			
sacrilegious	sacrifice	safety	salary
satellite	scary	scenery	schedule
secede	secretary	seize	sentence
separate	sergeant	several	shepherd
shining	similar	simile	simply
sincerely	skiing	soliloquy	sophomore
souvenir	specifically	specimen	sponsor
spontaneous	statistics	stopped	strategy
strength	strenuous	stubbornness	subordinate
subtle	succeed	success	succession
sufficient	supersede	suppress	surprise
surround	susceptible	suspicious	syllable
symmetrical	synonymous	skillful	

T			
tangible	technical	technique	temperature
tendency	themselves	theories	therefore
thorough	though	through	till
tomorrow	tournament	tourniquet	transferred
truly	twelfth	tyranny	threshold
tomato	tomatoes		

U			
unanimous	undoubtedly	unnecessary	until
usage	usually	unfortunately	

Romance a Book

Alda
Noronha-
Nimmo

I browsed around bookstores to find what reading material is on display shelves. I
have also asked about the kind of selections local high school teachers have assigned
students. Additionally I have checked into the type of books popular among young
adults. To my delight, I discovered that these popular books included a number of
classics. The following is a compilation of book titles from my "research" at the local
bookstores:

1. *To Kill a Mockingbird* by Harper Lee

2. *October Sky* by Homer Hickam

3. *Heart of Darkness* by Joseph Conrad

4. *Twelfth Night* by William Shakespeare

5. *All Quiet on the Western Front* by Erich Maria Remarque

6. *Go Tell It on the Mountains* by James Baldwin

7. *Hunger of Memory: The Education of Richard Rodriguez* by Richard Rodriguez

8. *Fahrenheit 451* by Ray Bradbury

9. *Pride and Prejudice* by Jane Austen

10. *A Raisin in the Sun* by Lorraine Hansberry

11. *Anne Frank: The Diary of a Young Girl* by Anne Frank

12. *One Flew over the Cuckoo's Nest* by Ken Kesey

13. *Othello* by William Shakespeare

14. *Ethan Frome* by Edith Wharton

15. *Bless Me Ultima* by Rudolfo Anaya

16. *The Time Machine and the Invisible Man* by H. G. Wells

17. *Hamlet* by William Shakespeare

18. *The Chosen* by Chaim Potok

19. *Hiroshima* by John Hersey

20. *The Awakening* by Kate Chopin

21. *The Importance of Being Ernest* by Oscar Wilde

22. *Three Cups of Tea* by Greg Mortenson

23. *What Is the What* by Dave Eggers

24. *The Castle of Otranto: A Gothic Story* (Oxford World's Classics)
    by Horace Walpole

25. *The Boy Who Harnessed the Wind* by William Kamkwamba

26. *The Glass Castle* by Jeannette Walls

27. *Angela's Ashes* by Frank McCourt

28. *Things Fall Apart* (50th Anniversary Ed.) by Chinua Achebe

29. *I Am Nujood Age 10 and Divorced* by Nujood Ali

30. *The Tipping Point: How Little Things Can Make a Big Difference* by Malcolm Gladwell

31. *The Glass Menagerie* by Tennessee Williams

32. *In Cold Blood* by Truman Capote

33. *The Secret Life of Bees* by Sue Monk Kidd

34. *The Brief Wondrous Life of Oscar Wao* by Junot Diaz

35. *Night* by Elie Wiesel

36. *A Yellow Raft in Blue Water* by Michael Dorris

37. *The Collector* by John Fowles

38. *Cry, the Beloved Country* by Alan Paton

39. *All the King's Men* by Robert Penn Warren

40. *A Mountain of Crumbs* by Elena Gorokhova

41. *The Picture of Dorian Gray* by Oscar Wilde

42. *A Long Way Gone: Memoirs of a Boy Soldier* by Ishmael Beah

43. *Mountains beyond Mountains* by Tracy Kidder

44. *And Then There Were None* by Agatha Christie

45. *Twenty Thousand Leagues under the Sea* by Jules Verne

46. *A Farewell to Arms* by Ernest Hemmingway

47. *Crazy Weekend* by Gary Soto

48. *Ordinary People* by Judith Guest

49. *Utopia* by Thomas More

50. *Committed* by Elizabeth Gilbert

51. *The House on Mango Street* by Sandra Cisneros

52. *A Thousand Splendid Suns* by Khaled Hosseini

53. *The Kite Runner* by Khaled Hosseini

54. *The Bluest Eye* by Toni Morrison

55. *The Elegance of the Hedgehog* by Muriel Barbery

56. *Pygmalion* by George Bernard Shaw

57. *Oedipus The King* by Sophocles

58. *How to Read Novels Like a Professor* by Thomas C. Foster

59. *The Color of Water: A Black Man's Tribute to His White Mother* by James McBride

60. *Gifted Hands: The Ben Carson Story* by Ben Carson

Note: You could search the Internet to obtain information about the book before you buy it or check it out of the library. Sometimes you may have the opportunity to read an excerpt online. This could help you determine whether you will like the author's style and whether you would find the reading interesting. You will also recognize some of these titles to be titles of movies. If you find a book that has been made into a movie, you will realize that it is usually better to read the book first. If you have watched the movie already, I encourage you to read the book. You may find that your experience with the book is more enriched because your imagination plays an important role. Besides, often movies are not true representations of the material in books. Directors like to add to and delete from the plot to please their audiences.

3   You, or someone you know, may be interested in reading material that is written with ESL (English as a Second Language) students in mind. The Penguin Readers are simplified versions of classics and other texts that are published at seven levels of difficulty. Once you browse through these books, you will learn what level is appropriate for you. To obtain more information, go to www.penguinreaders.com. Also, Dominoes are simplified texts at four reading levels of difficulty. They include graphic novels. For more information, go to www.oup.com/elt. Similarly, reading material in the Footprint Reading Library series is content-based reading in simplified text. Material is available in three formats (print, audio, and video). Visit elt.heinle.com for more information.

4   Let today be the day that you allow a book the opportunity to talk with you!

Read Your World

Alda
Noronha-
Nimmo

I am providing you with a list of ways you can intentionally apply the reading skills you have learned in this book while "reading your world" (making sense of the world around you). Recall that the kinds of critical thinking required for the application of the reading skills are similar to the type of thinking we all do to solve problems and to make sense of things in our everyday life. Language is the common denominator. We read in a language and we think and communicate in everyday life in a language. Therefore, you can easily recognize similarities of reading skill application to the thinking we do in situations such as those in the following list. This should not take up too much of your time. In fact, in most cases, all you have to do is analyze the situation and, as you know, this takes milliseconds of your time.

1. When you are at the doctor's office and pick up a magazine to browse through, think about predicting what the titles reveal about the material, and whether you can predict main idea, tone, author's purpose, and pattern of organization before you begin to read. Then read to check if you are right. Ask yourself what kind of thinking you did to select the magazine that you did.

2. When you pick up a prescription from the pharmacy, ask the pharmacist to provide you with a printout. Read it. Identify major supporting details. Are there words that you are unfamiliar with? How did you make sense of them? Sometimes medication comes with its own printout in the package. Often this is more difficult to read since it is written with pharmacists and doctors in mind. Look to see if you can make some sense of it. Can you find topic sentences for the paragraphs? If you are uncertain about your understanding, check with the pharmacist.

3. When you are signing paperwork at the doctor's office, the hospital, an outpatient facility, and such, particularly before a procedure, read what you are signing. Stop to check for understanding at the end of each paragraph. In other words, what is the implied main idea or main idea of each paragraph? If you are uncertain, ask the person who is requesting your signature. This way you can be sure that you understood the material. After all, your health is important to you, is it not?

4. When you fill out forms at the doctor's office, are you reading the questions correctly? If you are confused, ask. This means that you will then be sure to provide the right answers.

5. When you are signing a contract with a new cell-phone company, for a credit card, a car, a house, or for renovations, and such, read the contract. Most times salespeople's primary objective is to sell and, therefore, what you hear them tell you may not be what is on the contract or they may not have informed you of all the other things that are on the contract, that, had you

known about them, you may not have signed. Remember that the salesperson's purpose is to persuade you to buy. Therefore, do not rush into signing any contracts until you have read and understood what you are signing. For example, you must ask yourself whether the argument presented in favor of buying a particular car is sound (Is support relevant and adequate?) and what has motivated the salesperson to convince you that the car is the best of its kind (Is his commission higher if you purchase that particular car?). What kind of propaganda techniques were used, if any, about other car dealerships or car manufacturers?

6. Before you open your e-mails, bring to mind your background knowledge of the person who sent it and the title (in the "Subject" line) and then try and figure out what you think that e-mail is going to be about (predicting an implied main idea based on topic and background knowledge). Then read it, and see if you were right. If the e-mail went out to others, call them and ask them to tell you what the e-mail is about in one sentence (after you all have read it) and see if all of you had a similar answer.

7. After a meeting on your job, ask yourself what the meeting was about (main idea). Then ask another couple of coworkers who attended the same meeting and check if you had a similar answer.

8. When you have watched a movie, figure out an implied main idea. Check with friends to see what they came up with for an implied main idea. Do the same when watching sitcoms. See if you could tell about the movie in a few sentences (implied main idea and major supporting details—a summary).

9. When your friend or relative is relaying information to you about something, ask yourself at the end of his conversation what it was about in one sentence (implied main idea), ask yourself what pattern of organization(s) he used to relay that information. Do you think that he thought about how he was going to organize the information that he was going to give you? He did, but not on a conscious level. If he did not organize the information, you would not have understood what he was talking about. Also, ask yourself if he used any transition words (We usually do not use too many when we are talking to someone.) to express the connection between his thoughts (relationship between sentences/thoughts). What tone did he use? You not only "heard" the tone but also you could tell based on his choice of words.

10. When you are trying to fix something in your house that is broken and what you are trying to do based on your prior knowledge is not working, do you not stop and problem solve and think about how you can fix it using a different approach? Similarly, when you are studying or reading, if you are not comprehending or learning, you have to stop and use other strategies. You will recall that the reading comprehension process is not a one-size-fits-all!

11. When you are watching debates between and among political candidates, look for fallacies (false reasoning) that result from unsound arguments. Analyze whether support is irrelevant and/or inadequate. In an election year, when you are bombarded on television and radio with advertisements about candidates, think of what kind of propaganda techniques are being employed to influence the viewers.

12. When you are waiting at the subway, bus station, mall, or any place where people frequent, look at the people around you. What kind of inferences are you drawing based on how people look, how they are dressed, how they are speaking, etc.? I call this "reading people." Are your inferences based on solid, verifiable evidence or on factors such as emotion, intuition, preconceptions, or prejudice?

13. When you listen to sports commentators discussing the same game, but stating different perspectives, can you determine who is biased and who is objective? Are you inclined to agree with the "biased" commentator because she is speaking in positive terms about your favorite team although they lost the game? If you are, does that also make you biased?

14. As you continue with your college education, you will analyze what students tell you about instructors, courses, programs of study in the context of their perspectives and their ability to present a sound argument, and your ability to determine soundness of an argument.

2   I think by now you have realized that we use the same sort of reasoning to figure out the answers to reading comprehension questions as we do in reasoning through our everyday life situations. The difference is that the everyday thinking we do to solve problems is usually done on a subconscious level, but when we are taught reading comprehension in reading courses, we learn to do our thinking on a conscious level without realizing that reading comprehension is not

very different from how we make sense of our world. Once we realize the connection between our 'reading' world and our everyday world, we begin to process reading comprehension more naturally and holistically. Hence the informal expressions: "Do you read me?" And "Why are you reading so much into this situation?" Therefore, we have to make a conscious effort to identify these everyday comprehension processes that take a few seconds of our time—if that—and apply them to our reading comprehension tasks. (Of course, one important difference is that in reading we must first learn how to decode our language.) Now, do not take my word for it. Try these reading encounters for yourself!